The New York Times

Light & Easy Crossword Puzzles

Edited by Will Shortz

St. Martin's Paperbacks

THE NEW YORK TIMES LIGHT AND EASY CROSSWORD PUZZLES

Copyright © 2005 by New York Times Company.

Puzzles originally appeared in *The New York Times* daily editions from December 31, 2001, to March 25, 2003. Copyright © 2001, 2002, 2003, by The New York Times Company, Reprinted by permission

Cover photo © Johnner/Photonica

For information address St. Martin's Press, 175 Fifth Avenue, New York, NY 10010.

ISBN: 978-0-312-93773-7

Printed in the United States of America

St. Martin's Paperbacks edition / June 2005

St. Martin's Paperbacks are published by St. Martin's Press, 175 Fifth Avenue, New York, NY 10010.

20 19 18 17 16 15 14

The New York Times

Light & Easy
Crossword
Puzzles

ACROSS

1 Pointed a pistol
6 Blockhead
10 Quantities: Abbr.
14 Mix-up
15 Nabisco cookie
16 Epitome of redness
17 Teetotaler's New Year resolution?
19 Cotton unit
20 Best guess: Abbr.
21 "___ Can" (Sammy Davis Jr. book)
22 French explorer La ___
23 ___-do-well
25 Comment of approval
28 Light touch
29 "Get lost!"
31 Bootlegger's New Year resolution?
33 Highlands hat
35 ___ ès Salaam
36 French girlfriend
37 Came in
41 "I'm a Believer" band, with "the"
43 Monopoly card
44 Singer's syllable
46 Born: Fr.
47 Executioner's New Year resolution?
50 Making sounds
54 Oils and watercolors
55 Lady-killers
57 Seward Peninsula city
58 All set

60 Pack away
62 ___ Quentin
63 100-meter, e.g.
64 Scrabble player's New Year resolution?
67 Cruise stopover
68 Use a beeper
69 Donnybrook
70 Choreography move
71 Not barefoot
72 Has a need for Rogaine

DOWN

1 Trembling trees
2 Shortly
3 Guru
4 Flunking letters
5 Assigned task
6 Has some success
7 Circled the sun
8 Meadow
9 Bare peak
10 Palindromic pop group
11 When to eat
12 Fib
13 Places for church bells
18 Rooster's mate
22 60's radical org
24 Family-friendly, in cinema
26 Smile widely
27 Cook's cover-up
30 Ruin
32 Hire
34 "Same here"

Puzzle 1 by Nancy Salomon and Harvey Estes

37 John Glenn player in "The Right Stuff"
38 Biblical lands
39 Octopus's arm
40 Bongo, for one
42 Carson City's state: Abbr.
45 Way back when
48 Have a go at
49 Greenhouse area
51 Sportscaster Howard
52 Dumbfounded
53 Telescope parts

56 "H-E-L-P!"
59 Hard to fathom
61 Embryo's site
64 Family M.D.'s
65 "Yay, team!"
66 ___ culpa

ACROSS

1 Small batteries
4 Theme of this puzzle
8 Skedaddled
12 Neuters
15 One of the Durbeyfields
16 Small songbird
17 Check endorser
18 Has an at-bat
19 Makes a choice (for)
20 Chew the fat
21 Silent performer
22 Notwithstanding that, briefly
23 Baker's dozen quantity
25 Industrial solvents
28 Adapt machinery
29 Antebellum Dixie
31 Dating from
32 Pro ___ (like some lawyers' work)
34 Kitty-cat
35 Holier ___ thou
37 Talk a blue streak?
39 Island greeting
42 Berkshire school
44 Saudi, e.g.
48 The Left
50 Overlook
52 Panama and others
53 Modern
55 Lao-Tzu's "way"
56 Mysterious letter

58 Longfellow bell town
59 Child of fortune?
60 Take ___ (snooze)
61 60's dance craze
63 Travelers' stops
64 Jamaican exports
65 Whale finder
66 To be, to Tiberius
67 See 4-Across
68 Safari animal

DOWN

1 Cleopatra biter
2 Cochise and Geronimo, e.g.
3 Greet
4 Cheat on
5 Gets closer to, as a target
6 Having nothing lost or gained
7 Pretty basic bike
8 See 4-Across
9 Traveler to Hades to rescue Eurydice
10 Comebacks
11 Wearer of a half-inch gold stripe: Abbr.
13 See 4-Across
14 Sharp fight
23 "The flowers that bloom in the spring, ___ la"
24 Napoleon exile site
26 Sugar amts.
27 Wallflowerish
30 Wacky

Puzzle 2 by Manny Nosowsky

33 Like Nash's lama
36 Mischief
38 Troop group
39 Biopic starring Will Smith
40 Takes heed
41 Gets possession of
43 Salt shaker?
45 Like the 1920's
46 Crafty person?
47 Honey maker
49 Military wing with wings
51 Ibexes

54 "Gotta have it" sloganeer, once
57 E pluribus ___
59 Shake a leg
62 Capote nickname

ACROSS

1 Speaker's platform
5 Thailand, once
9 Used a broom
14 "Tickle me" doll
15 Part of S.R.O.
16 Spine-tingling
17 1966 Beach Boys hit
20 Possible reply to "Will you take out the trash?"
21 Chinese restaurant drink
22 Class head
24 Seek the affection of
25 Morse code bits
29 U.S./U.K. divider
31 Back of the neck
35 Actor Hawke
36 It'll knock you out
38 Neon or freon
39 Was completely indifferent
42 Last word in the Pledge of Allegiance
43 Fine sheet material
44 "The Divine Comedy" poet
45 Sixth word in the Pledge of Allegiance
47 Gangster's gun
48 "The Joy Luck Club" writer
49 Fraternity letter
51 Long ago
53 Have in mind
56 February 29

61 Comment from a recipient of an extravagant gift
63 "Tomorrow" musical
64 "Star Wars" princess
65 Steel ingredient
66 Adhesive
67 Tells it like it isn't
68 Microscope part

DOWN

1 Moist in the morning
2 Hand lotion ingredient
3 Radio host Don
4 Auctioneer's final word
5 Submarine detection systems
6 Foreword
7 Rope-a-dope boxer
8 Legendary story
9 Take care of
10 Continued
11 Buffalo's lake
12 Type size
13 Golf bag item
18 Relies (upon)
19 Derby hat
23 Where Easy Street is?
25 Coffee order
26 Lagoon surrounder
27 Longtime Dolphins coach Don
28 "2001" computer
30 Lighter ___ air
32 Insurance seller

33 It might be cooked al dente
34 Ruhr Valley city
36 ___ Kett of old comics
37 Beef, e.g.
40 1998 Winter Olympics site
41 Put down
46 Understands
48 Sites for fights
50 Giggle
52 Blast from the past
53 New Rochelle college

54 Women in habits
55 Uninteresting
57 Pop singer Collins
58 Truth or ___ (slumber party game)
59 Stratford's river
60 Desires
61 Pound sound
62 Luau souvenir

ACROSS

1 Soreness
5 Snakes do it
9 Hitter's problem
14 Wheedle
15 Put one ___
16 Medieval invader
17 Maryland athlete, for short
18 Neighbor of Sumatra
19 Bandleader Shaw
20 Scenic park in 58-Across
23 Gather together for stitching
25 18-Across, e.g.: Abbr.
26 In medias ___
27 Noted bridge in 58-Across
32 Record
33 Operatic soloist
34 Pulitzer novelist Anne
38 High cards
40 Olympian's quest
43 Wedge in a bottleneck?
44 Purposely lose
46 Roman date
48 Sharp turn
49 Museum house in 58-Across
53 Columbus Day mo.
56 What Austrians speak: Abbr.
57 Teacher's charges
58 European cultural center

63 Muslim ascetic
64 River spanned by 27-Across
65 Misfortunes
68 Clear the tape
69 Nick at ___
70 Lexicographer Webster
71 Like sunflowers
72 Hall-of-Famer Slaughter
73 "___ La Douce"

DOWN

1 Play part
2 British runner Sebastian
3 Sign of things to come
4 Send abroad
5 Voodoo
6 Certain coffee table shape
7 Jeans maker Strauss
8 Calamitous
9 Like night skies
10 Shortening
11 Express
12 Sen. Snowe's state
13 Decrease?
21 Word with pure or standard
22 Cigar residue
23 Accident sound
24 Bootlegger's product
28 Pep
29 A 1950 film was "all about" her

Puzzle 4 by Janet R. Bender

30 Spanish naval base site
31 Olive in the comics
35 Actress with many exes
36 Gives off
37 Patron saint of marriage
39 Appeasement
41 Wood-dressing tool
42 Sign of summer
45 Bet
47 Pet lovers' org.
50 Football's Dawson
51 Esoteric
52 The Big Ten's Fighting ___
53 Bid
54 Red Cross organizer Barton
55 Hungarian wine
59 Stand
60 "___ go bragh"
61 Fascinated by
62 Nail holders
66 Make tracks
67 ___ Na Na

ACROSS

1 Little lies
5 "___ 'er up!"
9 Yuri's love, in a Pasternak book
13 Fit of fever
14 Most qualified to serve?
15 Wind-borne toys
16 Nick's wife in "The Thin Man"
17 2002 Olympics locale
18 W.W. II sub
19 Response to a vet, maybe
22 Motorist's org.
23 "This ___ test . . ."
24 Sacred song
27 Phone hook-up
29 Mischievous
32 B.M.I. alternative
33 Designer Chanel
34 McGwire's onetime home-run rival
35 "Quiet, please!"
38 Weapons in shootdowns, for short
39 "___ kleine Nachtmusik"
40 New coins
41 Couple
42 Grain holders
43 Artist Max
44 Long time
45 Suffix with absorb
46 Hive output?
55 Children's song refrain
56 Mysterious: Var.
57 Woodwind
58 Gyrates
59 Composer Khachaturian
60 Narrow street
61 London's ___ Gallery
62 Mislay
63 Greek war god

DOWN

1 Cobra's weapon
2 Frankenstein's assistant
3 Extra–short haircut
4 Burn
5 Early time to arise
6 Prefix with venous
7 Shakespearean king
8 Bert of "The Wizard of Oz"
9 Person born October 1
10 Suffix with origin
11 Bring up
12 Study of the stars: Abbr.
15 Ill-fated Russian sub of 8/12/00
20 Designer Lauren
21 Big copier company
24 "I don't believe it!"
25 Jerk
26 Satisfied sounds
27 ___ Hopkins University
28 Fluish feeling
29 Father-and-son Nobel Prize winners in physics

Puzzle 5 by Michael Shteyman

30 Like ___ in the dark
31 Partners of dits
32 Aide: Abbr.
33 Where a sock goes?
34 Stay away from
36 Ketchup brand
37 Avis rival
42 Clowns
43 Pepsin, e.g.
44 Online publication
45 Poet Pound and others
46 Tops
47 "___-Dee-Doo-Dah"
48 Time: Ger.

49 Ardor
50 Nil
51 Writer Émile
52 Letter-shaped construction piece
53 Part of DMZ
54 Sleep symbols

ACROSS

1 Truck name
5 Unlike Charles Atlas
9 With 55-Down, Soap Box Derby home
14 Screen image
15 BB's, e.g.
16 Sawyer of TV news
17 With 32-Across, a hackneyed joke start
20 "Any ___?"
21 Cool quality
22 Engraving tools
23 Hint for a hound
25 Peach or plum
27 What's hot
32 See 17-Across
36 La-di-da
37 ___ synthesizer
38 Overact
40 Sharer's word
41 Let ride, at the track
43 With 59-Across, a heckler's interruption
45 Like some lingerie
46 "Nifty!"
47 Cratchit, for one
49 ___ firma
54 Superskillful sort
58 Oater brawl site
59 See 43-Across
62 Raga instrument
63 Presque Isle lake

64 Mark permanently
65 Like Santa on Christmas Eve?
66 Split apart
67 Classic cars

DOWN

1 Hands, slangily
2 Have ___ with (speak to)
3 Like the taste of some bad wine
4 Use a prie-dieu
5 Quipsters
6 Aussie runner
7 A Vanderbilt
8 Legit
9 Get comfortable with
10 Place for a firing
11 Gardener's tool
12 Till fillers
13 Beatty and Rorem
18 Author Jong
19 Take the cake
23 Bridge feat
24 Final exam giver?
26 Do as directed
28 Dig like a pig
29 Pin's place
30 Average guy?
31 Two capsules, say
32 Little rascals
33 Genesis skipper
34 Went like the dickens
35 Look like a wolf
36 TelePrompTer filler

Puzzle 6 by Kelly Clark

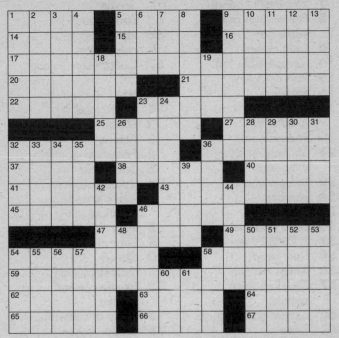

39 Shipbuilder's wood
42 Tell's forte
44 Demolish
46 Infernal
48 Shipload
50 Church official
51 Delivery person's beat
52 Marciano's given name
53 Pharaohs' crosses
54 Radiator sound
55 See 9-Across
56 Dorothy's dog

57 Cross words?
58 Runners carry it
60 "___ pales in Heaven the morning star": Lowell
61 Yang's opposite

ACROSS
1 Norway's capital
5 Person in a puffy white hat
9 Latin dance
14 Comparable (to)
15 Part of U.A.W.
16 Farewell
17 Contents of some tablets
20 Popeye's son
21 Shakespeare's last play, with "The"
22 Muscle quality
24 Blubber
25 Was forced
29 Do a great job
31 P. Diddy's music
34 Courtyard
36 Attila, for one
37 Opening in a sweater?
38 Classic parlor game
41 Effortless
42 Total
43 Bothers greatly
44 Salk and Pepper: Abbr.
45 Have the helm
47 Passover staple
48 Take to court
49 Relief pitcher's goal
51 "Top Hat" star Fred
55 Boo-boo
60 Hit 1980's–90's series
62 Chutney fruit
63 Whole bunch

64 Creme-filled cookie
65 See-through
66 Handicapper's calculation
67 Delicatessen loaves

DOWN
1 Horse feed
2 Distort
3 Queue
4 Fairy tale opener
5 Small role
6 Compassionate
7 Pilot's prediction, for short
8 Type choice
9 Bear or hare, e.g.
10 Skilled
11 Outfielder's cry
12 Handicappers' actions
13 Remove from office
18 Decide not to take part
19 Side on a football field
23 Disinters
25 Detested
26 Battling
27 Slip cover?
28 Very small
30 Billiard stick
31 Fowl pole?
32 "I Love Lucy" star
33 Basil-based sauce
35 Whodunit
37 Falafel bread

39 "___ Sera, Sera"
40 Least wild
45 Pitcher of woo
46 Rear-ended
48 Boot camp boss
50 Opinions
51 Cash dispensers, for short
52 Former Iranian leader
53 Fork part
54 A gas from the past
56 God of thunder
57 Full of breezes

58 Patella's place
59 Freudian topics
61 Aged

ACROSS

1 Queens's ___ Stadium
5 Big Mama
9 Made eyes at
14 Mooring place
15 Cornerstone word
16 Colt's sibling
17 Big Apple cardinal
18 1934 Mae West tune
20 Pipsqueak
22 Mars and Milky Way
23 Debussy's "La ___"
24 Poke fun at
26 Tries again
28 Groundhog Day's mo.
30 Human equivalent of a 16-Across
32 Côte-___, France
33 The rain in Spain
35 New Mexico artists' home
37 Killer whales
41 Has an Olympics honor
44 Ferber and O'Brien
45 School founded in 1440
46 The Eternal City
47 Misbehaving
49 Assns.
51 Coral ___
52 Spotted beetle
56 "Spare" things
58 Exist
59 Earthbound avians
61 Like extra-lite ice cream
64 Be an innovator
67 Callas, for one
68 Locks locale
69 Arctic ice
70 "___ Brockovich"
71 Serengeti scavenger
72 Merlin, e.g.
73 Place to work

DOWN

1 Big galoots
2 Sound of relief
3 Nora Ephron best seller
4 Bert's "Sesame Street" pal
5 Tent spot
6 "___ takers?"
7 Snooty sort
8 Kind of energy
9 Descendant
10 Dodger great Hodges
11 Four-legged Andean
12 "___ Gantry"
13 Batik artisans
19 ___ Scott Decision
21 YM or GQ
25 Wipe clean
27 Dropped pop-up, e.g.
28 Turn toward
29 Old oath
31 Kin of keno
34 Sheikdom of song
36 One way to be caught
38 CNN debate show

Puzzle 8 by Richard Chisholm

39 Peak
40 Queens's
   ___ Stadium
42 Sponsor of Columbus
43 Casey Jones, for one
48 Hardly Einsteinian
50 B'way notice
52 Gate closer
53 Orderly grouping
54 Diplomat Silas
55 Chasms
57 Finito
60 Mall event
62 Famous #2

63 Bazooka target
65 Bond creator Fleming
66 Actress Wanamaker

ACROSS

1 "The Wizard of Oz" dog
5 ___ Island (immigration point)
10 Birdbrain
14 On ___ with (equal to)
15 Lasso loop
16 Decorative pitcher
17 Ten: Prefix
18 French fashion designer
20 Like bagpipes
22 First month in Madrid
23 Actress Skye
24 Emulate Salt-N-Pepa
26 Room with an easy chair
27 Spinning competition
31 How checks are signed
32 Regarding
33 ___ de cologne
36 Litter members
37 Tropical ray
39 Islamic ruler
40 Road wiggle
41 King ___
42 Ogling
43 1925 hit musical with the song "Tea for Two"
46 Lawn base
49 Letter after zeta
50 Bunches
51 Madison Square Garden, e.g.
53 Hearty breakfast
57 Performer in a cage
60 Historic periods
61 Med school subj.
62 Funny-car fuel
63 Quirks
64 Mediocre
65 Lip application
66 Cry from Santa

DOWN

1 Little ones
2 Oil grp.
3 ___ Bell
4 They're given at graduations
5 Community next to Van Nuys
6 Ease up
7 ___ Ness monster
8 Prefix with metric
9 Instant, for short
10 Student overseer
11 Had
12 Tractor maker John
13 Synthetic fabric
19 Aware of, slangily
21 Clock sound
24 Take five
25 "The Thin Man" canine
27 "Egad!"
28 Burden
29 Sounds made by 36-Across
30 Fancy ballroom steps
33 Give off
34 "___ She Sweet"

35 Impel
37 No longer worth debating
38 Ballerina Pavlova
39 Valuable things to give?
41 Work, as dough
42 Organic compound
44 Ones pointing fingers
45 Some Oldsmobiles
46 Long stories
47 Maine college town
48 "Le Viol" painter
52 Say ___ (deny)

53 Eight: Prefix
54 Quartet minus one
55 R.P.M. indicator
56 Old Standard Oil brand
58 One of four for a square: Abbr.
59 Nothing

ACROSS

1 "Boris Godunov" singer
6 Egg holder
10 Man in Eden
14 Whirling
15 "___, Brute?"
16 Back of the neck
17 Girl in the family
18 Blasé
20 Stick in pick-up-sticks
22 Collect
23 Light switch settings
24 As well
25 Well-bred horse
26 1966 Rolling Stones hit
31 Primitive fishing tool
34 Table scraps
35 Ocean
36 Impose, as taxes
37 It can follow the end of 20-, 26-, 43- or 54-Across
39 One of the Ivies
40 Jackie O's husband
41 Helvetica, e.g.
42 Wallop
43 Respected person
47 M.D.'s
48 Galley implement
49 Profs' helpers
52 Over
54 Burrower
57 Quick rests
59 Vietnam's capital
60 Arctic Ocean hazard
61 Gaelic
62 Tennis star Chris
63 Facility
64 Menial laborer
65 Father-and-daughter Hollywood duo

DOWN

1 Bluegrass instrument
2 From 59-Across, e.g.
3 Glasses, for short
4 Not well
5 Poor movie rating
6 Brain cell
7 11,000-foot Italian peak
8 Fret
9 Formal wear, informally
10 Mole or mule
11 Stores of information
12 Forest swingers
13 Club ___ (resorts)
19 Atkins diet no-nos
21 You, on the Riviera
25 A.B.A. member: Abbr.
26 Treat
27 Dessert not for the diet-conscious
28 Like some sale clothes: Abbr.
29 Division of a euro
30 Welles character
31 Eastern European
32 Prefix with scope or meter
33 Demons
37 Peat sources

Puzzle 10 by Zack Butler

38 67.5 deg.
39 Target score
41 Aspect
42 Sat
44 European herb used in soups
45 Unbuckle
46 Pop
49 Piano technician
50 Squirrel's staple
51 Sketches
52 French cleric
53 La ___ tar pits
54 "Now ___ talkin'!"

55 Approximately
56 Be bound (to)
58 Jivey

ACROSS

1 Bank job
6 Forest opening
11 Fore's opposite
14 God, in Mecca
15 "Bye!"
16 ___-tzu
    (Taoism founder)
17 1994 Winter
    Olympics site
19 On the other
    hand
20 Bit of chicanery
21 Boxing venue
23 Buckles on
27 Chemical-free
29 Find not guilty
30 Part of U.S.S.R.
31 Butter maker
32 Archeological find
33 Kilmer who played
    Batman
36 Furniture wood
37 Soup go-with
38 Clamp
39 Salt Lake City-to-Las
    Vegas dir.
40 Witches' assembly
41 "Beer Barrel ___"
42 Biblical passages
44 AT&T customer
45 Army outfit
47 Oriental
48 Belt features
49 "___ fair in love
    and war"
50 Tool for making
    48-Across

51 1928 Winter
    Olympics site
58 Spectate
59 Grassy plain
60 Set free
61 Suffix with station
62 Aden's land
63 Discrimination

DOWN

1 "2001" computer
2 ___ Lilly & Co.
3 Down with the flu, say
4 "My gal" of song
5 At that place
6 Window pane
7 Hobbling
8 Convenience store
    convenience: Abbr.
9 Sandra of "Gidget"
10 Inconsistent
11 1992 Winter
    Olympics site
12 Animals collectively
13 General Mills cereal
18 Follow a fox, say
22 Bemoan
23 What to face
24 Partner of pains
25 1960 Winter
    Olympics site
26 Istanbul native
27 Actor Lloyd ___
28 Zealous
30 Tennis ace Monica
32 Shade of black
34 Prosecutor,
    at times

Puzzle 11 by Gregory E. Paul

35 Memorize
37 Middling
38 Electric unit
40 In an angry way
41 Faint
43 Summer in Paris
44 Storm preceder
45 New moon or full moon, e.g.
46 Farther down
47 Friend of Dionne in pop music's Dionne & Friends
49 Elizabeth I's mother

52 Stout
53 "___ shocked— SHOCKED!"
54 Genetic letters
55 Part of T.G.I.F.
56 Small bird
57 Last letter

ACROSS

1 Tel ___
5 Sired, biblically
10 Hits with phaser fire
14 Ankle-showing skirt
15 Play ___ in (be involved with)
16 Quod ___ faciendum
17 Folk singer Burl
18 Suppress
19 Indian music
20 Critique roughly and unfairly
23 Cryptologic grp.
24 "Fat chance!"
25 Increase the price of at auction
28 $$$ provider
31 Ideal for dieters
35 Web address ender
36 Destination from Dover
39 Press
40 Harbor personal motives
43 Extent
44 Covetous
45 Actress Tilly
46 Hardly modern
48 "___ Miniver"
49 "Touched By an Angel" star Della
51 Unruly head of hair
53 German name starter
54 Gulf war weapon
63 Five-star Bradley
64 Run on a bank
65 A party to
66 Like some amateurs
67 Indicator of freshness, perhaps
68 June celebrant
69 80's rock band from Australia
70 Ed Norton's workplace
71 Beatty and Buntline

DOWN

1 In the thick of
2 In ___ (type of fertilization)
3 Inspiration
4 The Preserver, in Hinduism
5 "Enough, Enrico!"
6 Speedskater Heiden
7 Early Black Sea settler
8 Burn healer
9 Metric portion
10 Blastoff time
11 Resident of 55-Down
12 When repeated, a Samoan city
13 "South Park" kid
21 Org. that shelters strays
22 Feb.'s predecessor
25 "The View" co-host Joy
26 "Do ___?" (words of indecision)
27 Comforter
28 It might scream after being tripped

Puzzle 12 by Alan J. Weiss

29 Internal Revenue Service, e.g.
30 Small arachnids
32 Fiction genre
33 "___ of God" (1985 film)
34 Precarious perch
37 "The Ice Storm" director Lee
38 Outfield surface
41 Sets aside (for)
42 Spinning toys
47 "How exciting!"
50 Naval standard

52 Dads
53 "The ___ of Wakefield"
54 3-D figures
55 Muscat is its capital
56 Kind of cat
57 Ending with hard or soft
58 Be wise to
59 Quiet type?
60 Concerning
61 Amount of work
62 Goes no further

ACROSS

1 ___, beta, gamma . . .
6 Like skyscrapers
10 Not fully closed
14 Lulu
15 Creme-filled cookie
16 Stubborn beast
17 With 37- and 56-Across, where "God Save the Queen" is the national anthem
20 Heavy weight
21 Dancer Charisse
22 Hoodwinks
23 No-no
26 Arcade game name
28 Improvement
30 Wharf
31 76ers' org.
34 Jawaharlal of India
35 Fourth-down option
36 Middle Brady Bunch girl
37 See 17-Across
41 Superlative suffix
42 Is sick
43 Parish priest
44 ___ Speedwagon
45 Almanac datum
46 Torment a stand-up comedian
47 Egg beater
49 Abstract artist Albers
50 Forearm bones
52 It's bottled in Cannes
53 "7 Faces of Dr. ___" (1964 flick)

56 See 17-Across
61 Apple or maple
62 Cry like a banshee
63 Kind of question
64 & 65 Miscellany, when separated by "and"
66 Obsolete anesthetic

DOWN

1 Be adjacent to
2 Letterman rival
3 Celebrate
4 Simple shelter
5 Gobbled up
6 1964 Olympics host
7 Dry
8 Football great Dawson
9 Nautical journal
10 Love affair
11 Rolling Stones hit of 1968
12 Lotion ingredient
13 They keep track of pins
18 Pesticide brand
19 W.W. II turning point
24 Surrounding glow
25 Very dry, as Champagne
26 Some wedding guests
27 "Toodle-oo!"
28 Felix of "The Odd Couple"
29 Intrinsically
30 Colorful cover
32 Hackneyed

Puzzle 13 by Peter Gordon

33 Wrestling's
___ the Giant
35 Puncture
38 Sheepish sounds
39 Currier's partner
40 Heading on
Santa's list
45 Ichthyologist's study
46 Daylight savings
saving
48 Despises
49 Puts behind bars
50 Golden rule word
51 "___ of the Flies"

52 Novelist Bagnold
54 Game show
host Robinson
55 Stink
57 Emitter of 38-Down
58 Competed in a 10K
59 Needle part
60 Tennis call

ACROSS

1 Race car guages, for short
6 Mesa dweller
10 "No way, ___!"
14 González from Cuba
15 Soon, to a bard
16 Third afterthought in a letter: Abbr.
17 Even if, familiarly
18 Big cat
19 Butcher's goods
20 What 2002 was, according to the 38-Across
23 Temperature
24 Clairvoyant
25 Mournful trumpet sound
28 Soak (up)
30 Prepares for a tough battle
34 Took the cake?
35 Fan mags
37 Laissez-___
38 See 20-Across
41 Book that refers to "People of the Book"
42 Kind of power
43 Inc., abroad
44 Historic London theater
46 Sow's pen
47 Gets the picture
48 Thingy
50 Part of a smoke screen?
52 Annual greeting appropriate to this puzzle
58 What the fat lady sings
59 Goal in musical chairs
60 Go for another 12 issues, say
62 Treaty
63 Fictional Jane
64 Field of play
65 Actress Sommer
66 Does and bucks
67 Disorganized

DOWN

1 It may be high in the afternoon
2 Friend in war
3 Refer to
4 Big laugh
5 "Zzzzzz . . ."
6 Intermediate shades
7 "Put a lid ___!"
8 Exclamations of disdain
9 Like a have-not
10 U.S. Steel founder
11 Phone abbr.
12 Hot tubs
13 Italy's Villa d'___
21 Rest area
22 Member of a herd
25 Off the wall
26 Playwright Fugard
27 Kooky
29 River to the Rio Grande

Puzzle 14 by Manny Nosowsky

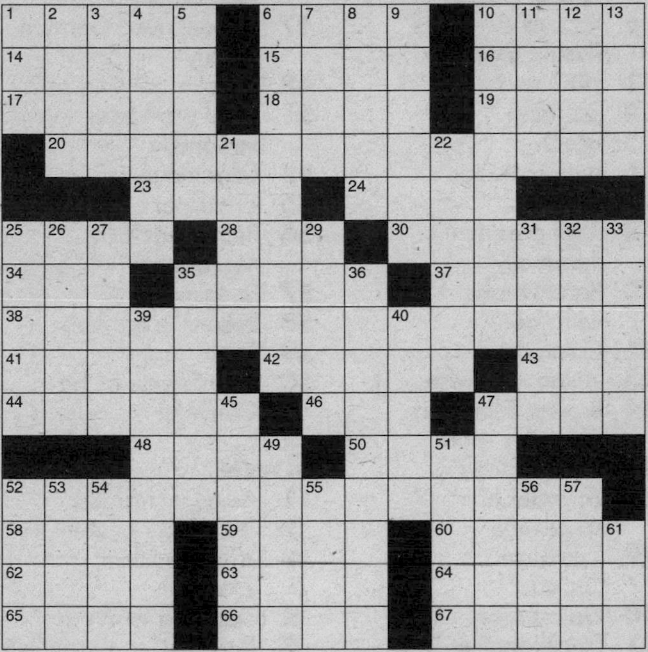

(Crossword grid)

31 Move crabwise
32 Fit to be tied
33 Unpopular ones
35 Highest point
36 Kind of taffy
39 Find a route
40 ___ on the line
45 Discontinued
47 Place for influence?
49 "That's nonsense!"
51 "Begone!"
52 Stare agog
53 ___ Mountains
(Asian border)

54 Short cut
55 Taxi rider
56 Snake eyes
57 Hankerings
61 Road to take

ACROSS

1 Greets the day
6 "___ of the Times" (Petula Clark hit)
11 HBO rival
14 ___ acid
15 Beach
16 Lens protector
17 For rent
18 16th president, informally
20 Barely make, with "out"
21 Colored
23 Italian or Jewish, e.g.
24 Braves, Mets and Cubs, for short
26 Join the service
27 By order of succession
29 ___ Motel, in "Psycho"
30 Go by bike
31 Stuck together
32 "For shame!"
35 He sold his birthright to Jacob
36 43rd president, informally
37 Waiflike
38 No. on a business card
39 ___ toast
40 Tractor maker
41 Eucalyptus eater
42 Daredevil's cord
43 How fast-talkers talk
45 Desert plants
46 Early game in a tournament
47 Discontinued German money
48 Popular cooking spray
51 23rd president, informally
53 Litter member
55 ET carrier
56 Refrain in "Old MacDonald"
57 Bungling
58 Everest, e.g.: Abbr.
59 Catch
60 Grant's side in the Civil War

DOWN

1 Amount charged
2 "Nothing's broken"
3 30th president, informally
4 Opposite WSW
5 "Told ya!"
6 Gray flakes
7 Like show horses
8 Charged particle
9 Beverage at a Japanese restaurant
10 Got comfy
11 Pictures put into computers
12 A bad one should be kicked
13 Oil cartel
19 "Get a load of ___!"
22 Samovar
25 Humdinger

26 Class that doesn't require much studying
27 "Original Gangster" rapper
28 Nasdaq rival
29 42nd president, informally
31 Throughout
32 40th president, informally
33 Father
34 Midleg
36 Request for a hand
37 Circus site
39 Hanging sculptures
40 Bowling target
41 Bit of Scottish attire
42 Sot's spot
43 Cheat, in a way
44 Reveal
45 Dugout, e.g.
46 Prune, before drying
47 Israel's Golda
49 Date with a D.D.S., e.g.
50 Story from Olympus
52 "Don't ___ stranger"
54 One, to Juan

ACROSS
1 Drive back
6 Halloween decorations
10 Scent
14 Helpful
15 Cross to bear
16 Mooring spot
17 Last-place team's infielders?
20 Czech or Serb
21 Inventor's starting point
22 On one's toes
23 It's pumped
25 In the past
26 Podiatrist's one-time charge?
35 Bar garnishes
36 Some surgery patients
37 Egg cells
38 Platte River people
39 Clear the whiskers
40 Keg party locale
41 Coffee holder
42 Swiftly
43 Shake off
44 Army exercise routine?
47 Not pre- or post-
48 Hack (off)
49 Ruhr city
52 Pooch's name
55 Kismet
59 Envoy's sheepskin?
62 Tickled pink
63 Province
64 Dr. Salk
65 It's active in Sicily
66 Lucci's award, finally
67 Used up

DOWN
1 Chafes
2 Bibliographical abbr.
3 Italian tourist city
4 Puts on a pedestal
5 "Solaris" author Stanislaw
6 Dr. No foe
7 Poker stake
8 Big brass
9 F.I.C.A. funds it
10 Spotted wildcat
11 Rotunda feature
12 [see other side]
13 Landlord's due
18 Dublin's land
19 Heroic tales
24 Conditions
25 Sheltered, at sea
26 Gold Medal product
27 Petrol unit
28 In with
29 Revolutionary Allen
30 Place to build
31 Flu symptom
32 Public meeting
33 Dodge
34 Moth or worm follower
39 Hotfooted it
40 Policy reversal
42 Acid in proteins

Puzzle 16 by Arlan and Linda Bushman

43 Conceit
45 Marcos of the Philippines
46 "The Time Machine" people
49 Barely beat
50 River deposit
51 Wings' measure
52 Old MacDonald's place
53 Part of a list
54 Time to attack
56 First-class
57 Eliot Ness, notably
58 Sunrise direction
60 Dogpatch's Daisy ___
61 Bedwear, briefly

ACROSS

1 ___ Mayer (wiener maker)
6 Doe's mate
10 Poker action
13 Great Plains tribe
14 San Diego baseballer
16 Holiday preceder
17 Informer
19 Nothing
20 Is in danger of sinking
21 Prophecy giver
23 U.K. news source
26 Mineral suffix
27 Mennonite group
28 Pennsylvania university
30 Like some Chinese cooking
33 Overflowing (with)
34 Rocket engine
35 Hubbub
36 Mangle
37 Nickels-and-___ (bothers with trivialities)
38 Last year's sr.
39 Misjudge
40 Military doctor
41 Unloads
42 Corrupts
44 100 centimos
45 Like a beaver
46 Minister: Abbr.
47 Letters after Q
48 "Aeneid" poet
50 Like ghost stories
52 Koch and Asner
53 Habitual boob tube watcher
58 "Do Ya" rock grp.
59 Extra
60 The "U" in U.S.S.R.
61 Ballpoint, e.g.
62 Gone across a pool
63 Barker of military orders

DOWN

1 Gives a thumbs-up
2 Dog command
3 Make dove sounds
4 Person missed by a 63-Across
5 North Carolina's capital
6 Volleyball kill
7 License plates
8 Summer cooler
9 Ones using brushes and combs
10 Substitute
11 Worse than knavery
12 Prefix with phone
15 Singer Caruso
18 Trodden track
22 ___ Wednesday
23 Held responsible
24 "___ the Ides of March"
25 Committee head
27 Ancient Mexican
29 Suffix with organ or patriot
30 Games before finals
31 Modifies

Puzzle 17 by Christina Houlihan

32 Signals, as to an auctioneer
34 Document amendment
37 Unfolds
38 Film director Van Sant
40 Voodoo and wizardry
41 Crafty
43 Scott Joplin tune
44 Whom a copper apprehends
46 Fix, as cuffs
48 Prez's #2
49 Inactive
50 Creamy shade

51 Sicilian spouter
54 Big Detroit inits.
55 Lungful
56 Coat, informally
57 "You're Still the ___" (1998 Grammy winner)

ACROSS

1 Funnyman Fox
6 Wallop
11 Little demon
14 Lagoon surrounder
15 Suffix similar to -ish
16 ___ es Salaam
17 2001 50-Across nominee
19 "Exodus" hero
20 Gush
21 ___ vez (again, in Spanish)
22 Virtuoso
23 2001 50-Across nominee
27 Bygone Spanish dictator
30 Regret
31 2001 50-Across nominee, with "The"
37 Thurman of "Even Cowgirls Get the Blues"
38 It merged with Time Warner
39 Brazilian city, familiarly
41 2001 50-Across nominee
48 650, Roman-style
49 Said
50 See 17-, 23-, 31-, 41- and 63-Across
56 Wacky
57 Race in "The Time Machine"
58 Sidle
62 Pewter component
63 2001 50-Across nominee

66 Palindromic preposition
67 "Tomorrow" musical
68 Relative worth
69 Watergate prosecutor Archibald
70 Like visiting teams, often
71 ___ and drabs

DOWN

1 Plays impromptu
2 Above
3 Pouting grimace
4 It "blows no good"
5 Yalie
6 Capital of Western Australia
7 Stick out like ___ thumb
8 Young pigeon
9 Yank
10 Wide shoe width
11 Its license plates say "Famous Potatoes"
12 Former governor Cuomo
13 Geo model
18 ___ this earth
22 Small songbird
24 Sgt., e.g.
25 Mess up
26 It makes MADD mad
27 Winter ailment
28 Capital of Italia
29 Saudi, e.g.
32 Tit for ___
33 ___ polloi
34 Little toymaker
35 Indomitable spirit

Puzzle 18 by Peter Gordon

36 Cosecant's reciprocal
40 Strange
42 Small whirlpool
43 Point of no return?
44 Where Einstein was born
45 Old Pan Am rival
46 Env. contents
47 Finished a round even
50 Dweller at Tenochtitlán
51 Nile city
52 Wing
53 Kind of question

54 "What's it all about?" guy
55 Courted
59 Noted Surrealist
60 Food that is "rustled up"
61 Scrapes (out)
63 Yak
64 Lennon's love
65 Blockbuster rental, perhaps

ACROSS

1 Whole bunch
5 Letter before 29-Down
10 Heavy mists
14 Cincinnati's home
15 Lose ignominiously, in slang
16 "For Your Eyes ___"
17 1952 Gene Kelly classic
20 Film director's cry
21 Pub pints
22 Altar vow
23 One-named New Age singer
25 Walked in
27 Remodeled Clay?
30 P.D.Q.
32 "Wailing" instrument
33 "Gentlemen Prefer Blondes" writer Anita
35 Metallic rocks
37 To the point
41 1929 Irving Berlin song
44 Death row reprieves
45 Scruff
46 Ivan or Nicholas
47 Old Ford
49 Alan of "Shane"
51 Pitcher's stat.
52 This could raise a pitcher's 51-Across
56 End-of-the-week cry
58 Ailing
59 "___ my words"
61 Got around

65 1963 Peter, Paul and Mary hit
68 Capital of Peru
69 First month on a calendario
70 Émile Zola novel
71 Grandson of Eve
72 Gain a monopoly over
73 Knock 'em dead

DOWN

1 Slugger Sammy
2 Voguish
3 "___ it the truth!"
4 Ponderosa stray
5 "Ulysses" poet
6 "Bali ___"
7 2001 erupter
8 Name
9 2004 Olympics site
10 Voting yes
11 Studio sign
12 Fly without an engine
13 Church council
18 Inner Hebrides island
19 Kind of sale
24 Vice President Burr
26 Put out, as effort
27 Austrian peaks
28 Oaf
29 Letter before kappa
31 Serving to punish
34 Vogue
36 March 17 honoree, for short
38 ___ and shine
39 Headliner

Puzzle 19 by Randall J. Hartman

40 Old Testament book
42 Panama and others
43 Fly a crop duster
48 Keaton and Sawyer
50 Ring fix?
52 Holy book
53 Tuckered out
54 Replay feature
55 Father, Son and Holy Ghost
57 Baby deer
60 Was in on
62 Obsolescent phone feature

63 Sicilian resort
64 June 6, 1944
66 Lived
67 1990 one-man Broadway show

ACROSS

1 Nav. officers
5 Muscle contraction
10 Madcap
14 Con ___ (vigorously)
15 Nametag word
16 Soothing plant extract
17 China/Korea border river
18 Disney's ___ Center
19 Church seating
20 Brainy
23 Kind of orange
24 Tex-Mex restaurant dip
28 Surgery locales: Abbr.
29 Gridiron great Groza
31 "You've got mail" co.
32 Words from Caesar
35 "Beyond Good and Evil" author
38 Brainy
41 Egotistical
42 Mindless repetition
43 Biblical verb ending
44 Attorneys' org.
45 Bring to bear
47 Coup ___
49 Symbol of Americanism
54 Brainy
57 Guitarist Hendrix
60 "Secrets & Lies" director Mike
61 Roman 152
62 Vicinity
63 "Exodus" actor Sal
64 "___ in Full" (Tom Wolfe novel)
65 Succotash tidbit
66 Uneasy feeling
67 Summoned help, maybe

DOWN

1 Vast gulf
2 "Law & Order," e.g.
3 Where to see "The Last Supper"
4 San Francisco bread
5 Clippers
6 Coke competitor
7 Highway to Fairbanks
8 Gradual
9 Sweater eater
10 Inventor of the Mothers of Invention
11 Ginger ___
12 Right away
13 "You bet!"
21 Roofer's supply
22 Rodeo producer
25 Milk: Prefix
26 Not ___ (mediocre)
27 Coeur d'___, Idaho
29 One of two ballroom dancers
30 Horse picker's hangout, for short
32 Flowed back
33 Clichéd
34 Too snug
35 Zip, to Zapata

Puzzle 20 by Marjorie Richter

36 Suffix with expert
37 San Francisco transport
39 Shrubby land
40 Keyboard key
45 Outcome
46 Patty Hearst's kidnap grp.
48 From the Orient
49 Imitating
50 Buzzes, say
51 Director Brian De ___
52 Suffix with beaut-
53 Stretching (out)

55 ___ mater
56 Jockey strap
57 Abrupt thrust
58 Wrath
59 ___ culpa

ACROSS

1 Sixth Greek letter
5 Short hit, in baseball
9 Specialized vocabulary
14 Tennis great Lendl
15 "___ bitten, twice shy"
16 Crystal-lined stone
17 Barbershop call
18 Place for "junk"
20 Emergency situation that an Egyptian goddess experiences?
22 Spell-off
23 Golf ball peg
24 Down's opposite
28 ___ and aahs
30 Head-butt
33 Three-wheeler
34 Thin wedge of wood
35 Stew holders
36 Fruit that grandma dubbed?
39 Rooney of "60 Minutes"
40 Place to stroll
41 Refrain in "Old MacDonald"
42 Magic 8-Ball answer
43 Sherlock Holmes prop
44 Beauty parlors
45 "Thar ___ blows!"
46 Permit
47 Ornate clone of designer Chanel?
55 Big political contest
56 Buckeye's home
57 Foreword, for short

58 Slender nail
59 Child with no siblings
60 Parts of houses and mouths
61 Shopper stopper
62 ___ pony

DOWN

1 Metal in brass
2 ". . . happily ___ after"
3 Way around town
4 Aardvark's fare
5 Supervisors
6 Loosen, as laces
7 Sgts. and cpls.
8 Actress Hatcher
9 Texas A&M's team
10 Baseball great Pee Wee
11 Mongolian desert
12 Scandinavian god
13 Royal flush card
19 Breathing woe
21 "A Doll's House" playwright
24 Unable to flee
25 Origami bird
26 Orange covers
27 Approve
28 Chicago airport
29 Sound in "Old MacDonald"
30 One of Shakespeare's "star-crossed lovers"
31 Didn't go out to a restaurant

Puzzle 21 by Peter Gordon

32 Forerunner of
   Windows
34 Rice Krispies sound
35 Bucket
37 Each
38 "Cool!"
43 Wedding album
   contents
44 Withdraw (from)
45 Winter wear
46 Making all stops
47 Nevada city
48 "I'm ___ you!"
49 Spheres

50 Singer Irene
51 Condo's cousin
52 Speed skater Apolo
   Anton ___
53 Tablet
54 It has its ups
   and downs
55 Knight's title

ACROSS

1 Artist Chagall
5 Rams' mates
9 Hairy-chested ones
14 Former Expos manager Felipe
15 À la mode
16 Use a soapbox
17 Scorch
18 Frequent quarreler with Zeus
19 Chop finely
20 Oil container #1
23 On the briny
24 Melody
25 ___-de-France
28 Oil container #2
33 Neighbor of Syr.
36 Downfall
37 Pitcher Ryan
38 "The Intimate ___" (1990 jazz album)
40 Disgusted
43 Capone's nemesis
44 English actors Bates and Rickman
46 Granola bits
48 Play thing
49 Oil container #3
53 "Naughty!"
54 Many a crossword clue
55 Follow
59 Oil container #4
64 Novel or essay
66 Desert bordered by steppe land
67 French cleric
68 "The House of the Seven Gables" locale
69 Place for a spending spree
70 Apple throwaway
71 Nobel, for one
72 One way to orient a boat
73 Greek H's

DOWN

1 Tuscan city noted for its marble quarries
2 Alaskan native
3 Dappled horses
4 A time to remember?
5 Reverberate
6 "That was a close one!"
7 Leprechaun's land
8 Sacred beetle
9 Big hit
10 Enemies of the Iroquois
11 Lower jaws
12 Often-repeated abbr.
13 Maiden name preceder
21 Bert of "The Wizard of Oz"
22 The "S" in R.S.V.P.
26 Rent
27 Young's partner in accounting
29 ___ Wiedersehen
30 Tell tall tales
31 At the ___ one's rope
32 "___ voyage!"

Puzzle 22 by Sarah Keller

33 Vaulted
34 "Less Than Zero" novelist
35 Very attractive body?
39 Queen's subject, possibly
41 Old Mideast inits.
42 "Harper Valley __"
45 Above all others
47 "Peter Pan" character
50 Capek play
51 Riddle
52 Unite threads
56 Wooden shoe

57 Planetary shadow
58 Fencing needs
60 Secondhand
61 Brat's stocking stuffer
62 Highly adroit
63 Blue or White follower
64 Supp. writings
65 Untreated

ACROSS

1 Players in a play
5 Tobacco smoke component
8 Scottish Gaelic
12 Commedia dell' ___
13 Visibly dumbstruck
15 Trust, with "on"
16 Wheedle
17 Stick-on
18 Not fully closed
19 Puccini opera Web site?
22 Unlatch, to bards
23 Intl. cultural org.
24 Saigon's former enemy
26 60's campus grp.
27 Exact-time Web site?
32 "Don't go!"
33 Post-Crucifixion sculpture
34 Humid
38 Milky gems
41 Farmer's output
42 Violinist Stern
44 "Bye-bye"
46 Document miniaturization Web site?
49 Kwik-E-Mart clerk on "The Simpsons"
52 Where Goodyear is headquartered
53 Brunch dish
55 Tavern
57 Printed clothing Web site?
60 Elvis ___ Presley
62 Painter Rivera
63 Prefix with scope or logical
64 With 11-Down, Brontë heroine
65 Particle in electrolysis
66 R. & B. singer Redding
67 Reached ground
68 "___ Rosenkavalier"
69 Points per game, e.g.

DOWN

1 It has points in Arizona
2 "I Get ___" (Beach Boys hit)
3 Rubbernecks
4 Lubbock's home
5 Discretion
6 Attack helicopter
7 Insert fresh cartridges
8 Silent ___ (time before the talkies)
9 Celebrant
10 Response to an affront
11 See 64-Across
13 Expand, as a house
14 Pres. Washington
20 Sgts. and such
21 Alphabet series
25 Suffix with psych-
28 Spigot
29 Marriott competitor
30 Great Plains Indian
31 Treasure hunter's aid
34 Slow-witted

Puzzle 23 by John Greenman

35 "___ was saying"
36 Food that can be strung on a necklace
37 Driving test directive
39 Fond du ___, Wis.
40 Was atop
43 Company: Abbr.
45 Bullets
47 Thingamabob
48 Part of AOL
49 "Little Women" writer
50 Bradley University site
51 Maximum extent
54 Group's character

55 ___ California
56 Asia's ___ Sea
58 Actor Dullea
59 In times past
61 After-tax take

ACROSS

1 Locker room handout
6 Alma ___
11 Madison Avenue products
14 Post of etiquette
15 Line to the audience
16 Dog doc
17 News host, e.g.
19 Gabor or Perón
20 It may be bitter
21 "Uh-uh"
22 Token of respect
24 Gossip's attribute
28 Sandal feature
30 Former partner?
31 Sauce with basil
32 Toast toppings
33 Grub
34 Part of LED
36 Grub
40 Whittle down
41 Reporter's question
42 Deejay's bribe
45 32-Across, e.g.
47 Sign of unfaithfulness
49 Angelic strings
50 Long, long time
51 Misfortune
54 Simile's center
55 Bit of aid
59 Hamster, e.g.
60 Bay window
61 Bathed
62 Wind dir.

63 Aquarium favorite
64 Poem of lament

DOWN

1 Head of France?
2 Muscat's land
3 Kind of show
4 Lodge member
5 Deceiving
6 Noisy bird
7 White-faced
8 Haberdashery item
9 Author LeShan
10 Cinnamon treats
11 Exact retribution for
12 Gobble up
13 Glassy look
18 NASA scrub
23 N.Y. neighbor
25 Small colonists
26 Garden bloom, informally
27 Hardly racy
28 Reveal, poetically
29 Stew item
32 ___ Six-Pack
34 Painter of limp watches
35 Farsi-speaking land
36 "Believe" singer
37 Dog days phenomenon
38 Former California fort
39 Director Craven

Puzzle 24 by Louis Hildebrand

40 Aimless bit of gunfire
41 Quarrel noisily
42 Moon stages
43 Make bubbly
44 Big mouth
45 Aussie lassie
46 Lowly laborer
47 Rodeo wear
48 Slack-jawed one
52 Force on earth, briefly
53 MacDonald's partner in old movies
56 Bard's before

57 Inebriated
58 "2001" computer

ACROSS

1 Tail motions
5 Wheelchair-accessible route
9 Harvest
13 Needlecase
14 Braga from Brazil
15 "Cogito ___ sum"
16 Columnist Bombeck
17 Sweethearts of Sigma Chi
18 Losing effort?
19 Light modifiers
22 Utter
23 Big wine holder
24 Aussie hopper, for short
25 Goal
26 Leave earth?
31 Scarlett of Tara
34 Pharmacist's weight
35 "Get it?"
36 Temptations for spouses
40 Hawaiian wreath
41 "Put ___ on it!"
42 Some tests
43 Europe, Asia and Africa
46 Yea's opposite
47 Mich. neighbor
48 Brillo pad competitor
49 ___ Khan
52 Some thrown baseballs
57 Home run hitter Ruth
58 Surf sounds
59 "___ if you . . ." (bumper sticker)
60 Kiln
61 Feared eel
62 French friend
63 Dampens
64 Alteration canceler
65 Oboe, for one

DOWN

1 Grass chokers
2 Skylit lobbies
3 Like envelope seals
4 Thailand, once
5 Night stick?
6 All over again
7 Skirt that goes below the knee
8 Deli meat on rye
9 Extremely popular
10 New York's ___ Canal
11 Many moons
12 Flower holder
14 "Git!"
20 Perrier rival
21 Businesses: Abbr.
25 "Roses ___ red . . ."
26 Hair feature
27 Fat
28 Govt. watchdog
29 Touch
30 Own (up to)
31 Norway's capital
32 Shoe part
33 Gung-ho
34 Wooded valley
37 Rigging supports

Puzzle 25 by Gerald R. Ferguson

38 Words to a bride and groom
39 Have a bawl
44 Adds a lane to
45 Lonely number
46 Clamorous
48 Jack of nursery rhyme
49 "A House Is Not ___"
50 Wish granter
51 Invited
52 Goalie's action
53 "Oh, sure"
54 Cheer (for)
55 Stallion's mate
56 Blacken
57 Arrow shooter

ACROSS

1 Dogpatch cartoonist
5 Prefix with byte
9 Book after Hebrews
14 Away from the wind
15 "Oh dear!"
16 10% taker
17 Job enders
19 Dweebish
20 Christmas season
21 Singer DiFranco
23 Actor's prompt
24 Writer/director Nicholas
26 Tours within tours
29 G.P.'s grp.
30 Phaser setting
32 Go a-courting
33 Sound in the head
35 Concern of 41-Down: Abbr.
36 Stingless flier
39 Descending into ruin
43 Bruce of comedy
44 Singer Sumac
45 Chem. and bio.
46 Back on board
47 Kinks song of 1970
49 Newt
50 Malibu menaces
54 Some stereos
56 "Double Fantasy" musician
57 "What Kind of Fool ___?"
58 Auctioneer's "Sold!"
59 "Hit the road!"
61 Idaho city
66 Crème de la crème
67 Scotch partner
68 Martinique et Guadeloupe
69 Splinter groups
70 "That hurts!"
71 Clancy hero Jack

DOWN

1 Upper limit
2 Thrilla in Manila boxer
3 Small-time
4 Sri Lanka export
5 Shopaholic's heaven
6 Gin-maker Whitney
7 Clothing store, with "The"
8 Syrian president Bashar al-___
9 They have sweeping responsibilities
10 Secret stat, sometimes
11 French thanks
12 Eventually become
13 Eye sores
18 Sun. talks
22 F.D.R. program
24 Sitcom set in Korea
25 Messages via modem
26 Like anthems
27 Chic
28 Movable castles
31 Dickens boy
34 Old lab heaters
37 Bluenose
38 Instruct morally

Puzzle 26 by Nancy Salomon
and Harvey Estes

40 One way to go down
41 Managed care grps.
42 Boom producers
48 Beginning on
50 He took two tablets
51 "That's enough!"
52 Classical column style
53 Addlebrained
55 Studio sign
58 Bite like a beaver
60 A.B.A. member:
   Abbr.
62 Misery

63 Promising words
64 Grazing locale
65 Tax form datum:
   Abbr.

ACROSS

1 Scrounges (for)
6 Antlered animals
10 New Testament book
14 Move rapidly toward
15 Wordwise Webster
16 When doubled, quickly
17 ___ Sam
18 Dog in Oz
19 "___ Lee" (classic song)
20 Like some figures
22 Dad, slangily
24 Part of a process
25 Luau memento
26 Skater Babilonia
27 1986 sci-fi sequel
30 Fundamental
34 Free access
37 Third word in "America"
39 Pitcher's stat
40 See eye-to-eye?
44 Krazy ___
45 "Sprechen ___ Deutsch?"
46 Seas
47 Model's session
50 Like salmon, often
52 Certain retriever, briefly
54 Knock off, to a mobster
55 Statutes
59 Maine's ___ National Park

62 Stop signal
64 Buddy
65 Medical liquids
67 Playing marble
68 ___ Bora (Afghan region)
69 Numbered club
70 Part of an egg
71 Bridge
72 Train segments
73 Prepare, as tea

DOWN

1 Beetle larvae
2 Charge
3 "I give!"
4 Shea, for one
5 Footfall
6 Meat dish, often
7 Examine oneself
8 Kit ___ bar
9 "Darn!"
10 "Evangeline" setting
11 Fish scraps
12 When tripled, a W.W. II movie
13 Nine inches
21 Ones with green cards
23 Igor's place
28 Hawaii's ___ Day
29 You: Ger.
31 "Will be," to Doris Day
32 Unwrinkle
33 "Shake It Up" band, with "the"
34 Fraternal members

35 Man famous for doing a double take?
36 In ___ (entirely)
38 Had Marlboros, say
41 Notes after las
42 "Rocks"
43 Kind of district
48 Hemingway title character
49 Mai ___
51 "___ Eleven" (Sinatra film)
53 Microsoft's first product
56 Texas A&M player
57 Like a surrender flag
58 Very expensive
59 Does stage work
60 Cut of lamb
61 Radiant glow
63 Samuel ___, inventor of the stock ticker
66 Paleozoic, for one

ACROSS

1 High land
5 Brewers' needs
9 Red Cross supplies
13 Spoken
14 Got close to
16 With 37- and
   57-Across, a
   common warning
18 Taco holders
19 Sudden burst
20 Friend of Pooh
21 Six-pointers,
   for short
24 Cold war foe
25 Corn bread
28 Spy's device
31 Italian dramatist
   Pirandello
33 Prize that Pirandello
   won in 1934
34 Pitcher's asset
37 See 16-Across
40 Pilot's announcement,
   briefly
41 Haughty ones
42 Kind of blade
43 Cuff site
45 The Big Board: Abbr.
46 Choir member
49 WNW's opposite
50 Make stuff up
52 Bow parts
54 Present and future
57 See 16-Across
62 More than great
63 Covered
64 Sound of a leak

65 In ___ (existing)
66 Bowlers and boaters

DOWN

1 Swab
2 Memorable times
3 Obi
4 Mr. Hyde,
   to Dr. Jekyll
5 One of a pair of
   vanity plates
6 Not working
7 Favoring
8 "My dear man"
9 Take quickly
10 Ferber and others
11 Four-sided figs.
12 "Doe, ___ . . ."
14 Not on deck
15 Dash lengths
17 Arafat's grp.
21 What ignoring this
   puzzle's warning
   may mean
22 Knock down
23 Suffix with young
25 Ballet bend
26 Depose
27 Ship of 1492
29 Gold bars
30 Winglike
32 Guy Lombardo's
   "___ Lonely Trail"
34 A.B.A. member:
   Abbr.
35 Classic cars
36 A ___ child
38 Author Rice

39 Paragon
43 Easy outs
44 Unaccompanied part songs
46 At ___ for words
47 Upper levels
48 Soy foods
51 Elected ones
53 Sault ___ Marie
54 Align
55 Singer Fitzgerald
56 Urgent in the E.R.
58 French one
59 Hwys.

60 Goddess of the morning
61 1960's radical grp.

ACROSS

1 Decoration on an Indian moccasin
5 Sound of astonishment
9 Relative of a croc
14 Therefore
15 Long (for)
16 Blazing
17 "You said it!"
18 Tall tale teller
19 Like property for businesses
20 "Good Will Hunting" actress
23 Beneath
24 Ferdinand's queen
28 Shooter pellet
29 Compete (for)
32 Storage places
33 Theater district
35 Helps out
36 St. Paul's twin
39 Kindergartners learn them
41 Competed at Henley
42 Least healthy
45 6-0 or 7-6, in tennis
46 Opponent
49 Nylon and others, chemically speaking
51 180° reversal
53 Electronic development of the 1960's
56 Thread holder
59 Mafia boss
60 Latvian capital
61 The "L" of AWOL
62 Choir voice
63 Sorry failure
64 "Holy cow!"
65 For fear that
66 Transmitted

DOWN

1 Transport to the Enterprise, say
2 Luxury fur
3 "To do" list
4 "No man is an island" writer
5 Forceful wind
6 Citric ___
7 Puppeteer Lewis
8 U-boat features
9 Garden structure
10 Previously mentioned
11&12 Source of metal for cans
13 Scarlet
21 Rea ___, noted New Yorker cartoonist
22 Actor Kilmer
25 Oahu wreaths
26 Inc., abroad
27 Ninny
30 James Bond creator Fleming
31 Like house wiring
33 Double-crossing a Mafia boss, e.g.
34 Blacken
36 1250, in old Rome
37 Be indebted to

Puzzle 29 by Richard Chisholm

38 Abate
39 Nile biter
40 Life lines?
43 Writer Zola and others
44 Member of Cong.
46 Pointless
47 Salem's home
48 Transported
50 Climb
52 Home territories
54 Chooses
55 Not worth debating
56 Foxy
57 Rock and Roll Hall of Fame architect
58 Durable wood

ACROSS

1 Impertinent talk
5 Shopaholic's binge
10 Pond organism
14 Taxing trip
15 Popular golf event
16 Satiric Sahl
17 Comrade in arms
18 Shred
19 Frankenstein's assistant
20 Source of sudden wealth
22 Dracula portrayer, 1931
24 "___ a traveler from an antique land": "Ozymandias"
25 Source of sudden wealth
26 Exceed
29 Central American Indians
30 Green Gables girl
31 Peter, pumpkinwise
32 Watchdog's warning
35 Possible title for this puzzle
39 Hosp. sections
40 Itsy-bitsy biters
41 "___ Was a Rollin' Stone"
42 Lip-___ (fakes singing)
43 Made use of
45 Source of sudden wealth
48 Drops from the sky
49 Newsman Peter

50 Source of sudden wealth
54 Feline line
55 Wrinkle removers
57 "Mm-hmm"
58 ___ noire
59 Tropical fruit
60 It's the geologist's fault
61 Musher's transport
62 Incite
63 Young newts

DOWN

1 All-male
2 Folk singer Guthrie
3 Pitch
4 High jumper?
5 Relatively agile
6 Word processor command
7 Hitchcock film
8 Vichy water
9 One on the payroll
10 Guadalajara girlfriends
11 Access the Web
12 100th of a zloty
13 Skylit lobbies
21 Marseille Mrs.
23 Take a revolver from
25 Bubbling waters
26 Marvin of Motown
27 ___ about (roughly)
28 Burden
29 Damon and Lauer

Puzzle 30 by Nancy Salomon and Harvey Estes

31 Put on the books
32 Nibble away
33 Seized vehicle
34 "Saving Private ___"
36 Pharaoh's land
37 Lickety-split
38 "Shoot!"
42 Distorted
43 "Cheers" star
44 Purge
45 Doorway sides
46 Staggering
47 100 smackers

48 Fab Four drummer
50 "The World of Suzie ___" (1960 movie)
51 "Like, no way!"
52 Took a powder
53 Polite response to an invitation
56 Unprestigious paper

ACROSS

1 1692 witch trials setting
6 Alan of "Manhattan Murder Mystery"
10 Blues singer James
14 Run off together
15 Archaeological site
16 Claim on property
17 Dieting?
20 Lady of Spain
21 Haley who wrote "Roots"
22 Function
23 Distance runner
25 Made big cuts
27 Scottish cap
30 Siamese ___
31 Pal from Down Under
32 Utah city
34 Cry made while the reins are pulled
36 Silly
40 Going in a pit without a helmet?
43 Mecca resident
44 Allergic reaction
45 Florence's river
46 Many a Cecil B. DeMille film
48 It may have an extra electron
50 "Absolutely"
51 Leftovers
54 ___ Antoinette
56 Live
57 Misplace

59 Does figure eights, e.g.
63 Inn mergers?
66 "What's gotten ___ you?"
67 Wrapped up
68 Minimal
69 Superlative
70 "Like taking candy from a baby!"
71 Pompous ones

DOWN

1 Stitches
2 Wings: Lat.
3 Cut of meat
4 English racetrack site
5 Like grams and liters
6 Coach Parseghian
7 Moon-related
8 Obsolescent phone part
9 Actress Lansbury
10 "A Nightmare on ___ Street"
11 Traffic jam
12 Drawn tight
13 Chipped in
18 Neighbor of Zambia
19 Rare and wonderful
24 Like some humor
26 Five: Prefix
27 Male turkeys
28 Operatic song
29 Waiter's card
31 One of TV's Brady girls
33 Mythical sorceress

Puzzle 31 by James P. Sharp

35 Frequently, to Frost
37 Breezy
38 Zero
39 Slaughter of baseball
41 Miniwave
42 What Richard III offered "my kingdom" for
47 Tristan's love
49 Inventor Tesla
51 Sir, in India
52 Witch
53 Catches one's breath
54 Intends

55 Overhangs
58 Ancient portico
60 Afternoon socials
61 Scottish Gaelic
62 Concordes
64 Preschooler
65 Shift, tab or caps lock

ACROSS

1 Understand
6 Ill-gotten gains
10 One of the Three Bears
14 With 59-Down like some winds
15 Mimic
16 Shortstop Rodriguez
17 Invalidate
18 Beaujolais, e.g.
19 Swamp
20 Something followed on a screen
23 Sun or moon
26 64-Across and others: Abbr.
27 Blots out
28 Bet taker
30 Light snack
32 Astronomer Hubble
33 Jacques of "Mon Oncle"
34 Lazarus or Goldman
38 Something followed in a classic movie
41 Mediocre
42 Diner sign
43 Very angry
44 Violins and violas: Abbr.
45 Shoe part
46 French city on the Strait of Dover
50 Inc., in London
51 Boozer
52 Something followed at school
56 Medicine bottle
57 It goes across the board
58 Make into law
62 "Cómo ___?"
63 Dialing need
64 Whence the Ten Commandments
65 Dick Tracy's Trueheart
66 Try at roulette
67 It may follow a split

DOWN

1 Govt. property overseer
2 Accepted the nomination, say
3 ___ Darrow of "King Kong"
4 Not much of a pencil
5 Trigger, e.g.
6 Hocks
7 Michael Jackson's record label
8 Filmmaker Riefenstahl
9 Not just fast-paced
10 Deadly African snake
11 Son of Sam, e.g.
12 Blackbird
13 Skating jumps
21 Colorado native
22 College sr.'s test
23 Follows
24 Roping venue
25 Some championship games
29 Narc's find, maybe

Puzzle 32 by Sarah Keller

30 St. ___ (New York church, informally)
31 Inflammatory suffix
33 Aid to skiers
34 Goofs
35 Castle protectors
36 San ___, Calif.
37 Skilled
39 Divers' garb
40 Benevolence
44 "To ___ With Love"
45 Ice skater Midori
46 Spotted cat
47 Liqueur flavoring

48 Exams for would-be attys.
49 Book that readers think the world of
50 It's kept in a closet
53 Clip
54 Singer Tennille
55 Scissors sound
59 See 14-Across
60 Saturn or Mercury
61 Dead heat

ACROSS

1 Whittler's material
5 Church benches
9 Knuckleheads
14 "Say it isn't so!"
15 Yoked beasts
16 Arcade game maker
17 Denver, the ___ High City
18 Humdinger
19 French Impressionist
20 Comment from a parent of rowdy sons
23 Diplomacy
24 Feel sick
25 Regard highly
28 Commercials
30 "Baseball Tonight" channel
34 Studies frantically
35 Insomniac's need
37 Bunion's place
38 Be unrealistically optimistic
41 Night bird
42 Earnings
43 Exposed
44 Binary digits
46 "Whew!"
47 Simple and unpretentious
48 $20 bill dispenser
50 Tennis's Steffi
51 Mellow person's motto
58 Reef material
59 Company V.I.P.'s
60 Brain wave
61 Grammarian's concern
62 The "A" in Chester A. Arthur
63 Sharp's counterpart
64 County of Newark, N.J.
65 Kind of sax
66 Snaky swimmers

DOWN

1 Prebirth berth
2 Where the Reds and the Browns play
3 The "O" in ROM
4 Serves a sentence
5 Cry before "Open up!"
6 Rejoice
7 In good health
8 Give the cold shoulder
9 Disney deer
10 Peter of "My Favorite Year"
11 Kooky
12 Loads from lodes
13 Dog command
21 Poland's capital
22 Simplifies
25 Sound before "Gesundheit!"
26 Audibly overwhelm, with "out"
27 Syrup flavor
28 From another planet
29 Family rooms
31 Baby bird?

Puzzle 33 by Peter Gordon

32 John, Paul and John Paul
33 Impoverished
35 Long story
36 Small, fast U.S. Navy craft
39 Beta's follower
40 Radioactive decay measure
45 Barbaric
47 California city
49 Old-fashioned news transmitter
50 Be a bad winner

51 What red ink indicates
52 Accts. for old age
53 Final Four org.
54 Brand of computer
55 Inactive
56 Calves' meat
57 Stops fasting
58 Pool stick

ACROSS

1 Light bulb unit
5 Up and about
10 Gung-ho
14 Like a 911 call: Abbr.
15 Captain Nemo's creator
16 Playing with a full deck
17 Group of packers?
19 High school breakout
20 Tiny bit
21 Afrikaner
22 Heavy smoker's voice, maybe
23 Use for expensive wood
25 Summer show, often
27 Certain sports event
30 Not on the up and up?
33 They may be picked up in bars
36 ___ McAn shoes
38 Casals's instrument
39 Friend of François
40 Group of freezer repairers?
42 The Buckeyes, briefly
43 You use gray ones
45 Think (over)
46 Have the lead
47 Borrowed
49 Michelangelo masterpiece
51 Toys on strings
53 Closing number
57 Down with something

59 Hostilities ender
62 Newsman Newman
63 Buddies
64 Group of masseurs?
66 Fluish feeling
67 N.B.A.'s Shaquille
68 Nonsmoking ___
69 After-bath wear
70 Humor columnist Dave
71 Lady's man

DOWN

1 Modern news and entertainment source
2 Dean Martin's "That's ___"
3 George Bush, for one
4 Arm muscle
5 Student's stat.
6 Belgrade native
7 The Magi, e.g.
8 ___ circle
9 Wish undone
10 Usually
11 Group of airheads?
12 Rural retreats
13 Like a billionaire's pockets
18 ___-do-well
24 Some campus marchers: Abbr.
26 "Casablanca" cafe owner
28 Interrupter's word
29 Clean, as a spill
31 Designer Schiaparelli

Puzzle 34 by Bob Peoples and Nancy Salomon

32 Sullen
33 Crunchy munchie
34 End of grace
35 Group of male goats?
37 Timbuktu's land
40 "My word!"
41 Staff symbol
44 Visual survey
46 Bank fortifier
48 "Piece of cake!"
50 Seating section
52 Spa spot
54 With it

55 Some bedding
56 Conclude by
57 Practice punching
58 "Othello" villain
60 Smokey spotter
61 Way uphill
65 Noted cathedral town

ACROSS

1 Steals from
5 Inferior, as writing
11 1936 candidate Landon
14 Norway's capital
15 Certain apartment
16 Hair styling stuff
17 Robert Mitchum drama, 1958
19 "___ Got You Under My Skin"
20 "Beetle Bailey" character
21 Big I.R.S. mo.
22 Out of the wind
23 Home of Bert and Ernie
27 Educ. group
30 Mal de ___
31 Feather's partner
32 Seniors' org.
34 Golf targets
37 Michelangelo masterpiece
41 Billy Wilder film starring Gloria Swanson
44 Fulton's power
45 ___ mater
46 Buffalo's lake
47 Kind of service
49 Charlottesville sch.
51 Chaney of horror films
52 A trusting person may be led down it
58 Millions of years

59 Calif. airport
60 Lhasa's land
64 In the past
65 Source of many old pop songs
68 Baseball score
69 Eight-armed creatures
70 Frolic
71 Rocker Tommy
72 Pop maker
73 Brake part

DOWN

1 Goes bad
2 Dept. of Labor watchdog
3 Make less clear
4 The 40 in a "top 40"
5 Mao ___-tung
6 Karel Capek play
7 The "A" in James A. Garfield
8 Slippery ___
9 Citizen Kane's real-life model
10 Balance sheet abbr.
11 Spry
12 Embankment
13 Naval force
18 Consider
22 Get there
24 Small group of believers
25 Popular vacation isle
26 Cash register output
27 Quarterback's option
28 Drawn tight

Puzzle 35 by Holden Baker

29 "Rule Britannia" composer
33 Writings by David
35 D.C. type
36 Recapitulate
38 "Duke of ___" (1962 hit)
39 Wynken, Blynken and Nod, e.g.
40 Mideast's Gulf of ___
42 40-Down V.I.P.
43 Popular hand soap
48 Constabulary
50 Lead-in to girl

52 Oyster's prize
53 Scalawag
54 Hole ___ (golfer's dream)
55 "Ho ho ho" crier
56 Montreal team
57 "Rolling" things
61 Dull
62 Architect Saarinen
63 Toddler
65 Pull along
66 Gibbon, for one
67 Zippo

ACROSS

1 Lash of oaters
6 Buccaneers' home
11 Iranian city: Var.
14 Bowl
15 "Are you calling me ___?"
16 Actress Merkel
17 Very best
19 "___ bin ein Berliner"
20 Gas of the past
21 Gore's "___ My Party"
22 Lullaby rocker
24 Amigo of Fidel
26 More acute
27 Scores for Shaq
31 Pianist Nero
32 Renée's pal
33 Police offer
35 Scattered
38 Wash cycle
40 Detergent brand
41 Close-fitting hat
42 Journey for Kirk
43 Where 17- and 61- Across and 11- and 29-Down might be used
45 Olympics chant
46 "Shush!"
48 Consumer's bottom line
50 Academic AWOL's
52 Gloppy stuff
53 Friars' fetes
54 Wilder's "___ Town"
56 Location
60 Swabber's org.

61 Ceaselessly
64 A.F.L.'s partner
65 ___ Kid of early TV
66 Like helium, chemically
67 Barbie's beau
68 Heads overseas?
69 Job extras

DOWN

1 Lois of the Daily Planet
2 God of war
3 Sales force, for short
4 Use a key on
5 ___ Claire, Wis.
6 Ex-lax?
7 Word before fair or well
8 Cambridge univ.
9 More than thirsty
10 Noah's landfall
11 Fair exchange
12 Cry of surrender
13 Mr. Politically Incorrect
18 Pedro's lucky number?
23 Playground retort
25 "Take one!"
26 Wrist injury, maybe
27 Homer's boy
28 Mideast chief: Var.
29 Prerequisite
30 Gym garb
34 Tate collection
36 Hardly a he-man
37 Without ice

Puzzle 36 by John F. Hughes

39 Gull-like predators
41 Josip Broz ___
43 Makes no attempt to save
44 Actress Pola
47 Not damaged
49 Trig function
50 Teamster's transport
51 "Sweet" O'Grady of song
54 Long ago
55 Roswell sightings
57 Roman's way
58 Istanbul native

59 CPR pros
62 Believer's suffix
63 Quick drink

ACROSS

1 Maker of Space Invaders
6 Cut with scissors
10 Verdant
14 Batman's sidekick
15 "Voilà!"
16 Gazetteer datum
17 Punch in the mouth
20 Locale
21 Clean air org.
22 Lovers' secret meetings
23 "___ está usted?"
25 Roller coaster cry
26 Token punishment
32 Not tacit
33 Billy Joel's "Tell ___ About It"
34 Sgt., e.g.
35 Pooped out
36 Boeing 747, e.g.
37 The Jetsons' dog
39 Royal flush card
40 Cheerios grain
41 Bordeaux wine
42 Having drinks
46 They're exchanged at the altar
47 "So what ___ is new?"
48 Sitting room
51 Iceland's ocean: Abbr.
52 It's $24 on Marvin Gardens
56 Item for an armed detective, maybe
59 Chimney grime

60 Lake touching four states
61 French city, in song
62 Moppet
63 Caboose's spot
64 Dag Hammarskjöld, for one

DOWN

1 Clumsy boats
2 Singer Braxton
3 Border on
4 Low-calorie snack
5 Calligrapher's purchase
6 Walk over
7 Shuttle org.
8 Neighbor of Wyo.
9 Black cat
10 Perry Mason or Ally McBeal
11 "QB VII" author
12 Splinter group
13 Triumphant cries
18 Iced tea garnish
19 Didn't stand pat
24 Newspaper's ___ page
25 Sharpen
26 It might be put on the rack
27 "Two Women" star Sophia
28 Letter before iota
29 Preface
30 It has a groovy head
31 Choo-choo's sound
32 Pierce

Puzzle 37 by Peter Gordon

36 Fancy sports cars,
for short
37 "___ fair in love . . ."
38 Portable cutter
40 Not in stock yet
41 String quartet
instrument
43 Weaken with water
44 Screen favorite
45 Infernal
48 "Hey, you!"
49 Sailor's greeting
50 Piece next to a knight
51 Opera highlight

53 French 101 verb
54 Require
55 Orchard unit
57 Poetic preposition
58 Turntable turners,
briefly

ACROSS

1 Plays the ponies
5 Dads
10 Suitcase
14 Part of Hawaii
15 Make amends
16 Philosopher Descartes
17 Unleashes
19 Penny ___
20 What the neophyte jester didn't feel like?
22 Building addition
24 Bagel topper
25 Officeholders
26 Curtain holder
27 Fashion
30 Relative of a rabbit
32 Common term for strabismus
35 Bill
36 What the part-time abacus user didn't feel like?
40 Likely
41 And so forth
43 Relative of a rabbit
45 God of war
46 Tire filler
47 Hold up
48 German cathedral city
50 Castaway's place
52 What the queasy rodeo rider didn't feel like?
57 Savior, to Bach
58 "Family Affair" star of 1960's–70's TV
61 "Jeopardy!" host Trebek
62 Reached in a hurry
63 Rock band Better Than ___
64 Gardener's need
65 Thrown for ___
66 Pond duck

DOWN

1 Big Apple subway inits.
2 ___ de cologne
3 Puccini's last opera
4 Because
5 Magician's hiding spot
6 At the peak of
7 Gene group
8 Founder of Scholasticism
9 Take care of
10 Tennis's Steffi
11 "Le Moulin de la Galette" artist
12 Chant
13 Strips
18 White ___
21 Sigh with relief, say
22 Bow
23 Writer Ephron
27 Accomplishment
28 Popeye's Olive ___
29 Direct (to)
31 Touch
33 Get really wet
34 A twin city
35 Twitches

37 Dined
38 Not shrunk or enlarged
39 Tribe with palisaded villages
42 "Jeopardy!" host Fleming
43 Big citrus fruit
44 Sacred birds, to some
45 Unprincipled
47 Indian prince
49 The Balance
50 Opposite of "Yum!"

51 Trapshooter's target
53 Elegance
54 Boy, in Barcelona
55 Flying mammals
56 Spanish articles
59 ___-la-la
60 Shakespearean prince

ACROSS

1 Pilfer
6 Mars' counterpart
10 Waiflike
14 French wine valley
15 Expert
16 Texas city on the Brazos
17 Bearer of the heavens, in myth
18 Memo abbr.
19 Bullfight cheers
20 Craziness
23 Pigs' digs
24 French friend
25 Lowly abode
28 Stomach muscles, for short
29 Talk like th-th-this
33 Most-wanted invitees
35 "___ bin ein Berliner"
36 Rubik of Rubik's cube fame
37 No-goodnik
41 ___ a one
42 Observe
43 Any Time
44 Happy-go-lucky syllables
46 ___ Francisco
48 Men
49 Money for old age: Abbr.
50 South-of-the-border friend
52 Slight hoarseness
59 "I do" or "Drat!"
60 One way to settle a dispute
61 It's just over a foot
62 Sandpaper coating
63 And others: Abbr.
64 Alfred E. Neuman, for one
65 Back talk
66 Former mayor Giuliani
67 Sports figures

DOWN

1 Extra fat
2 Tiny bit
3 Cheerful tune
4 Vulgar
5 Say "um . . ."
6 Some marbles
7 Baseball's Babe and others
8 Old Harper's Bazaar designer
9 Lie on the beach, perhaps
10 Common soda bottle capacity
11 Football game division
12 Cake decorator
13 Prying
21 Penpoint
22 Earthbound bird
25 Lacks, briefly
26 Of an armbone
27 Princess' headwear
29 Coll. or univ.
30 Reduce to ruins

Puzzle 39 by Patrick Merrell

31 Result
32 Tournament of ___
34 Features of some bright rooms
35 Suffix with Israel
38 New York hockey player
39 Teachers' org.
40 Cotton fabrics
45 Jackie's second
46 Odoriferous
47 Spot in a river
50 Leading
51 "Ready ___ . . ."

52 Reasons for lighthouses
53 ___ avis
54 Singer Redding
55 Ballerina's dress
56 Gumbo ingredient
57 Tons
58 Column next to the ones

ACROSS

1 Purple bloomer
6 Hardly tanned
10 Vegan's no-no
14 Staffordshire stench
15 Factual
16 First name in scat
17 Dire early morning warning?
20 Sort
21 Ga. neighbor
22 Takes potshots
23 Used up
25 Cools down
26 Doll's cry
28 Big cheeses
32 Author Jong
34 Do damage to
35 To and ___
38 Joey's place?
42 "Lah-di-___!"
43 Kauai keepsakes
44 Pan-fry
45 Most fearless
48 Golfer's selection
49 Hood's blade
51 Snitches (on)
53 Orbital high point
55 Blood fluids
56 Jefferson Davis's org.
59 Buzz over New York City animals?
62 Powerful shark
63 Enlarge, as a hole
64 Spooky
65 Gaelic tongue
66 ___ a soul
67 Lively dances

DOWN

1 Centers of activity
2 Teen fave
3 Yale person?
4 Diving bird
5 Rugged box
6 "Right away!"
7 Long, long time
8 Little shaver
9 New wings
10 Army docs
11 Skip the big wedding
12 Balm additives
13 Highland hats
18 Fender blemish
19 Riddles
24 Nafta, for one
26 Pinochle combo
27 Diva's delivery
29 Part of a lunar cycle
30 Newsman Rather
31 Nonprofit's U.R.L. ending
33 Here, there and everywhere
35 Gettysburg Address opener
36 Old newspaper section
37 Foreboding
39 Fish caught in a pot
40 Tease
41 Alternative to air or highway

Puzzle 40 by Barry Callahan

45 Often-stubbed digit
46 Hot and humid
47 Status before statehood: Abbr.
49 Asparagus unit
50 Sounds of frustration
52 Los Angeles hoopster
53 Pinnacle
54 Make, as money
55 Debate (with)
57 Make dirty

58 Home of Iowa State
60 Pasture
61 Tappan ___ Bridge

ACROSS

1 Garage sale tag
5 The whole spectrum
9 Sea creatures with claws
14 Worker's ___ (insurance)
15 Catch rodeo-style
16 "Scheherazade" locale
17 Knight's protection
19 Quite sharp
20 Marisa of "What Women Want"
21 Bad firecracker
22 James Dean persona
23 Econ. yardstick
25 Letter distribution on base
27 "Close, but no cigar"
31 Mermaid's home
32 Phone the folks
34 Despot
38 ___ Khan
39 Sheetful of cookies
41 Twinings product
42 Italian cheese
45 Money for the house
48 Fellows
49 Certain spiders in "Spider-Man"
50 Linguistic borrowing
55 Moo ___ pork
56 Fouled up
57 "___ you sure?"
59 Ice house
63 Treat badly
64 Theme of this puzzle
66 "Hasta la ___, baby!"
67 NBC's peacock, e.g.
68 Sitting on one's hands
69 Gas additive
70 Smudge
71 Loch ___

DOWN

1 It's got your number: Abbr.
2 London shopping district
3 Muslim holy man
4 Big name in catalogs
5 Pitcher's pride
6 Warty hopper
7 Poppy product
8 Mrs. F. Scott Fitzgerald
9 Pride of country music
10 Indy entry
11 Island near Curaçao
12 Tropical nut
13 Whiff
18 Final inning, usually
24 Gratis, to a lawyer
26 Land bridge
27 Raleigh's state: Abbr.
28 Othello's undoer
29 Chowder morsel
30 Vocalist Sumac
33 Biblical verb ending
35 Plenty, and then some
36 In apple-pie order
37 Shades from the sun

Puzzle 41 by Nancy Salomon and Harvey Estes

40 See 65-Down
43 General pardon
44 F.D.R.'s plan
46 Code of conduct
47 Rowan & Martin's show
50 Sailor's shore time
51 Planet's path
52 In ___ (hurriedly)
53 R&B singer Lou
54 Start to wilt
58 It follows that

60 Put on board, as cargo
61 Lubricates
62 Small bills
65 With 40-Down, a modern company

ACROSS

1 High school outbreak?
5 Afternoon affairs
9 Witty Wilde
14 Person of action
15 Sitar master Shankar
16 Fern-to-be
17 Rapscallions
18 McCain's state: Abbr.
19 Spills the beans
20 Thomas Mann classic
23 Home of the Braves: Abbr.
24 Photo ___ (camera sessions)
25 See 48-Across
28 Bakes, as eggs
30 Place for pennies
32 Inc., abroad
33 Angry
35 Classic toothpaste
37 Halving
40 Partner of dined
41 Golfer's concern
42 Jiffy
43 "Gotcha!"
44 "ER" extras
48 With 25-Across, speaker of the quote hidden in 20-, 37- and 53-Across
51 Watch chain
52 Abba's "Mamma ___"
53 Nearby
57 Dunkable treat
59 Hamlet, e.g.
60 Old English letters
61 Grenoble's river
62 Astronaut Shepard
63 Newshawk's query
64 Passover supper
65 Tuna ___
66 Newbie

DOWN

1 Nike competitor
2 O'Neill title ender
3 Himalayan denizen
4 Start with while
5 Walked about
6 Brings in
7 Tel ___
8 XXL, e.g.
9 Old port on the Tiber
10 #, to a proofreader
11 Deli dish
12 Object of Indiana Jones's quest
13 In medias ___
21 Abominable
22 A.T.M. maker
26 ___ time (never)
27 Nutritional fig.
29 Tear apart
30 Coup d'état group
31 Seaweed, for one
34 Drop a line?
35 Spirits that victimize the sleeping
36 Wing: Prefix
37 Prie-___ (prayer bench)

Puzzle 42 by Paula Gamache

38 Not level
39 Like a lamb
40 Financial daily, initially
43 Bat wood
45 Shop with an anvil
46 Choice word
47 Refuses
49 Habituate
50 Out-and-out
51 Big test
54 Dutch cheese
55 Greece's ___ of Tempe

56 Adult eft
57 Speak ill of, in slang
58 Sugar suffix

ACROSS

1 Listened to
6 Nickname for a good ol' boy
11 Entrepreneur's deg.
14 "The Goat" playwright Edward
15 Zones
16 Seek office
17 Etiquette expert
19 Wager
20 They're not yet adults
21 Conductors' sticks
23 Head of a fleet
26 Colorful crested bird
27 Photocopier attachment
28 Rice dish
29 Part of a printing press
30 Least good
31 Actress Peeples
34 Solicits for payment
35 Organ features
36 10-percenters: Abbr.
37 W.W. II region: Abbr.
38 Eiffel Tower's home
39 Falling sound
40 Rabbit's home
42 Mississippi city where Elvis was born
43 Alcohol
45 Reveals secrets about
46 "I'm in a rush!"
47 Lessen
48 Suffix with schnozz
49 Language mangler

54 ___ and vinegar
55 Boner
56 Weeper of myth
57 Office seeker, for short
58 Raises, as children
59 Not on the perimeter

DOWN

1 Popular Easter dish
2 Inventor Whitney
3 Stomach muscles, briefly
4 Breathers
5 More reserved
6 Trite
7 Coffee vessels
8 "Busy" one
9 Free of pointed parts
10 Military offensive
11 Famous tap-dancer
12 ___ Vista Lake, Calif.
13 Anxious
18 On ___ with (equal to)
22 ___ Aviv
23 Parenthetical comment
24 Food with a hole in the middle
25 One with encyclopedic knowledge
26 Exposes
28 Stop by
30 Electrical lines
32 From Rome: Prefix

33 ___ Martin (auto)
35 Back section of seats
36 Dessert often served à la mode
38 More fastidious
39 Islamic chiefs
41 Bush spokesman Fleischer
42 Dabbling duck
43 Busybody
44 Old disease
45 Skiers' transports
47 Love god
50 Mex. lady.

51 Rubbish
52 ___-Wan Kenobi
53 Paper Mate product

ACROSS

1 Not that
5 Plods along
10 Take it easy
14 Open to inspection
16 Showy flower
17 Citrus fruit waste
18 Coal deposits?
19 Thieves' hangout
20 Employee's reward
21 Hippie's catchword
22 Intrinsically
23 Place for a cold one
24 Play time
27 N.L. or A.L. division
31 A criminal may go by it
32 Stomach filler
34 Log-burning time
35 D.E.A. operative
36 Theme of this puzzle
37 Ship lockup
38 Allergy consequence
39 Field of expertise
40 The "L" in 51-Down
41 Erne or tern
43 Radio talk show participant
44 L.B.J.'s successor
45 Tree knot
47 Throw out
50 April forecast
51 Santa ___, Calif.
54 Lena of "Havana"
55 Q-Tip, e.g.
57 Come down
58 Ruin a shot, in a way
59 Water swirl
60 Mexican bread
61 "Ah, me!"

DOWN

1 Walked (on)
2 Call to Fido
3 "Terrible" czar
4 Lust, for one
5 Takes an oath
6 ___ lazuli
7 More than heavy
8 Jubilation
9 French seasoning
10 Philadelphia tourist attraction
11 Pavarotti specialty
12 Brass component
13 North Carolina motto starter
15 Exit
21 Give a scathing review
22 Sweet drink
23 Hospital capacity
24 Indian royalty
25 Make jubilant
26 Around
27 Drink with fast food
28 Like Mayberry
29 Well's partner
30 Cubist Fernand
32 Explorer maker
33 Be beholden to
36 Country dance spot

40 Adam's apple's place
42 Dennis the Menace, e.g.
43 Rapids transit?
45 Microsoft honcho
46 Explosion maker
47 Shoe bottom
48 Decked out
49 Cheese coating
50 Wander
51 Mil. truant
52 Canaveral letters
53 Beame and Saperstein
55 ___ a plea
56 Baden-Baden or Évian

ACROSS

1 Eye amorously
5 No ifs, ___ or buts
9 Partners
14 Place for seagulls to sit
15 Not shallow
16 Oven emanation
17 "What ___ is new?"
18 Dance in a grass skirt
19 Neglected neighborhoods
20 Classic Salinger novel, with "The"
23 Poi root
24 Yang's complement
25 Favorite project
28 Make, as a guess
31 Land for a house
34 Without help
36 Tijuana gold
37 Celebration
38 Behave promiscuously
42 Erupt
43 Bemoan
44 Put back to zero, say
45 Electric fish
46 Goulash seasoning
49 Make an effort
50 1040 initials
51 Old-fashioned containers
53 Repeated lyric in a children's song
61 Clay brick
62 "Incredible" one
63 Follow orders
64 Neighbor of Earth
65 Comedic actress McClurg
66 Took a train, say
67 Beauty, brawn or brains
68 "I haven't a thing to ___!"
69 Egg holder

DOWN

1 Letters from the Persian Gulf?
2 Southwestern river
3 For fear that
4 Put up
5 Cling (to)
6 Brain cell
7 Supermarket part
8 C-___
9 #5 iron
10 "Over the Rainbow" composer Harold
11 Studio visit
12 TV honor
13 Enclosure with a MS.
21 Any port in a storm
22 Mountainous area of Austria
25 No longer in fashion
26 Secretly tie the knot
27 Dry (off)
29 ___ of London
30 Mentalist Geller
31 Opposite of most
32 Playful animal

Puzzle 45 by Gregory E. Paul

33 Cantankerous
35 This instant
37 Goliath, to David, e.g.
39 Use the backspace key
40 Break bread
41 Toped
46 Mass figure
47 Firenze's land
48 Field goal specialist
50 Fill (with)
52 Heap ___ upon
53 Coffee, slangily

54 Middle of March
55 Starts of workweeks: Abbr.
56 Not just swallow whole
57 Ill-mannered
58 Clarinet's kin
59 Cincinnati nine
60 Russian rejection

ACROSS

1 Underwater predator
5 Letters on a Soyuz rocket
9 October stones
14 Fermented honey drink
15 Bona fide
16 Running wild
17 Indigo dye source
18 School for a future ens.
19 NBC staple since 1/14/52
20 Either 38- or 53-Across
23 Privy to
24 Pizarro's prize
25 Clod buster
28 Priests' subordinates
31 Automobile sticker fig.
34 Boredom
36 Trucker's truck
37 Fly high
38 "The Last Supper" artist
42 Battering wind
43 Out ___ limb
44 Largish combo
45 In the style of
46 Tableland
49 Hosp. units
50 Iron man Ripken
51 Ten: Prefix
53 "The Divine Comedy" author
60 Canon competitor
61 Grease monkey's job
62 The "S" in CBS: Abbr.
63 Muse of poetry
64 Bruins' sch.
65 First name in jeans
66 Surrenders
67 Deportment
68 "Baseball Tonight" channel

DOWN

1 Barbra's "Funny Girl" co-star
2 Philosopher Descartes
3 Genesis son
4 He finished second to Ike
5 Friend of Friday
6 Big name in small planes
7 Scene of Jesus' first miracle
8 Blueprint
9 Many John Wayne films
10 TV teaser
11 Verdi heroine
12 It can generate a lot of interest
13 Porker's pad
21 Land of a billion
22 Line dance
25 Hägar's wife, in the comics
26 N.B.A.'s Shaquille
27 ___ Gay (plane)
29 Zagreb resident
30 Suffix with fact

Puzzle 46 by Matthew J. Koceich

31 Three-card hustle
32 Indiana hoopster
33 Dixie dish
35 Arles article
37 [not a typo]
39 Esther of "Good Times"
40 Heredity helix
41 ___ for (substantiate)
46 Feeling of pity
47 Unlike toadstools
48 Cyclades' sea
50 Big bill
52 Airplane seat option
53 Calamitous
54 Part of 18-Across: Abbr.
55 Reunion attendee
56 ___ Baines Johnson
57 Ogles
58 Invitation letters
59 "Put ___ writing"
60 Boom box button

ACROSS

1 Male voice
5 Destroy
9 Ralph ___ Emerson
14 Gem with a play of colors
15 Scores to shoot for
16 Love affair
17 Lawman of the Old West
19 Hindu queen
20 Home on the range
21 Old West cemetery
23 Off-road transport: Abbr.
25 Family girl, for short
26 Burn
30 Construction piece
33 Winter clock setting in S.F.
36 Grand lineup
37 Location of 21-Across
39 Weaver's apparatus
40 Durable fabric
41 Upon
42 Location of 51-Across
44 Explorer Sir Francis
45 Music with jazzlike riffs
46 Electric dart shooter
47 Twisty turns
48 ___ tai
49 Boo-hoo
51 Site of a famous gunfight
56 Squiggly marks
61 Not suitable
62 Legendary lawman of the Old West
64 Mow down
65 Art Deco artist
66 Poet Pound
67 Neighbor of a Finn
68 Nostradamus, reputedly
69 Take five

DOWN

1 Boxing match
2 Church alcove
3 Ditto
4 Smack
5 Discombobulate
6 "Count me out"
7 Lackluster
8 Capital once known as Christiania
9 1941–45, for the United States
10 Nanking nannies
11 Actress Anderson
12 Event done at 20 paces, maybe
13 Pitcher Hershiser
18 Word before "set, go!"
22 Missouri river
24 MTV features
26 Seasons, as steak
27 Petty thief
28 Wonderful smell
29 Suckling sheep
31 Shouldered
32 Trimming tools

Puzzle 47 by Sherry O. Blackard

33 Sandwich breads
34 Stir up, as a fire
35 Uses a Smith Corona
38 Mustang and Impala
40 Connector of floors
43 Scare suddenly
44 Amount to subtract
48 Bike that zips
50 Glossy brown fur
51 Fixes a squeak
52 Had a gut feeling
53 Bat's hangout
54 Amazes

55 Instrument for a Muse
57 Wanton look
58 Muddleheadedness
59 Flubs
60 Tiff
63 Gobbled up

ACROSS

1 Lady's shoe
5 Diamond measure
10 Prefix with legal
14 Phone button below the 7
15 Egg-shaped
16 Lighted sign
17 Delhi wrap
18 Information-gathering mission
19 Gin flavoring
20 Wall Street Journal beat
23 Many a legal holiday: Abbr.
24 Bill-blocking vote
25 Sapporo sash
28 Spoon-___
30 Part of a play
31 Call to Bo-peep
34 Macintosh and others
38 Deep sleep
39 Luau dish
40 Fly traps
41 Those not on the guest list
46 King: Lat.
47 Fire remnant
48 Stud site
49 Things that go together
50 To's reverse
51 Chest protector?
53 What 20-, 34- and 41-Across have in common
61 Photographed
62 Newsman Newman
63 One for the road
64 Keokuk's home
65 Chaucer pilgrim
66 Diver Louganis
67 Legally invalid
68 Not so crazy
69 What fellers need

DOWN

1 "Hey, you!"
2 D-Day beachhead
3 Filly's mother
4 Spectrum creator
5 Princess topper
6 ___ plaisir
7 Billiard hall item
8 Proton's place
9 Period of occupancy
10 Annoying, as a gnat
11 Wheel connector
12 Side-splitter
13 Polished off
21 Soy product
22 "Darn it!"
25 Come about
26 Wilderness Road blazer
27 Blend
29 Pool measure
30 In reserve
31 Sounds from R2-D2
32 Stroll along
33 Good thing
35 Zero-star review
36 Fish eggs
37 It's "company"
42 Diversify

Puzzle 48 by Nancy Kavanaugh

43 Certain similar chemical compounds
44 Burns, to Allen
45 ___ the Red
50 Of the unborn
52 Acts the blowhard
53 Biblical pronoun
54 Vigorous protest
55 Creative spark
56 Verdon of "Damn Yankees"
57 Honeycombed home
58 Atmosphere
59 Ragout or burgoo
60 Takes most of
61 Pride or lust

ACROSS

1 Instrument with a bow
6 Trucker with a handle
10 Like stallions and bulls
14 Heavenly hunter
15 Sharpen
16 Touched down
17 Two for breakfast?
20 Play ___ (do some tennis)
21 Deuce, in tennis
22 Baltimore player
23 Mink or sable
24 Not as dusty
25 Taiwan's capital
29 Stout drinks
30 Money in the bank, say
31 A ___ apple
32 Mailed
36 Two for dinner?
39 Ponies up
40 Summer coolers
41 Redhead's dye
42 "You said it!"
43 Diviner, of a sort
44 All-night studier
48 "Psst!"
49 What cable TV renders unnecessary
50 Bambi's mother, for one
51 Without cost
55 Two for dessert?
58 Isle of exile
59 Pro or con, in a debate
60 Dumbwaiter, essentially
61 Radiator sound
62 "Don't move!"
63 Actress Moorehead

DOWN

1 ___-Cola
2 Libido, in psychiatry
3 Vitality
4 Place for hay
5 Loved ___
6 Head of a meeting
7 Radius or rib
8 Finale
9 Aromatic
10 Craze
11 "March comes in like ___ . . ."
12 Fine thread
13 It'll knock you out
18 Needle case
19 War god
23 Crumbly white cheese
24 Ad biz awards
25 Push (down)
26 Away from port
27 Brit's exclamation
28 Beloved animals
29 Colorado town on the Roaring Fork River
31 Venomous snake
32 Fret
33 Almost forever
34 State bird of Hawaii
35 Peter I, II or III

37 How some shall remain
38 Chips ___! (cookies)
42 Asian nurse
43 Owner's proof
44 Sleeveless wraps
45 Spools
46 Riyadh residents
47 Flaky minerals
48 Sweetie pie
50 Bit of baby talk
51 Symbol of the WB network
52 Bit attachment

53 Relieve
54 Ambulance grp.
56 "Take a load off!"
57 When repeated, a Latin dance

ACROSS

1 Shoe blemish
6 Sean Connery, for one
10 Plod along
14 Trivial objection
15 Grandma
16 Like some tales or orders
17 Mountain ridge
18 Uzis and AK-47's
19 Columnist Bombeck
20 Barely wound Lee's men?
22 Affirm
23 Math course, briefly
24 Intertwine
26 ___ room (place for tots)
30 Van Gogh home
32 Skater's jump
33 Ricky player
35 Skylit lobbies
39 Elude capture
41 Primal therapy sounds
43 Beachhead of 1/22/44
44 Dance at a barn dance
46 Braun and Gabor
47 "Julius" in Gaius Julius Caesar
49 Join the navy, say
51 Major publicity
54 Weight not charged for
56 Airline to Ben-Gurion
57 Examine an Eastern European language?
63 Moreno of "West Side Story"
64 To laugh, to Lafayette
65 One-tenth payment
66 Oast
67 More than
68 Per ___ (yearly)
69 Bohr or Borge
70 Many a Bosnian
71 Lots and lots

DOWN

1 Heroin, slangily
2 Mystery writer John Dickson ___
3 Iris's place
4 Irish surname starter
5 Lamb's cover
6 Traffic problem
7 Venezuela's capital
8 "Gentle ___ Mind" (country classic)
9 Mortarboard attachment
10 Pilfer I-beams?
11 Caterpillar, e.g.
12 Ancient Mexican
13 Menacing look
21 Italy's largest lake
25 In the area
26 Sitar selection
27 Yoked pair
28 City on the Moselle
29 No-frills Cessna?
31 Greet the day
34 Brontë heroine

Puzzle 50 by Eugene W. Sard

36 26-Down player Shankar
37 "__ corny . . ."
38 Kind of prof.
40 Moth's temptation
42 Office worker
45 One on the way in
48 Computer shortcuts
50 Sweet stuff
51 Judean king
52 Three-time batting champ Tony
53 Like Cheerios
55 Sour-tasting

58 Busy place
59 Fan's publication, for short
60 Sicilian spouter
61 Ground-up bait
62 Clothes lines

ACROSS

1 West Point institution, for short
5 Made a gaffe
10 Bathroom powder
14 Enter
15 Exit
16 Is in arrears
17 Quick race
20 Sisters' daughters
21 It's connected to the left ventricle
22 Sportscaster Garagiola
24 Sault ___ Marie
25 Basketball hoop
27 Patriotic women's org.
28 Insurance company with a duck in its TV ads
30 Lament
32 Engine additive letters
33 Munchie in a brownie, perhaps
35 Doesn't wander
37 Rock band with the platinum album "The Downward Spiral"
41 Sleeping disorder
42 Kind of valve in a car
44 "Leaving ___ Vegas"
47 Commit to memory
49 Spacey of "American Beauty"
50 Granola morsel
51 Egyptian reptile
52 Praiseful poem
54 Big galoot
55 Eventual oak
57 Imaginary
59 1979 nuclear accident site
64 Pay attention to
65 Gift recipient
66 Onetime Atlanta arena
67 At loose ___
68 Oodles
69 Light blade

DOWN

1 "How revolting!"
2 Old French coin
3 Liza . . . with a Z
4 "Me, myself ___"
5 Put into power
6 Cash in
7 Suntanners catch them
8 Sister of Zsa Zsa
9 Architect Mies van ___ Rohe
10 Kind of list
11 Medals and trophies, e.g.
12 Vampire in Anne Rice novels
13 D flat's equivalent
18 Salvation for someone stranded in the Arctic, say
19 "Whatever Lola Wants" musical
22 Long feature of a crocodile
23 In the blink ___ eye

Puzzle 51 by Trip Payne

25 Book after Judges
26 Citizen of Tehran
29 Ballerina Pavlova
31 Recognition from "the Academy"
34 Food spearers
36 Location
38 ___ tide
39 Groovy light source
40 Gambol
43 Chemical suffix
44 Despise
45 German city near the Belgian border
46 In an attic
48 "Really, you don't have to"
53 Towels off
56 Dark wines
57 Bone by the humerus
58 Balm ingredient
60 Physicians, for short
61 Quadrennial games org.
62 SSW's reverse
63 Casino cube

ACROSS

1 Lines on a musical staff
6 Froth
10 Man trapper
14 Maui veranda
15 First name in scat
16 Needle holder
17 Muscle
18 Tibetan monk
19 Launch agcy.
20 Columnist for the lovelorn
23 Part of U.C.L.A.
24 Square-dancing call
25 Maximally
29 Strike callers
31 Shot out of a sand trap
32 Columnist for the lovelorn
38 Citadel student
40 Texas tea
41 Pago Pago's place
42 20-Across, to 32-Across
45 Rumor generator?
46 "Trick" joint, maybe
47 Brunch dish
49 Beverage that soothes a sore throat
53 "Be Prepared" org.
54 Entreaty to 20- or 32-Across
61 Popeye's tooter
62 High time?
63 Autumn drink
64 Ode or haiku
65 Shirt brand
66 Go ___ with
67 Addition column
68 Addition column
69 Trappers' wares

DOWN

1 Napoleon was banished to it
2 Dress
3 ___ B'rith
4 Deputy ___ (cartoon canine)
5 Important exams
6 Chops down
7 Norwegian saint
8 ___ mater
9 The Kettles
10 Morning Star
11 Video game pioneer
12 Pondered
13 Softly, on scores
21 Teeny bit
22 Petty officers
25 Depositor's holding: Abbr.
26 Spring occurrence
27 Longish skirt
28 Dentist's direction
29 Bring together
30 Fr. miss
33 Beak
34 Title for Agatha Christie
35 Actor Jannings
36 Something to play
37 Put (away)

39 Expressed disapproval
43 Irritated
44 Parks on a bus
48 Like the Marx Brothers
49 Hulking herbivore
50 Burger topper
51 Portable dwelling
52 Abounds
53 Gives a bit
55 Seep
56 It may be new or blue

57 Awful-tasting
58 Britney Spears, to teen girls
59 Euro part
60 Work units

ACROSS

1 North Pole assistant?
4 Military bases
9 Lowly workers
14 Misstatement
15 In the upper berth
16 Brightest star in a constellation
17 Holiday ___
18 Postal device
19 Scent
20 Star of 36-Across
23 Insurance company worker
24 What an actor waits for
25 Terrier or retriever
28 Deli sandwich
29 Trails
32 Titled lady
33 Use an 18-Across
35 Kind of position
36 Series set at 328 Chauncey Street in Brooklyn
41 Wise one
42 Computer shortcut
43 All over
44 Put up, as a building
46 Sharp flavor
50 Sun. speaker
51 Wrath
52 "I agree!"
53 Co-star of 36-Across
58 About 39 inches, in England
60 Multiflavor ice cream
61 Touch of frost
62 Letter opposite 16-Across
63 Conspicuous success
64 WNW's opposite
65 Mass transit vehicles
66 Spicy sauce
67 Wilmington's state: Abbr.

DOWN

1 Hebrew prophet
2 Amount of space in a newspaper
3 Foil user
4 Suggest
5 First word in a fairy tale
6 Male deer
7 Turnpike charge
8 Oration
9 Not in anymore
10 Tickle Me ___
11 When no games are scheduled
12 Flyers' and Rangers' org.
13 Mule of old song
21 Ability
22 Vienna's home: Abbr.
26 Sharif of "Doctor Zhivago"
27 Hair goops
29 Wrestling win
30 Six, say, for a first-grader
31 Herb in soups
32 Signified

Puzzle 53 by Allan E. Parrish

34 Long, long time
35 In favor of
36 Leader opposed by the Bolsheviks
37 Sharpen
38 Boosts
39 Bub
40 World Series mo.
44 "To ___ is human . . ."
45 ___ Pieces
47 Made good
48 In any way, in dialect
49 God's honest truth

51 Think tank output
52 Mediterranean land
54 Goad
55 Blue Triangle org.
56 Steelmaking site
57 Gay 90's and Roaring 20's
58 Mafia
59 Big bird

ACROSS
1 Lay to rest
6 Up to, informally
9 Zest
14 Riyadh resident
15 Prefix with cycle
16 According to
17 Black Panthers, e.g.
19 Like Valhalla's heroes
20 "A-Tisket, A-Tasket" singer
22 "___ a deal!"
23 Victor's booty
24 "We want ___!" (baseball fans' cry)
26 ___ Speedwagon
27 Piece of field artillery
31 Was ill with
34 Faint with beating heart
36 Place for a béret
37 Like the Tower of Pisa
39 Hardship
40 Stuck in Pamplona?
41 Pro ___
42 Old Ford flop
44 Draft dodgers' bane: Abbr.
45 This puzzle's theme
48 Fallen space station
50 Concerning, in memos
51 Nail-___ (tense situations)
54 Catch some rays
56 Rite of passage, for some
59 ___ Fountain

61 Pertaining to tautness
63 Black ink item
64 Bard's before
65 Barely managing, with "out"
66 They're sometimes stolen
67 Match part
68 Actress Zellweger

DOWN
1 Doctrine
2 Artless ones
3 Dutch bloomer
4 Perry White, e.g.
5 Most elegant
6 Counterparts to lyrics
7 Verb type: Abbr.
8 Actress Kudrow
9 Father of independent India
10 Hope's road show org.
11 Wine drinks
12 Dry run
13 Miners' finds
18 Luminous
21 Some post-graduate study
25 "Tell ___ the judge!"
27 Young toughs
28 Teller's stack
29 Vacation times in Verdun
30 Some M & M's
31 Mata ___

32 Rat-___
33 Blonde's quality, in jokes
35 Ran a tab
38 Croquet area
40 More showy
43 Broadcasts
46 Asteroids' paths
47 New Deal org.
49 Annul
51 Stanford-___ (I.Q. rater)
52 Arrested
53 Classic Ladd western

54 Attempt
55 Celestial bear
57 Numbered hwys.
58 Insignificant
60 Neckline shape
62 T-shirt size: Abbr.

ACROSS

1 Fraud
5 Yemeni or Qatari
9 Coffee lightener
14 Show bravery
15 Over hill and ___
16 Oscar-winning Berry
17 Coal waste
18 Stir up
19 French clerics
20 Symbol marking a composer's music?
23 Early form of bridge
24 Waikiki wreath
25 Leave
28 Crossword solving, for one
32 Make happy
33 Land of O'Kelly and O'Keeffe
35 Woman's hairstyle
36 Composer's popular works?
40 Choose
41 Emulated Pinocchio
42 Close, in poetry
43 Gets hot under the collar
46 Spirited
47 Publicize
48 Powell of the Bush White House
50 Like the dog days of summer, for a composer?
56 Brilliance
57 One of five Norwegian kings

58 Thoroughly
60 Portion
61 Cry of greed
62 Writing of Chaucer
63 Marine detector
64 Ages
65 Verve

DOWN

1 60's protest grp.
2 Baby elephant
3 Asia's ___ Sea
4 It can provide a big jolt
5 Skillful
6 What the monsoon season brings
7 Parcel out
8 "It's ___ real!"
9 Pursues
10 Cottontail
11 Exile isle for Napoleon
12 One of the Baldwins
13 Fit well together
21 Flung
22 African antelope
25 Show cars
26 Leave via ladder, maybe
27 Stickum
28 ___ Piper
29 "Peer Gynt" dramatist
30 Background sound in a store
31 Door
33 Oklahoma city
34 1 or 95: Abbr.

Puzzle 55 by Sheldon Benardo

37 Heads-up
38 10-Down fur
39 Deluge
44 Noted Las Vegas casino
45 Disorderly one
46 Toils (away)
48 Hue
49 John who wrote "Butterfield 8"
50 Hardy heroine
51 Cuatro + cuatro
52 Pearl Buck heroine
53 Volume

54 And others, for short
55 "Damn Yankees" seductress
59 Kind of Buddhism

ACROSS

1 "Whatcha ___?"
5 Madonna musical
10 "Yikes!"
14 Big name in oil
15 Assaults with a spray
16 "Adam ___" (Eliot novel)
17 Elvis Presley hit of 1956
20 Hippie
21 Without support
22 Like Coolidge's utterances
23 Letter adornment
25 Volcanic spew
27 Gist
29 Portly plus
32 Record player
34 Losing tic-tac-toe row
35 Pre-stereo
36 Stared at
37 Busy airport
38 Gluck's "___ ed Euridice"
39 Hanging on every word
40 Standard
41 Ralph Kramden, for one
42 Sturdy tree
43 Bluesman McClinton
45 Mos. and mos.
46 Workout venues
48 Purple ___, New Hampshire's state flower
50 Very, to Verdi
52 Reject, as a motion
55 Beatles hit of 1967
58 "The Little Mermaid" baddies
59 Pitchfork wielder
60 Diversion
61 Box that crackers go into?
62 Hair-raising
63 British P.M. before Macmillan

DOWN

1 Children's author Roald
2 Nabisco cookie
3 Four Tops hit of 1965
4 Scandinavian land, to natives
5 Mission
6 Fluctuates
7 Cake finisher
8 Kind of party
9 One way to get directions
10 Carlo Levi's "Christ Stopped at ___"
11 Rolling Stones hit of 1965
12 Yemeni port
13 Expunge, as text
18 Sewer line?
19 Fast runner
23 Stuck-up sort
24 Prefix with system
25 Really love
26 "Love Story" author

Puzzle 56 by Robert Malinow

28 Outlying community
30 Words after bend or lend
31 Cel mates?
33 Widebody, e.g.
35 ___ Smith's pies
37 Haarlem painter Frans
38 Start-up costs
40 Shooter pellet
41 Easily provoked
43 A fifth of MMMX
44 Medicine show purchase

47 Parson's estate
49 Actress Woodard
50 Impresses
51 Long Island Railroad stop
52 Opera persona
53 England's Great ___ River
54 Plump songbird
56 E.R. workers
57 "Hold on a ___"

ACROSS

1 Slice (off)
4 Indoor camera attachment
9 Rand McNally book
14 Gay 90's, e.g.
15 Spooky
16 One of the Allman Brothers
17 Prefix with puncture
18 Alfalfa's love in "The Little Rascals"
19 A-list group
20 "Freeze!"
22 Leader of reformers' 31-Down
24 Wet, weatherwise
26 Charged particle
27 Processes, as ore
29 Daily Hollywood publication
33 Signals goodbye
34 Sent a letter by phone
35 Playboy Mansion guy
37 The best three in a three-of-a-kind
38 Goofed
39 Concrete
40 One over a birdie
41 Use
42 Succinct
43 Using a blowtorch
45 Give
46 Fill one's stomach
47 Oscar winner Marisa
48 Leader of football's 31-Down

53 Dutch cheese
56 Stadium
57 Farsi speaker
59 Dolly the clone, e.g.
60 Nobleman
61 Snooped (around)
62 Operated
63 Skew
64 Wagner work
65 Pink Floyd co-founder Barrett

DOWN

1 Mrs. Rabin of Israel
2 Killer whale
3 Leader of pop music's 31-Down
4 Prime rate setter, with "the"
5 Gets smart
6 Ordered set
7 Pie-cooling spot
8 Mound
9 Throat tissue
10 The Green Wave, in college sports
11 With 54-Down, in reserve
12 Poker stake
13 Crystal ball user
21 Grimm works
23 Employed
25 "___ in his kiss" (1964 pop lyric)
27 Exchange
28 Parrot's cousin
29 Airline to Rio

Puzzle 57 by John Leavy

30 Skater's jump
31 1960's group (in three different ways)
32 Brewer's need
34 Drescher of "The Nanny"
36 Turn tail
38 Musical with the song "Buenos Aires"
39 Girl's name meaning "born again"
41 Not budging
42 Mr. Turkey

44 "Instant Karma" singer
45 One of Santa's reindeer
47 Needle
48 Needles
49 Like some medicines
50 Zeus' wife
51 The Flintstones' pet
52 Plummet
54 See 11-Down
55 Darn
58 It borders Wash.

ACROSS

1 Argentine plains
7 "Some of this, some of that" dish
11 School advisory grp.
14 Everlasting, old-style
15 The "C" in U.P.C.
16 Serving of corn
17 1925 musical featuring "Tea for Two"
19 Opposite of post-
20 Blue books?
21 Stereo forerunner
22 Number 2's
24 Make jubilant
26 Fish organ
27 Of one's surroundings
30 Hard to miss
33 1950's–60's guitar twanger Eddy
34 Get ___ (start work)
36 Ed of "Daniel Boone"
37 Like Shostakovich's Symphony No. 2
38 "I've Got the Music in Me" singer, 1974
41 Eggs
42 March Madness grp.
44 Stet's opposite
45 Quiz show host, often
47 Make a point, in a way
49 White knights
51 Les États-___
52 UFO occupant
53 Barber chair attachment
55 Sashes in "The Mikado"

56 Opera set along the Nile
60 Reaction to a back rub, maybe
61 Polynesian treat
64 Brooklyn campus, for short
65 Furies
66 Off course
67 Shade tree
68 Cloud ___
69 Insufficient

DOWN

1 They used to be lowered into wells
2 Nuclear energy source
3 Restaurant handout
4 Amino acid chain
5 Lee who founded the Shakers
6 Mariner
7 Part of an act
8 Oz visitor
9 Summer D.C. setting
10 Crop-destroying beetle
11 1937 Jean Gabin title role
12 Infield cover
13 Mars' counterpart
18 Like a road in a Frost poem
23 Charles Lamb's pen name
25 Soup ingredient
26 Golden ___
27 Tennis scores after deuce
28 Chew (on)

29 Liquor-flavored cake
30 Go askew
31 Emphatic refusal
32 Winter Palace residents
35 ". . . ___ the cows come home"
39 Bad time for Caesar
40 House overhang
43 The New Yorker cartoonist Peter
46 Original "Ocean's Eleven" star
48 1972 Ben Vereen musical

50 Bridal paths
52 Invective
53 Store sign
54 Follow
55 Store sign
57 "I'd consider ___ honor"
58 Collision memento
59 Like would-be bohemians
62 Mentalist Geller
63 Semicircle

ACROSS

1 Comical Laurel
5 All excited
9 Knights' ladies
14 Sexologist Shere
15 Sandy slope
16 "Remember the ___!"
17 Service status
18 Damon of "The Bourne Identity"
19 Disinfectant brand
20 Wind pointer
23 D.D.E.'s command in W.W. II
24 Some household heads
25 Not Rep. or Dem.
26 Myrna of "The Thin Man"
27 The hoop in hoops
28 Having good posture
30 Hissy fit
32 Meal in a shell
33 Quoits target
35 One ___ kind
36 Lay ___ the line
37 "Changing the subject . . ."
41 Raid rival
42 Pi follower
43 China's Sun ___- sen
44 Take a load off
45 Part of CNN
47 Flies alone
51 Leave dumbstruck
52 Confederate soldier
53 Lobbying grp.
55 Before, of yore

56 Ford or Lincoln
57 1972 Carly Simon hit
60 City near Syracuse
62 Stink to high heaven
63 Brain wave
64 Russian Revolution leader
65 Patiently wait
66 Dryer outlet
67 Rival of ancient Sparta
68 Winter blanket
69 Pay to play

DOWN

1 Missourian's demand
2 Musical ineptitude
3 "Relax, soldier!"
4 Shipshape
5 Product pitchers
6 Some football linemen
7 Airing
8 "Stop worrying about picayune stuff!"
9 Big name in Chicago politics
10 Prince ___ Khan
11 Grand Prix racer
12 :-) or :-(
13 Wise king of Israel
21 Woo in an unwelcome way
22 ___ public
29 Rooters' refrain
31 At all, in dialect

Puzzle 59 by Harvey Estes and Nancy Salomon

1	2	3	4		5	6	7	8		9	10	11	12	13
14					15					16				
17					18					19				
20				21					22			23		
24				25				26				27		
28			29			30	31				32			
			33		34		35				36			
	37	38				39				40				
41					42				43					
44					45			46		47		48	49	50
51				52				53	54			55		
56				57			58				59			
60			61			62					63			
64						65					66			
67						68					69			

32 Connect with
34 Island on the Java Sea
37 Free serving at a restaurant
38 A bull may wear one
39 Many a commuter's base
40 Explorer ___ da Gama
41 Storied vampire
46 Popular swimwear
48 Hard to lift

49 Show the ropes to
50 100-member group
52 "___ Hope" (former soap)
54 Cockeyed
58 Horse halter?
59 Cheer starter
61 A.F.L.'s partner

ACROSS

1 Couch
5 Fail to act
10 Host before Carson
14 Grad
15 Think the world of
16 Light brown
17 Sask. neighbor
18 ___ palm
19 Whiz kids
20 Hoot at confined hooters?
23 Bank statement amt.
24 Have a bite
25 Eventually
27 Explorer Johnson
30 Captain's hook
33 Send via Western Union
34 Hamlet, in "Hamlet"
36 Bill Gates, to some
38 Supplies, as assistance
41 Claim Confederate leader has varied taste?
44 Winetaster's criterion
45 1970 Kinks hit
46 Triumphant cry
47 Room at San Quentin
49 Part of a basilica
51 Auction buy
52 Villain in Exodus
55 Response to a preacher
57 Tennis judge's cry
58 Entice W.W. II agents?
64 Racer Luyendyk
66 It's a fact
67 Site of the Taj Mahal
68 ___ suit (baggy outfit)
69 First name in cosmetics
70 "___ Over Beethoven"
71 Oscar winner Paquin
72 Takes five
73 Not just a five-minute jaunt

DOWN

1 German industrial region
2 ___ podrida
3 Play around (with)
4 Dumbfound
5 "Mission: Impossible" assignment, maybe
6 Thought: Prefix
7 Screen pooch of 1939
8 Makes suds
9 Shortest light
10 Unimpressive brain size
11 Unplanned
12 Rock concert venue
13 Out of practice
21 End of a two-part move
22 Request before a click
26 Build
27 Shamu, for one
28 Rise quickly
29 Divvying-up process

Puzzle 60 by Randall J. Hartman

31 Natural gas, for one
32 Common refrigerant
35 "___ Gantry"
37 Pac-10 team, for short
39 "Thank You" singer, 2001
40 Leave in a hurry
42 Steven Bochco series
43 Doesn't skimp with
48 Window smasher, maybe
50 Actors Begley and Begley Jr.

52 Public square
53 "Great white" bird
54 Preakness entrant
56 It's eye-grabbing
59 On the ___ (bickering)
60 Let stand, in editorial parlance
61 Aviation pioneer Sikorsky
62 ___ Stanley Gardner
63 Polio vaccine developer
65 LAX info

ACROSS

1 Old-time oath
5 Threaded fastener
10 Went out, as a fire
14 Auntie of Broadway
15 Fight site
16 Memo starter
17 Elvis's middle name
18 First line of a nursery rhyme
20 Creative guy
22 Make a goof
23 Matt of "Friends"
24 Delivery room doctors, for short
25 Hwy.
27 Symbol of slowness
28 Submarine sandwich
30 Colorado ski resort
31 Brother of Cain
33 Sign after Taurus
35 1961 Sinatra album
39 Divulge
40 He played Ricky on 50's TV
41 Took too much of a drug, briefly
42 Copycat
44 Japanese restaurant fare
49 "No ___" (Chinese menu phrase)
50 601, in old Rome
51 Place to play jai alai
53 Pamper
55 J. P. Morgan and others
56 Knocking sound
58 Cube inventor Rubik
59 Phoenix's state: Abbr.
60 Lab containers
61 Slippery part of a banana
62 Tennis great Sampras
63 White, to Latinos
64 Canvas bag

DOWN

1 Sends a message by computer
2 Madison Square ___
3 One-celled protozoan
4 National park in Alaska
5 Brand of wrap
6 Chewed noisily
7 Soldier in Dixie
8 Fill with love
9 All-Star third baseman, 1985–96
10 Have ___ on (claim)
11 Five-time Tour de France winner Miguel
12 Ejecting lava
13 Cotillion girl
19 Battleship letters
21 Spanish province or its wine
26 Yale player
29 Omit in pronunciation
30 Rival school of The Citadel: Abbr.
32 Skier's headgear

34 The Wizard of Menlo Park
35 Old anti-Communist reaction
36 "Eureka!"
37 Actor Beatty
38 Spongelike toy
39 CD-___
43 Frisbee's inspiration, supposedly
45 Given away
46 Not mono
47 Big stinger
48 Shoe part

50 Banned insecticide
52 "Midnight Cowboy" character
54 Stupefy
56 Run-D.M.C.'s music
57 "You're it!" game

ACROSS

1 Nile slitherers
5 Masked critter
9 Expecting, as a raise
14 Opportunity, so to speak
15 Dagger handle
16 Monica of the courts
17 1999 Meryl Streep movie
20 "___ not fair!"
21 Gardener's need
22 Craving
23 Master's requirement, often
25 Met or Card, for short
27 Gateway Arch city: Abbr.
30 Midleg
32 Viands
34 Negative vote
36 Foolhardy
38 Interminably
39 Ayn Rand book
42 Out-and-out
43 Accordingly
44 Gives the nod
45 Ethel Waters classic
47 Fall shade
49 Twitch
50 Shows one's human side
52 Things with ___ (theme of this puzzle)
56 Yiddish plaints
57 Bread spread
59 Matterhorn, e.g.

60 1988 John Cleese movie, with "A"
65 Action spot
66 Easily molded
67 Bumped off
68 Fortuneteller's card
69 Golden rule word
70 Nothing more than

DOWN

1 Own up to
2 Pole position?
3 Group that's rounded up
4 ___ Lanka
5 Picky people?
6 Meatheads
7 "Come here ___?"
8 Extreme
9 Leading down the aisle
10 Hammer part
11 It has many keys: Abbr.
12 Anthem preposition
13 Queue after Q
18 Goatee site
19 Gave the once-over
24 First U.S. space station
26 McNeil's longtime news partner
27 Built for speed
28 Looks after
29 60's turn-on
31 Egg roll time
33 Colombia's capital
34 One of the Judds

Puzzle 62 by Sherry O. Blackard

35 Storage spot
37 "Quiet, please!"
40 Back street prowler
41 Not familiar with
42 Make lace
46 ___ Minor
48 Flat-bottomed boat
51 Wise lawgiver
53 Cyclist Armstrong
54 Respected one
55 Gardener's need
56 "It can't be!"
58 Took off
60 "___ chance!"

61 Lyrical Gershwin
62 Sun. talk
63 Baton Rouge sch.
64 Prepare to shoot

ACROSS

1 Panorama
6 "I dare you!"
10 Meal-in-bed supporter
14 ___ and aahed
15 Upper hand
16 Hearty's companion
17 With 61-Across, a fictional pair who are hard to tell apart
19 Jane Austen heroine
20 Toward sunrise
21 Res ___ loquitur (legal phrase)
22 Face-valued, as stocks
23 Scurries
25 El ___ (Pacific phenomenon)
27 Family pair who are hard to tell apart
33 56-Across + 56-Across
34 For takeout
35 Enamored of
36 Writer Wharton
38 "___ about that?!"
40 Hertz competitor
41 Satellite TV receivers
43 ___ is to say
45 Court subject
46 Routine that's hard to tell apart from past routines
49 "It's c-c-c-cold!"
50 Minipie
51 Laugh-filled
54 Prefix with potent

56 Fair share, maybe
60 Song for a diva
61 See 17-Across
63 Dovetail
64 Powerful auto engine
65 Remove from the blackboard
66 Feathery scarves
67 Shipped
68 So far

DOWN

1 November catchword
2 Dubuque's state
3 The Rolling Stones' "___ a Rainbow"
4 Prepare to bite?
5 Say further
6 Sound that's heaved
7 Bookie's quote
8 Big lizard
9 Chairman pro ___
10 What a loser may throw in
11 Interstate entrance/exit
12 ___ mater
13 1776 or 1945
18 Deceive
22 Aardvark
24 On paper
26 Sort
27 Place for a sacred cow
28 Godly belief
29 Codgers
30 Counting everything
31 Wanderer

Puzzle 63 by Manny Nosowsky

32 Frequent Arctic forecast
33 British refs.
37 Malaise
39 "And then . . . ?"
42 Popular camera type, for short
44 ". . . the way of a man with ___": Proverbs
47 Be half asleep
48 Not these or those
51 Window's support
52 Creme cookie

53 Actress Bonet
55 Lo ___ (noodle dish)
57 24 hours ___
58 ___-majesté
59 Centipede's multitude
61 Show showers
62 Pasture

ACROSS

1. Breathless state?
6. Bach's "Mass __ Minor"
9. 1930's French P.M. Léon
13. Dixie talk
14. __-Day vitamins
15. Ambience
16. Record company
17. "Sense and Sensibility" actor, 1995
19. Altar vow
20. Works of Homer
22. Stimulate
23. 1960's–70's pop singer/actor
26. __ Wednesday
27. Dig in
28. Codebreakers' org.
31. Hectic episodes
34. Play starter
37. Most suitable
39. End of 17-, 23-, 50- or 61-Across
42. Severe lawgiver of Athens
43. Gave temporarily
44. Sticks up
45. Disney collector's item
46. Encyclopedia unit: Abbr.
48. Ground breaker
50. Rainbow Coalition founder
56. Signal enhancer
59. Confined, with "up"
60. "__ luck?"
61. "To Kill a Mockingbird" novelist
63. Welcome one's guests, maybe
65. Korea's home
66. Ogler
67. Family girl
68. In that case
69. Word of accord
70. English county bordering London

DOWN

1. Go off script
2. Madrid museum
3. Mover and shaker
4. Lamb ma'am
5. Back streets
6. Occupied
7. Photo envelope enclosure, for short
8. Grand __ (island near Florida)
9. Title for Münchhausen
10. Oahu wingding
11. Coffee holders
12. Chess ending
14. Cry of eagerness
18. Au __ (how some potatoes are served)
21. "No way!"
24. Fundamental
25. Monarch's rule
28. Claudius I's successor
29. Swedish car

Puzzle 64 by Ethan Cooper and Michael Shteyman

30 "___ Well That Ends Well"
31 Like some electric appliances
32 Potentially disastrous
33 Egg shape
35 Refs' decisions
36 Amount past due?
38 Shortstop Jeter
40 1956 Elvis hit
41 Filmmaker Coen
47 Fish hawk
49 Gas pump number

50 Sumo land
51 Blunt blades
52 Scoff (at)
53 "For goodness ___!"
54 In reserve
55 One of the original Baby Bells
56 First-rate, slangily
57 Skin problem
58 Cleveland's lake
62 Soapmaking need
64 Family girl

ACROSS

1 Signs of healing
6 File folder parts
10 ___ of Capri
14 Apportion
15 Airline that serves only kosher food
16 Financial aid criterion
17 "Oh boy!"
18 Writer Ephron
19 Lotion ingredient
20 One whose name can be followed by "Esq.": Abbr.
21 Good-looking guy
23 Ho-hum
25 Sis's sib
26 W.W. II prison camp
29 China's most populous city
34 They replaced francs, marks and pesetas
35 Goatee's place
36 Hostel
37 Casual clothing item
41 Flow back
42 Business phone button
43 Nostalgic song
44 Big game on January 1
47 Portray
48 Pop's partner
49 Unwakable state
50 Easy-park shopping places
55 Dressed
59 Neighbor of Afghanistan
60 Egyptian queen, for short
61 Aunt's little girl
62 Vito Corleone's creator
63 Yard sale tag
64 Silly
65 Crystal ball gazer
66 Carrot on a snowman, perhaps
67 Card game that's a hint to today's theme

DOWN

1 It's a long story
2 Coagulate
3 Plenty
4 Big hit?
5 Pork place?
6 Final frame for a bowler
7 Baseball's Moises
8 The ___ of Avon
9 Fast-paced, slangily
10 Dazed and confused
11 Prefix with defense and destruct
12 Fifth-century pope who was sainted
13 Adam's apple location?
21 Droop
22 Ornamental vase
24 Young woman
26 Passover meal
27 Sports car engine
28 Saudis, e.g.

29 Three-card monte assistant
30 Rear
31 Language in New Delhi
32 Prank
33 Atlas enlargement
35 Cornfield bird
38 Prominent shoe seller
39 Limerick, e.g.
40 "Scent of a Woman" star
45 Key of Tchaikovsky's Symphony No. 5

46 Fast-tempo jazz
47 Whoop-de-___ (big parties)
49 Tight-knit
50 Has a taste of, as wine
51 Test choice
52 Tear down
53 To boot
54 Luau necklaces
56 Plumbing problem
57 Pockmark cause
58 Bucks and does
61 Small bite

ACROSS
1 Sheep's cry
6 On __ (like some jobs)
10 Subject of a Sophocles tragedy
14 Video's counterpart
15 Waterfront sight
16 Standard
17 Amorous entanglement
20 Discipline that uses koans
21 Send out
22 Member of a secret order
23 Eye opening for a squint
24 Sic a lawyer on
26 Annoyance for dwellers near airports
33 Bond's "Casino Royale" foe
34 Randomizer
35 Govt. initiative
36 Subsists (on)
37 Person with a chest pad
38 String section member
39 Possible solution
40 "Just __ thought!"
41 Acted badly
42 Clothing label designation
45 Hertz offering
46 "Of all the luck!"
47 Posthumous donation
51 Actress Pitts of old films
52 Greetings

55 Mechanical impossibility
59 Nobelist Wiesel
60 Fairy tale opener
61 With 40-Down, seat of Orange County, Calif.
62 Wildcat
63 Jab
64 Readily available

DOWN
1 Singer/activist Joan
2 Renaissance instrument
3 TV genie portrayer
4 Put on TV
5 Without inflection or feeling
6 Cheerleaders' finale, often
7 British P.M. under George III
8 Always with an apostrophe
9 Dernier __
10 Ballet Russe star Pavlova
11 Helps, as a memory
12 Singer Guthrie
13 Marvel Comics group
18 Simple folk
19 "I agree completely!"
23 1996 horror film with sequels
24 Barbershop sound
25 Colorado native
26 Ammonia derivative
27 "Well, I __!"
28 Campus offices: Abbr.

Puzzle 66 by Robert Malinow

29 Thinks out loud
30 Fireplace tools
31 Treaded surfaces
32 "Good heavens!"
33 Boo-boo
37 Exploitative type
38 Musical artiste
40 See 61-Across
41 Fleeting muscle problem
43 Clearasil target
44 Irish port near Killarney
47 German automaker
48 Bank (on)

49 Alfred E. Neuman expression
50 Summit
51 "An Officer and a Gentleman" hero
52 Aid to the stumped
53 Smidgen
54 Say sharply
56 Blouse, e.g.
57 Game with "Draw Two" cards
58 Beachgoer's goal

ACROSS

1 Instruments at luaus
5 Island of Napoleon's exile
9 Was in the movies
14 Man with an ark
15 Harvest
16 Stage between egg and pupa
17 "Arsenic and Old Lace" star, 1944
19 Airedale, e.g., for dogs
20 Totally
21 Scottish miss
22 Electricians, at times
23 Creditor's demand
25 Numerous
26 Colony member
27 Japanese farewell
31 Demanding
34 Knee/ankle connector
35 Trojan War hero
36 Vehicle that's hailed
37 Astound
38 Capture
39 Song for a diva
40 Capitol feature
41 Ready to hit the sack
42 Shower accessories
44 Copacabana city
45 Manage
46 Gatherings where people hold hands
50 Horrified
53 Foreboding
54 Actress Gardner
55 Emergency light
56 "Liar Liar" star
58 Life of ___
59 Fix, as copy
60 Tricks
61 Follows the leader
62 One giving orders
63 Voice above bass

DOWN

1 Open, as a bottle
2 Eucalyptus eater
3 Like the bird that catches the worm
4 Timid
5 Straying
6 Minimum
7 Outlaws
8 Fitting
9 Lacking pigment
10 Noted anti-alcohol crusader
11 Elder or alder
12 "As ___" (letter closing)
13 June honorees
18 Shuttle-riding senator
22 Oscar winner for "True Grit"
24 Top-selling vocalist of the 1990's
25 Corn
27 Phonies
28 A bit cracked?
29 Tool with teeth
30 Fired
31 Attempt
32 Skater Lipinski
33 Departure

34 Struck hard
37 Change according to circumstances
41 Crownlike headgear
43 Ambles
44 Does a double take, e.g.
46 Round after the quarters
47 "Deck the Halls," e.g.
48 Episode
49 Authority
50 Bushy do
51 Smooth-talking
52 Robust
53 Pal of Spot
56 One of the Bushes
57 Big TV maker

ACROSS

1 Bit of street art
6 Taken wing
11 Toast topping
14 Japanese automaker
15 Part of a TV transmission
16 Have ___ at
17 Character actor in the Cowboy Hall of Fame
19 Modern: Prefix
20 Mandlikova of tennis
21 A.A.A. suggestion: Abbr.
22 Redecorate
24 Actress Long or Peeples
26 Jelly fruit
27 After-hours pool use, maybe
32 "Phooey!"
33 Regal headdresses
34 Social misfit
36 Pentium maker
38 Fivescore yrs.
39 Enter, as data
40 No longer working: Abbr.
41 Singer Twain
43 Number cruncher, for short
44 Boo-boo
47 Cultural values
48 Big inits. on the Net
49 Like a habanero pepper
51 Nabokov novel

53 Agenda, for short
57 Dory need
58 Panhandler's request
61 Joanne of "Abie's Irish Rose"
62 Guys' prom attire, informally
63 Continental divide?
64 Shade tree
65 Minute ___ (thin cut)
66 Down and out

DOWN

1 Moonshiner's mixture
2 Bruins' sch.
3 Totally trash
4 Cardin rival
5 Pool distance
6 It's the truth
7 Gospel writer
8 Poetic homage
9 They start pitches
10 "Uh-uh!"
11 15th-century Flemish painter
12 Pulitzer winner James
13 Drop anchor
18 Farsi speaker
23 Like Dolly the clone
25 Part of IHOP: Abbr.
26 Designer Versace
27 Trig figures
28 Orchestra percussion
29 Pleasure craft
30 Most of "The Wizard of Oz"
31 Be crabby
32 Cone bearer

Puzzle 68 by Bob Peoples

35 Kind of "fingerprint"
37 Designer Head
39 Green Hornet's sidekick
41 Decathlon event
42 Stern or Hayes
45 Halloween characters
46 ___-Lorraine
49 Took a tram, e.g.
50 James ___ Carter
51 Square mileage
52 Place to work
54 "Trick" joint
55 Dated expletive
56 Refuse
59 Woodcutter's tool
60 Snookums

ACROSS

1 Furrowed part of the head
5 Cougars
10 Door fastener
14 "The ___ Ranger"
15 Basketball Hall-of-Famer Thomas
16 Hitch, as oxen
17 Start of a free call
20 "___, humbug!"
21 Hair removal brand
22 Not stand steadily
23 New York's ___ Place
25 Letter before omega
26 From ___ Z
27 Switzerland's Zug or Zurich
29 Hammer and mallet
31 Conclude by
32 "To thine own ___ be true"
33 Pepsi rival
37 1943 Mary Martin musical
40 Marquis de ___
41 Turndowns
42 Like some gases
43 Move crabwise
45 Shrewd
46 "Mamma ___!"
49 El ___ (Spanish hero)
50 Not stale, as chips
51 "O Canada," e.g.
53 Dear one, in Italy
54 Split ___ with ham
57 Some gamblers' weaknesses

60 Like books
61 A Brontë sister
62 Burden
63 "My Friend" of old radio
64 Pacifists
65 Opposed to, in "Li'l Abner"

DOWN

1 1950's horror film creature, with "the"
2 Writer Jaffe
3 Like some baseball catches
4 Tiny
5 Easy mark, slangily
6 Theater worker
7 Baseball glove
8 "How nice!"
9 Stops, as electricity
10 Jekyll's counterpart
11 Cardiologist's concern
12 ___ shooting
13 California's San ___ Bay
18 Completely
19 Astronaut Armstrong
24 Roll call at a political convention
25 Some casual shirts
27 Corporate honchos, for short
28 The "I" of "The King and I"
29 Giggle
30 Perfumes
32 Bawl out

Puzzle 69 by Charles E. Gersch

34 Getting ahead of
35 Composer Weill
36 Villa d'___
38 Strong as always
39 Optometrist's concern
44 Bakery worker
45 Layouts
46 New Zealand native
47 Kind of tube or ear
48 1980's George Peppard series, with "The"
50 The "C" of CNN
52 "Mary ___ little lamb"

53 404, in old Rome
55 Carrier for needles and pins
56 Org.
58 Comedian Philips
59 ___ double take

ACROSS

1 Deck out
6 Sign of stitches
10 Found's partner
14 Donnybrook
15 Use a whetstone on
16 Aware of
17 Strips away
18 Composer Franz-Joseph's favorite 58-Across?
20 Clean-shaven
22 Ore deposit
23 Golf ball prop
24 "Woe is me!"
26 Nursling
28 Enough for former hurler Dwight?
32 Order before "Fire!"
33 Withered
34 From which gold is spun, in a fairy tale
38 Smooth-talking
40 Church council
43 Per
44 Late bloomer
46 ___-engine
48 "___ Loves You"
49 Actor Liam's younger kin?
53 Southwestern saloon
56 Bar order, with "the"
57 Champ who could "sting like a bee"
58 Go fish, e.g.
60 Sheepdog, by training
64 Presidential shaving goofs?
67 Spaghetti strainer
68 "___ plaisir"
69 Campsite sight
70 Florida keys, e.g.
71 For fear that
72 Do in
73 Stuffed item?

DOWN

1 Roadie's load
2 Judge
3 Toast topper
4 Put in fresh film
5 Snuggles down
6 Librarian's admonition
7 Kentucky resource
8 "___ home?"
9 Begin to blush
10 ___ Alamos
11 "___ a customer"
12 Beef on the hoof
13 Arcade coin
19 Efts grown up
21 Briefs brand
25 Peppy
27 Memory unit
28 Totally smitten
29 Softens, as leather
30 Pass over
31 Slowly, on a score
35 Allergy indication
36 Yearn
37 "That was close!"
39 Like the wire in a croquet wicket
41 Holds the deed to

Puzzle 70 by Denise M. Neuendorf

42 Washington who sang the blues
45 Wear the crown
47 Unbeatable foe
50 Puts on the books
51 Patriot Adams
52 Meet an untimely fate
53 Gondola's place
54 Still in play
55 Puts the kibosh on
59 Sicilian smoker
61 Sub shop
62 At any time

63 Take five
65 Fall mo.
66 Slop spot

ACROSS

1 "Peanuts" boy
6 Lady's man
10 Fizzling-out sound
14 Make amends (for)
15 Taj Mahal site
16 Title role for Peter Fonda
17 Tunneling tusker?
19 Sinn ___ (Irish organization)
20 Brown in the kitchen
21 Hurt or irritate
23 Suzanne of "Three's Company"
26 Sultry Hayworth
28 The "I" of T.G.I.F.
29 Fruity coolers
30 Central street
32 Brown on the beach
34 Basketball's Alcindor
35 Florida home of Busch Gardens
36 Not weighing much
39 Mauna Loa, e.g.
41 Bought
43 Bad breath cause, maybe
44 Exhaust
46 Prevaricate
47 Holiday quaff
48 New Jersey hoopsters
49 Clutter
50 Musician's date
52 Better ___ than never
54 Goodies
56 Playful child
58 Cook, as clams
60 Needle case
61 Grizzly doing a striptease?
66 Powder ingredient
67 Writing on the wall
68 Spine-tingling
69 Sailing
70 Amusement park lure
71 Small drinks of liquor

DOWN

1 Chem class
2 "How was ___ know?"
3 Common conjunction
4 Joins forces
5 One who may hear "Si, si!"
6 Yaks
7 Vain voyage?
8 Gunner's grp.
9 Fortuneteller's card
10 Bit of smoke
11 Pest that's beating it?
12 Misleading maneuver
13 Minds, as a bar
18 Certain meter reader
22 Result of a punch in the mouth
23 Artillery burst
24 Old-fashioned music hall
25 Big-earned blubberer?
27 Sulking
31 Quantity

Puzzle 71 by Norma Johnson and Nancy Salomon

33 Help
35 Snarl
37 Raise
38 Long lock
40 Dove's sound
42 "Pride and Prejudice" author
45 Boils over
49 Dues payer
50 Reclusive Garbo
51 Itsy-bitsy bits
53 Ann ___, Mich.
55 Showed fury

57 Typesetter's unit
59 Fork feature
62 French friend
63 End of an ___
64 Something to take, carefully
65 Lawyer's thing

ACROSS

1 Hit head-on
4 Peloponnesian War soldier
11 Milk supplier
14 Noshed
15 Awakening
16 Tankard filler
17 Great deal
18 ___ Mountains of the far West
19 Women's ___
20 37-Across, e.g.
22 Trumpet feature
24 Irish of old
25 Less verbose
26 "The Graduate" daughter
29 Metal in pennies
30 Like much writing paper
31 Big tournament
33 Soccer star Mia
37 Renaissance man
40 Jemima, e.g.
41 Contributes
42 Things
43 Wading bird
45 ___ acid
46 Talked back to
49 Worshiper of Tlaloc
51 ___ & Whitney (engine maker)
52 37-Across, e.g.
55 Epitome of slipperiness
56 In name only
58 Butter serving

60 See 2-Down
61 Cause of diminishing returns
62 Rap sheet abbr.
63 Sunbeam
64 Feasts
65 Chair part

DOWN

1 Despicable one
2 With 60-Across, 1960's TV cartoon hero
3 List of choices
4 Casa grande
5 It's a revelation
6 Assume for argument's sake
7 "Star Wars" director
8 "This ___ outrage!"
9 Bit
10 Time before midnight
11 Rings up
12 Popeye's gal
13 Composer Carl Maria von ___
21 37-Across, e.g.
23 37-Across, e.g.
25 Louise of "Gilligan's Island"
26 Vocalist Fitzgerald
27 Stead
28 In a bit
29 Alphabet ends, in Canada
31 Bookie's computation
32 Herd of seals

Puzzle 72 by Don West

34 Working without __
35 Year Queen Victoria died
36 Catchall abbr.
38 Police action
39 Quayle or Cheney: Abbr.
44 Person in a pool
45 After much delay
46 Asparagus unit
47 Field of endeavor
48 Like pretzels
49 BMW competitor
50 Boer fighters

52 Dance instructor's instruction
53 Fire __ (gem)
54 Autumn tool
57 "__ said it before . . ."
59 Put out, maybe, in baseball

ACROSS

1 Lauderdale is south of it
5 Leader of pre-1917 Russia
9 Look more prominent than the rest, with "out"
12 Learn to cope
14 Loft
16 Lennon's woman
17 Literary Cather
18 Lento or largo
19 "Ladders to Fire" novelist Anaïs
20 Lousy-car buyer's protection
22 Link between nations
24 Leadership of a co.
25 Liable to make one scratch
26 Lane Kirkland of the AFL-CIO, e.g.
31 Lie in bed, say
32 Like some verbs
36 Latitude/longitude shower
37 Lethargy
39 Losing tic-tac-toe row
40 Let spread
42 Louse-to-be
43 Lego precursor
47 Link
49 Land bordering Greece: Abbr.
50 Long-necked instruments
51 Light that oozes

56 Links org.
57 Lucy's landlady
59 Le ___ (Paris paper)
60 Lithe swimmer
61 Late princess
62 Lower leg joint
63 Lacking moisture
64 "Let's go!"
65 Loss's opposite

DOWN

1 Loudly cry
2 Likely foil for Garfield
3 Less than 1 m.p.h., as winds
4 Level-headedness
5 "Later"
6 "Little of this, little of that" dish
7 Location for 24-hr. banking
8 Lifeguards' dangers
9 Lunch for a whale, in a Bible story
10 Like-mindedness
11 "Les Misérables" award, 1987
13 Latin dance
15 Line of mourners
21 L, e.g.: Abbr.
23 Linen color
26 Libeler, almost by definition
27 Labrador food?
28 Light purple
29 Lyre-carrying Muse
30 "Little Mermaid"

Puzzle 73 by William I. Johnston

31 Loudness increaser, at a concert
33 Like a hippie's hair
34 Line on a graph
35 Ludicrous comments
37 Lutèce V.I.P.
38 Lacking faith in God
41 "Let me go!" e.g.
44 Like certain engineers: Abbr.
45 Lima animal
46 Lozenge-shaped
47 Lion's cousin

48 Lire used to be spent here
50 Lost no time
51 Letterman rival
52 Ladd or Greenspan
53 "Lonely Boy" singer Paul
54 Livy's 1,551
55 Light hammer part
58 Lunch meat

ACROSS

1 Grateful?
6 Way off
10 Fitted at the smithy's
14 Forestall, with "off"
15 All-or-___
16 Hefty volume
17 Divided land
18 Garden access
19 Havoc
20 Carney and Garfunkel
23 "___ takers?"
24 Not of the cloth
25 Blazing
29 Turn, as pancakes
31 Bit of baloney
34 Man of Steel portrayer
35 Tram loads
36 Enter only up to the ankles, say
37 Clinton and Bradley
40 Lyric poetry
41 Vittles
42 Money in the bank, e.g.
43 Fore site?
44 Zillions
45 Kennel club categories
46 Half a sawbuck
47 Sculler's need
48 Robinson and Thomas
56 Reed in a pit
57 Drinker's spree
58 Checkroom items
60 Microwave
61 Up to it
62 Nairobi's land
63 Porter's regretful Miss
64 Like Jack Sprat's diet
65 Shuteye

DOWN

1 "Don't ___" (comment after a bad day)
2 Station
3 Relative of a rabbit
4 Ending with "for" or "what"
5 Columbus, e.g.
6 Ticked off
7 Brew topper
8 Nay sayer
9 Do another hitch
10 Leave the herd
11 Lesson duration, often
12 Pass over
13 Bears' lairs
21 Fraction of a 46-Across
22 Popular clothing store, with "The"
25 Shoptalk
26 Crystal-lined rock
27 Flood insurance of sorts
28 Class that's for the birds
29 Fingerboard ridges
30 Monocle part
31 "F" on a quiz

Puzzle 74 by Wei-Hwa Huang

32 Puttered around
33 Outdoes in competition
35 Gulf sultanate
36 Like Solomon
38 Just-born
39 Recruit's home
44 Bit of advice
45 Slot machine symbol
46 Hightails it
47 "Come here ___?"
48 U2's frontman
49 Border on
50 Evil Norse god

51 Choir garb
52 Caffeine source
53 "Joyeux ___" (French greeting)
54 Classic Welles role
55 Eyelid woe
59 Chucklehead

ACROSS

1 Hot sauce
6 Van Gogh flower
10 This for that
14 To no ___ (fruitlessly)
15 Scarf material
16 Scarf material
17 Cardplayer's oxymoron
20 Place to stop
21 Stretched
22 Miniature golf club
23 Misplace
24 Golfer's cry
25 Pie cutter's oxymoron
29 School org.
32 Wanderer
33 Poem on an urn
34 Miseries
35 Unit of a molecule
36 Stares
38 Sprained, as an ankle
39 Hawaii's ___ Coast
40 Fish eggs
41 Shampoo step
42 Work unit
43 Shuffler's oxymoron
46 Dog's favorite part of a steak
47 Customer of Fabergé eggs
48 Portly
51 Standard
52 "His Master's Voice" co.
55 Polltaker's oxymoron
58 Suffix with poet
59 Iridescent gem

60 Big bang maker
61 Socially challenged person
62 Greek goddess of victory
63 First American in orbit

DOWN

1 She won a 2002 Grammy for "Lovers Rock"
2 Shakespearean stream
3 Extol
4 Bro or sis
5 With everything
6 Bank, to a credit card
7 Laughfest
8 Poorly
9 Sticks on a slope?
10 Political ticket
11 Word repeated before "Don't tell me!"
12 1/640 of a square mile
13 Nobleman
18 Slacken
19 Territory
23 Relative of a camel
24 Lose brilliance
25 Viper, for one
26 Machine powerer
27 Shirley Jackson's "Life ___ the Savages"
28 Wished (for)
29 Feared destination in "Lady and the Tramp"

30 Not wordy
31 Daisylike flower
34 Helicopter sound
36 Henry Ford II, to Henry Ford
37 Top-notch
41 Like some charges on a cell phone
43 Gossipy Barrett
44 "Lawrence of Arabia" star
45 Abbr. after an asterisk in a car ad
46 Erect

48 Tear down
49 "___ upon a time"
50 Way up a slope
51 Fargo's state: Abbr.
52 Baptism, for one
53 Common syrup source
54 Auth. unknown
56 Prefix with gram or center
57 Zilch

ACROSS

1 Bother
5 Be overthrown
9 Wear away
14 Square measure
15 Not in port
16 Wanders
17 Bad day for 25-Across
18 More or less follower
19 Ticket seller
20 Gridiron order
23 Egg maker
24 Take-home pay
25 Rubicon crosser
29 Armor-___
31 Grp. symbolized by an elephant
34 Sweater material
35 Thumb (through)
36 Enterprise helmsman
37 Griddle order
40 Clock sound
41 Like mellower wines
42 Stop in the Sahara
43 Band performance
44 It may give a shock on a ranch
45 French equivalent of the White House
46 Groceries holder
47 Playtex product
48 Gridley order
55 Tour of duty
57 "Purple ___" (song played at Woodstock)
58 Telegraph
59 Door part
60 Malt beverages
61 1950's British P.M.
62 Lightened (up)
63 Liquefy
64 1990 World Series champs

DOWN

1 Like some maidens of myth
2 Pakistani tongue
3 Realizes
4 "Miss America" appears on it
5 Priest's title
6 Pallid
7 Long spring
8 Turner who was called the "Sweater Girl"
9 Cleared the boards
10 Synonym compiler
11 Transmission closer
12 Lion's home
13 Superlative suffix
21 Acceptance speech word
22 Not just a tie-up
25 Business expenditures
26 Bandleader Shaw
27 Vote in
28 Drench
29 Relinquished
30 In place
31 "You'll never ___!"
32 Stan's partner in comedy
33 Sign of life
35 Plastic block maker
36 Influence

Puzzle 76 by Steven Dorfman

38 Bart's mom
39 Grinding tooth
44 Went in separate directions
45 One of the Gallo brothers
46 Eat to excess
47 Diagonal face of a chisel
48 $5 bills
49 Impact sound
50 Fit as a fiddle
51 Wide-mouthed pitcher
52 Assistant

53 Historic Scott
54 Desires
55 ___-wolf
56 Actress Carrere

ACROSS
1 Actor Guinness
5 Frolics
10 Beatles song or movie
14 Opera star
15 Foreword, for short
16 Tarzan's raisers
17 Tied
19 New Jersey hoopsters
20 Big name in chickens
21 Most forlorn
23 Check for fit, as clothes
24 Off the correct path
26 Winemaker Ernest or Julio
28 Corn
32 Inclined path for wheelchairs
36 Dictator Amin
37 ___ bender (minor accident)
38 Disney's "___ and the Detectives"
39 "First Blood" character
41 Give a hand?
42 Starbucks orders
44 Peanut butter holder
45 Ivy League school
46 Escargot
47 Recording studio devices
49 Generic
51 NBC morning show
56 "Les Misérables" hero
59 City on the Rio Grande
60 Opera song
61 Clownish one
64 Inert element used in lights
65 Extraterrestrial
66 Columbus's home
67 Not out of one's mind
68 Lab glove material
69 Penpoints

DOWN
1 Very skilled
2 Paté ingredient
3 "___ man for himself"
4 Enthusiastic, as an attitude
5 Religious ceremony
6 Early afternoon
7 Network with annual awards
8 Magician's word
9 Submarine detector
10 Repairman
11 Fencing sword
12 Response to "Shall we?"
13 Cousin of "ahem"
18 Belted out, as a tune
22 Honored woman
24 Emmy-winner Alan
25 Brand of beef jerky
27 Broadcasts
29 Brainstorm
30 Eagerness
31 Writer ___ Stanley Gardner
32 Many wines
33 End of a prayer

34 Translucent mineral
35 Hardly a beauty
37 Duffer's cry
40 Make a cake, e.g.
43 Ice sheet
47 Capital of the Philippines
48 Pierce
50 Like a whiny voice
52 Hunter of Greek myth
53 New ___, India
54 Improvise
55 Duncan toys

56 Some car-pooling vehicles
57 Carpet buyer's calculation
58 Animal on England's shield
59 Short-tailed wildcat
62 Turned on
63 Civil War general

ACROSS

1 Fudd of cartoons
6 Speeder's snagger
11 "The ___" (Uris novel)
14 Actress Téa
15 Carroll heroine
16 "Hooray, José!"
17 Litter in monkey cages
19 N.F.L. scores
20 U.N. Day mo.
21 Econ. yardstick
22 Solar storm
24 General Mills product
27 "What was ___ think?"
28 Toys with keys
33 Crooks crack them
36 "Now I get it!"
37 Black-tie dinner, say
38 Memorable age
39 Loafers, e.g., or a lighthearted description of 17-, 28-, 49- and 65-Across
43 Outdoor game
44 Sofer of soaps
46 Vow words
47 Actress Massey
49 Machine parts
53 Musical sense
54 More au courant
58 Colorful marble
62 Investment option: Abbr.
63 Corp. bigwig
64 D.D.E.'s predecessor
65 What clean kitchens often have

68 Versatile vehicle, for short
69 Bring joy to
70 Banks in Cooperstown
71 Scratch
72 Tapes for producers
73 Prescribed amounts

DOWN

1 Macaroni shape
2 TV host Robin
3 ___ Carlo
4 Bambi's aunt
5 Carnival game
6 Mountain-climbing technique
7 Potent potable
8 Fizzles out
9 Constitutional rights grp.
10 Astronaut Judith
11 Tough issue to handle
12 Actor Ray
13 Don't be serious
18 Indigo source
23 Party animal?
25 You ___ here
26 New York or New Orleans
29 Pi follower
30 ___ Andreas Fault
31 Oomph
32 Multigenerational story
33 Belgrade native
34 Neighborhood
35 Mail to a star
40 Truth decay?

Puzzle 78 by Sherry O. Blackard

41 Mount in Crete
42 Gave the high sign
45 "Ah, me!"
48 Timothy Leary's turn-on
50 Made 7-Down
51 Eye parts: Var.
52 Soft ball material
55 Graphic symbols
56 Like a Stephen King novel
57 Kentucky Derby prize
58 Good buddy
59 Terrier of film

60 Bush's alma mater
61 Reason to cram
66 D.D.E.'s command
67 "___ y Plata" (Montana's motto)

ACROSS
1 Place to moor a boat
5 "Pipe down!"
10 Say "%@&#!"
14 City south of Moscow
15 Rich cake
16 Poker pot primer
17 Removes squeaks from
18 Actress Samantha
19 "___ almost taste it!"
20 Elvis Presley title "corrected"
23 Suffix with percent
24 Thrilla in Manila boxer
25 Sonnets and such
27 Grand ___ National Park
29 1996 Madonna musical
33 Take to court
34 Lennon's widow Yoko
36 Environmentalist's prefix
37 Does hip-hop
38 Gershwin title "corrected"
41 Vacationers' stops
43 Hosp. units
44 "What'd I tell ya?"
45 Corn holder
46 Kennel club classification
48 Molten rock
52 Letters that don't need stamps
54 Alley-___ (basketball maneuver)
56 Nonsense
57 Fats Domino title "corrected"
62 Paul who sang "Diana"
63 Tricks
64 Start of an invention
65 One 'twixt 12 and 20
66 Like a gymnast
67 Eyeglass part
68 Dole (out)
69 Breakfast, lunch and dinner
70 After curfew

DOWN
1 Take a chill pill
2 Baltimore ballplayer
3 Luxurious fabric
4 "If all ___ fails . . ."
5 Pittsburgh product
6 Immobilize, rodeo-style
7 Craving
8 Laurel of comedy
9 Group of buffalo
10 Egypt's capital
11 He wants you
12 Bypasses bedtime
13 D.C. V.I.P.
21 Food from heaven
22 Fed. pollution monitor
26 "Absolutely!"
28 Cries at fireworks
30 Sonnets and such

31 "___ bin ein Berliner"
32 Hula hoops and yo-yos
35 Eggs ___ easy
37 Perlman of "Cheers"
38 Where many memos land
39 Before, once
40 Office subs
41 Skater's surface
42 Convention's choice
46 Sandwich, briefly
47 "Is that a fact!"

49 Like a good egg
50 "One ___, please"
51 Opposite of "Ten-hut!"
53 Absurd
55 Desert havens
58 Streetcar
59 Bigger than big
60 China's continent
61 Sledder's spot
62 $20 bill dispenser, briefly

ACROSS

1 Trojan War hero
5 Hawkeye's show
9 Serviceable
14 DNA carrier
15 To ___ (exactly)
16 Spoke irrationally
17 Drags along
18 Numbers to crunch
19 Fresh from
   the laundry
20 Keats work
21 Address book no.
22 Refrain from singing?
24 1999 Will Smith
   movie
27 Decay
28 Sought a seat
29 ___ von Bismarck
33 Laid-back,
   personalitywise
36 Unlike dirt roads
38 It's charged
39 Nightgown wearer
   of rhyme
42 Chowed down
43 Tom and Jerry,
   for two
44 "And there you are!"
45 Doesn't guzzle
47 Suffix with Manhattan
48 Teen's embarrassment
49 Modern research tool
55 Galileo ___
58 How the excited go
59 Corrida cry
60 Cara or Castle
61 Loch ___ monster

63 Pack it in
64 Exotic fruit
65 Rebuke to Brutus
66 Cancel
67 Obie candidates
68 Leak slowly
69 First couple's place

DOWN

1 Shining
2 Day after mercredi
3 Child who behaves
   perfectly
4 Illiterates' marks
5 Achieved success
6 In any way
7 Wimbledon unit
8 Scorching times
9 Oceanic killers
10 Get beaten by
11 Eye part
12 Navy commando
13 Poet ___ St. Vincent
   Millay
21 Small-time
23 Extend, as Time
25 Pulled a six-shooter
26 Emptied
30 "Kon-___"
31 Travail
32 Most qualified
   to serve
33 "Jabberwocky"
   starter
34 Hairy humanoid
35 Chick's sound
36 Drama essentials
37 Make fractions

Puzzle 80 by Michael Shteyman

40 France's longest river
41 Staff member?
46 Like Benny Goodman's music
48 Fastens pants, in a way
50 Dairy section selections
51 Fritter away
52 Twisted
53 Say "bo's'n," say
54 Back, as a racehorse
55 Hobbling gait
56 Asia's ___ Sea

57 Tuneful Horne
62 Summer on the Riviera
63 Can. province

ACROSS

1 ___ salts
6 ___-Japanese War
11 Car co. bought by Chrysler
14 Poem with 17 syllables
15 Full-length, as a movie
16 The facts of life?
17 "Beat it!"
18 World traveler from Venice
20 Nightly "NewsHour" airer
22 Skating venue
23 New York governor before George Pataki
28 Cries to bullfighters
29 Inits. on a toothpaste box
30 "___, Joy of Man's Desiring"
31 Dashboard abbr.
33 Priest's robe
34 Hands and feet
36 Like one of the two jaws
40 Post office workers
42 Polish remover
44 Half of an audiotape
45 Croc's cousin
47 Symbol of industriousness
48 "___ Skylark" (ode)
50 Dryer buildup
51 Snarling dog
52 G.I. addresses
55 Home of the AAA Mud Hens
58 Shiploads
60 Bobby of the N.H.L.
61 By its very nature
64 Home with a dome
68 Simon and Garfunkel, once
69 Japanese port
70 Director who won his first 56-Down in 1934
71 ___ Juan (capital of 32-Down)
72 Goose eggs
73 Beginning

DOWN

1 Sounds of doubt
2 ___-Man (arcade game)
3 What to call an officer
4 Relative of a giraffe
5 Gibberish
6 Piña colada ingredient
7 Article in La Repubblica
8 Theatrical drop
9 Assistance
10 Siouan tribe
11 Buzzing with excitement
12 Winnie-the-Pooh's creator
13 Does chef's work
19 Exactly on time
21 Public row
23 Sirs' partners
24 Stevenson who lost twice for president
25 More than fervent

26 Bringing into play
27 Not at home
32 See 71-Across
35 French composer Erik
37 Hunt illegally
38 The blahs
39 Backward-looking
41 "Hurry!"
43 Time-share unit, often
46 100%
49 "Relax, and that's an order!"
52 They have pH's of less than 7
53 ___ New Guinea

54 Director Welles
56 Screen award
57 Bach instrument
59 "The Wizard ___"
62 Bout stopper, for short
63 Western treaty grp.
65 CD predecessors
66 Source of iron
67 Stable staple

ACROSS

1 Hardly high-class
6 Tiny tribesman
11 Medicine givers, for short
14 Stan's partner in comedy
15 Ham's need
16 Feed bag tidbit
17 Callisto and Europa, to Jupiter
18 Borneo critter
19 Alcott of women's golf
20 "What's up, Doc?" speaker
22 The Dow, e.g.
24 Remote button
25 Building beam
26 Take turns
29 Tweak
33 "Laugh-In" actress
34 Plants
35 Cambodia's Lon ____
36 Mamie's man
37 Less ornate
39 Brokaw's network
40 Born, in bios
41 Bizarre
42 Sandwich shop
43 Completely accurate
45 Tied fast
47 Shoots the breeze
48 Return for a buck?
49 Cornered
51 "Sufferin' succotash!" speaker
56 Phi follower
57 Fly-catching bird
59 Oarlock
60 Cigarette ingredient
61 Brain waves
62 Sent flowers to, say
63 Norm: Abbr.
64 20 Questions turn
65 Held the deed to

DOWN

1 Egyptian pyramid, e.g.
2 Moises of baseball
3 Drano target
4 Father or brother
5 "Agreed. However . . ."
6 Lying facedown
7 Tall tale
8 Aussie greeting
9 Degree div.
10 "I'm smarter than the average . . ." speaker
11 "Beep, beep!" speaker
12 With 50- and 53-Down, apt title for this puzzle
13 Charon's river
21 Sport ____ (modern vehicle)
23 ____ King Cole
25 Memo phrase
26 African charger
27 Like some old buckets
28 "I tawt I taw a puddy tat!" speaker

Puzzle 82 by Sherry O. Blackard

29 Bat one's eyelashes, say
30 Actress Skye
31 High-minded
32 Heston epic
34 Lot in life
37 "Th-th-th-that's all, folks!" speaker
38 Schleps
42 Where a boxer might be champion
44 Directions-giving org.
45 Dallas hoopster, briefly
46 Pug's combo
48 Grace word
49 Play makers?
50 See 12-Down
51 Popeye's __'pea
52 Those for
53 See 12-Down
54 Robt. __
55 Funny Foxx
58 College Web site suffix

ACROSS

1 Sired, biblically
6 2002 Winter Olympics locale
10 Mafia head
14 Microwave brand
15 ___ the way (lead)
16 Scent
17 Hightail it
19 In the thick of
20 Put down
21 Do a second time, as a role
23 Anniversary unit
25 Fall flower
26 Deep sleep
30 Initial phase
33 "You can say that ___!"
35 What a vacuum cleaner vacuums
36 Keats piece
39 Stop suddenly
43 Sewn edge
44 ___ china
45 Belgian city in W.W. I fighting
46 Alternative to a taco
49 Hawaiian tuber
50 Gold star
53 Frisbee
55 Running behind schedule
58 In vino ___
63 French Sudan, today
64 Change one's mind
66 Stratford's river
67 Part of the eye
68 Quaker State: Abbr.
69 Kind of conference
70 Circus sight
71 Before surgery

DOWN

1 Ali ___ and the 40 Thieves
2 Flightless flock
3 "The World According to ___"
4 Green Gables girl
5 Hang back
6 Optimistic
7 Bar bill
8 Say it's so
9 "___ goes!"
10 Not fine-grained
11 Own up to
12 Grace under pressure
13 Word after mail or money
18 Depletes, with "up"
22 Canned goods closet
24 Carrot-top
26 Direct payment
27 Undress with one's eyes
28 Sir's counterpart
29 Sharpshooter's asset
31 Crusty dessert
32 Globe
34 "___ Does It Better" (1977 Carly Simon hit)
36 Soup pod
37 Veal : calf :: vension : ___

Puzzle 83 by Gregory E. Paul

38 "Happy Motoring" company
40 Tel. book listings
41 Blast maker
42 Suitable
46 Subway vehicles
47 Sell off
48 Riding the waves
50 Madison Avenue worker
51 Create a carpet
52 Permit
54 Germany's ___ Works
56 Give off

57 Throw down the gauntlet
59 Roman road
60 Jukebox choice
61 The New Yorker cartoonist Peter
62 Ginger cookie
65 Cousins and such

ACROSS

1 New Jersey NHLer
6 Top spot
10 Environmental toxins, for short
14 Like Bo-Peep's charges
15 Heister's haul
16 Israeli dance
17 Barkeep's woe?
19 Mayberry moppet
20 Allergic reaction
21 Sweeper's accessory
23 Ignore
26 Weed killers
27 Left on a liner
30 Bygone carrier
31 In bounds
32 "No way!"
33 Geometric fig.
34 "You can say that again!"
37 Chest protector
38 Boxer's woe?
40 Sense of self
41 Thief
43 Go (for)
44 Initials may be carved in it
45 Art Deco artist
46 Get the drop on
47 Midmonth time
48 See eye to eye
50 Sake
52 War planner
54 Takes off the leash
58 Don Juan's mother

59 Stunt man's woe?
62 Wingless parasites
63 Eight, for starters
64 Where to find sweaters?
65 Mice-inspired yelps
66 Warp
67 Sheep counter's quest

DOWN

1 I lids?
2 Having neither side ahead
3 Tarzan's transport
4 Very detailed
5 TV host Gibbons
6 Politico Landon
7 Pigeon patter
8 Temperamental
9 Caesar's accusation
10 It may be checked in a security check
11 Police officer's woe?
12 Pipe material
13 French composer Saint-___
18 Relief for the stressed
22 Alan Ladd classic
24 Deep drink
25 Without exception
27 Good engine sound
28 Akron's home
29 Masseur's woe?
31 Sizzling pitch
35 Folklore fiend

36 Pans for stir-frying
38 "___ Pan"
39 Colorful fish
42 Mild currents
44 Like some lenses
48 Quick-witted
49 Wish granter
50 City division
51 Windblown soil
53 Ruckuses
55 Elisabeth of "Leaving Las Vegas"
56 German article
57 Go ballistic

60 Colorado native
61 Reaction to applause

ACROSS

1 Klutzes
5 Ailments for which there is no known cure
10 Sharpen
14 Exchange
15 Early stage
16 London's ___ Park
17 Give a darn
18 Like chips that have been set out too long
19 The "Iliad" or "Odyssey"
20 Bristling with firepower
23 Lois Lane often needed one
24 One who's looked up to
25 Pick-up line?
28 Quick smells
32 PC key
35 ___ Strauss & Co.
37 ___ firma
38 Display contempt for
42 Apple tool
43 Feed the kitty
44 Hair colorer
45 Rob, as a stage
47 Progresso products
50 ___ of Man
52 Bitter resentment
56 Barely scrape by
61 Norwegian king
62 Rating units
63 Dog in "Beetle Bailey"
64 Where Korea is
65 Donnybrook
66 Multicolored
67 When leaves turn
68 First sign of the zodiac
69 Vaccines

DOWN

1 Prize awarded at the Kodak Theatre
2 Knowing
3 Grows crops
4 When repeated, a cry to an awardee
5 Half of a 1940's–50's comedy duo
6 Suspicious of
7 Exam for attys.-to-be
8 Indian city
9 Knights' horses
10 Cyclists pop them
11 Ballyhoo
12 Trim, as text
13 Part of M.I.T.: Abbr.
21 Expected
22 Scout's rider
26 Horne or Olin
27 Pizzeria fixtures
29 Landlord of Lucy and Ricky
30 Wear on, as the nerves
31 Fill nicely
32 Do art on metal, e.g.
33 Chase away
34 Ringlet
36 Analogy words
39 Like feudal times

Puzzle 85 by Peter Sarrett

```
┌──┬──┬──┬──┬──┬──┬──┬──┬──┬──┬──┬──┬──┬──┐
│1 │2 │3 │4 │██│5 │6 │7 │8 │9 │██│10│11│12│13│
├──┼──┼──┼──┼──┼──┼──┼──┼──┼──┼──┼──┼──┼──┤
│14│  │  │  │██│15│  │  │  │  │██│16│  │  │  │
├──┼──┼──┼──┼──┼──┼──┼──┼──┼──┼──┼──┼──┼──┤
│17│  │  │  │██│18│  │  │  │  │██│19│  │  │  │
├──┼──┼──┼──┼──┼──┼──┼──┼──┼──┼──┼──┼──┼──┤
│20│  │  │  │21│  │  │  │  │  │22│  │  │  │  │
├──┼──┼──┼──┼──┼──┼──┼──┼──┼──┼──┼──┼──┼──┤
│23│  │  │  │  │  │██│  │24│  │  │  │██│██│██│
├──┼──┼──┼──┼──┼──┼──┼──┼──┼──┼──┼──┼──┼──┤
│██│██│██│25│  │  │26│27│██│28│  │  │29│30│31│
├──┼──┼──┼──┼──┼──┼──┼──┼──┼──┼──┼──┼──┼──┤
│32│33│34│  │██│35│  │  │36│██│37│  │  │  │  │
├──┼──┼──┼──┼──┼──┼──┼──┼──┼──┼──┼──┼──┼──┤
│38│  │  │39│40│  │  │  │  │41│  │  │  │  │  │
├──┼──┼──┼──┼──┼──┼──┼──┼──┼──┼──┼──┼──┼──┤
│42│  │  │  │██│43│  │  │  │  │██│44│  │  │  │
├──┼──┼──┼──┼──┼──┼──┼──┼──┼──┼──┼──┼──┼──┤
│45│  │  │  │46│  │47│  │  │48│49│██│██│██│██│
├──┼──┼──┼──┼──┼──┼──┼──┼──┼──┼──┼──┼──┼──┤
│██│██│50│  │  │  │51│  │██│52│  │  │53│54│55│
├──┼──┼──┼──┼──┼──┼──┼──┼──┼──┼──┼──┼──┼──┤
│56│57│58│  │  │  │  │59│60│  │  │  │  │  │  │
├──┼──┼──┼──┼──┼──┼──┼──┼──┼──┼──┼──┼──┼──┤
│61│  │  │  │██│62│  │  │  │  │██│63│  │  │  │
├──┼──┼──┼──┼──┼──┼──┼──┼──┼──┼──┼──┼──┼──┤
│64│  │  │  │██│65│  │  │  │  │██│66│  │  │  │
├──┼──┼──┼──┼──┼──┼──┼──┼──┼──┼──┼──┼──┼──┤
│67│  │  │  │██│68│  │  │  │  │██│69│  │  │  │
└──┴──┴──┴──┴──┴──┴──┴──┴──┴──┴──┴──┴──┴──┘
```

40 Touch lightly
41 Emotional disorders
46 Transfusion liquid
48 Popular cooking spray
49 Busybodies
51 Go in
53 Adorable one
54 Sleek swimmer
55 "The Mary Tyler Moore Show" spinoff
56 Goof off
57 "Casablanca" woman

58 Colorado resort town
59 "The Persistence of Memory" artist
60 Shoe shaper

ACROSS

1 Immunizations
6 Places for tents
11 HBO rival
14 "The Planets" composer
15 Golden-___ (oldsters)
16 Ad-___
17 Nebraska's largest city
18 "Of course"
20 "Of course"
22 Memorial Day weekend event for short
23 Fork providers?: Abbr.
24 Leather from the sea
26 Float gracefully
29 Old Mideast inits.
32 Beehives and others
33 "Honest" man
34 "Sharp Dressed Man" band
36 Spring in the Sahara
40 "Of course"
43 Dined at home
44 Holy radiances
45 Bake sale organizer, for short
46 Costa ___ Sol
48 Hectic hosp. areas
49 Letters akin to P.D.Q.
50 Asian shrines
54 Drum locale
56 Baseball's Jesus
57 "Of course"
63 "Of course"
65 Confused

66 Fraction of a joule
67 Replays may be played in it
68 Newly waxed
69 Fish eggs
70 Family car
71 Upscale hotel room features

DOWN

1 Booted?
2 Web browser button
3 Regal Norwegian name
4 Underwear top
5 Request when the national anthem is played
6 Play group
7 Malaria symptom
8 Haggard of country music
9 Victimized, with "on"
10 Speedy jet to J.F.K.
11 Move sinuously
12 Language of Delhi
13 Future mom's doc
19 Condemn from the peanut gallery
21 Trooper maker
25 Untethered
26 "S.N.L." character Baba ___
27 Some
28 Grand banquet
30 "___ boy!"
31 Court game
34 Like land in a city

Puzzle 86 by Michael Shteyman

35 Petted pet's sound
37 Doesn't guzzle
38 Small quantity
39 "___ out of it!"
41 Avoided a dragnet
42 Painting holder
47 Apt to change
49 Franklin with soul
50 Harness racer
51 Oldsmobile model
52 Mountain climber's obstacle
53 Church council
55 Pile up

58 ___ mater
59 City on the Rhone
60 Like
61 Hawaiian bird
62 Simon ___
64 Ninny

ACROSS

1 Test episode for a TV series
6 Front's opposite
10 Yen
14 Came up
15 Israeli airline
16 Actress Irene of "Fame"
17 Expensive fur
18 Christie's "Death on the __"
19 Diplomat Abba
20 007's introduction
23 Kind of sauce
25 Shipping magnate Onassis
26 Screwball
27 Thin 1960's supermodel
29 Coil
32 __ the Cow
33 Mathematician Descartes
34 "Invasion of the Body Snatchers" container
37 Jungle declaration
41 Main, Elm, etc.: Abbr.
42 Sicilian volcano
43 Turkic speaker
44 Flower with colorful blotches
46 "Peter Pan" playwright
47 Tasty
50 Stadium cheer
51 Where Mindy's TV friend came from

52 First line of "Moby-Dick"
57 Spoken
58 Poker payment
59 President Nasser
62 Dog on the Yellow Brick Road
63 On the double, in the O.R.
64 Get around
65 Winter forecast
66 Civil wrong
67 Spanish kids

DOWN

1 Mas' mates
2 Lyricist Gershwin
3 Capitol Hill wheeler-dealers
4 Peace Prize city
5 Adolescent
6 Cinema canine
7 Inter __
8 Serene
9 Swiss artist Paul
10 Fridge, old-style
11 Forbidden
12 How to start up a Model T
13 Useful
21 Moistureless
22 Hit the slopes
23 What roots connect to
24 Young hooter
28 Italian actress Scala
29 Youngman of one-liners
30 "Orinoco Flow" singer

(crossword grid)

31 Sign before Virgo
33 Followers of the Pied Piper of Hamelin
34 Officer on the beat
35 Studio sign
36 Bo of "10"
38 Buddhist sect
39 Tony-winning actress for "The Country Girl"
40 Cookie holder
44 Feather-filled item
45 Navy bigwig: Abbr.
46 Crash sound
47 Glasgow residents

48 Composer Copland
49 Academy founder
50 Scarlett's love
53 Sunrise direction
54 Look ___ (study)
55 Constellation component
56 Icicle site
60 Citrus drink
61 "___ Misérables"

ACROSS
1 Nickname in the N.B.A.
5 Part of a musical refrain
9 Hill's partner
13 "To Sir With Love" singer
14 Majestic poem
15 They hold water
17 Mine: Fr.
18 Cauldron stirrers, maybe
19 Something pushed by a trailer?
20 Drink garnish
21 "___ bin ein Berliner"
22 Treat with carbon dioxide
23 Really taut
26 Where the outboard motor goes
29 Two-time
30 "Le ___ d'Arthur"
32 Royal wish
33 Resigned remark
37 Really self-satisfied
41 Thetis bathed Achilles in it, in myth
42 Battle of Britain grp.
43 Southpaw
44 Grow old
47 Link
48 Really stylish
53 Some Crimeans
54 Benzene source
55 "Hold ___ your hat!"
59 Isolated
60 Dr. ___, TV adviser on life and relationships
61 Pearl Harbor locale
62 Seaport south of Milan
63 Architect Saarinen
64 Bad spot for a nail
65 Tear
66 Formerly, formerly
67 They're sometimes candied

DOWN
1 Indication of indignation
2 "History of England" author David
3 Lotion ingredient
4 Coverlet
5 Tributary of the Delaware
6 Geronimo, e.g.
7 Really ethereal
8 Southern comforts?: Abbr.
9 Humiliate
10 "___ to the wise . . ."
11 Burton of "Star Trek: T.N.G."
12 Verdi aria
16 Appear to be
22 Unanimously
24 Like summer drinks
25 At the peak of
26 Some stage equipment
27 Construction of snow, maybe

28 City of Paris
31 Prom wear
33 Do well on
34 Garret
35 Start of a play
36 Hebrides island
38 Regions
39 ___ souci
40 Actor Baldwin
44 Two-page ad
45 Link between stories?
46 Where trade-ins
   are made
48 Just for men

49 More healthy
50 Make amends
51 Talked and talked
52 Weirdish
56 Mom's mom
57 ___ McAn shoes
58 Inning closers
60 ___ Dee river

ACROSS

1 Tony winner Minnelli
5 Not all
9 Leg bone
14 Author unknown, for short
15 List-shortening abbr.
16 Upturned, as a box
17 Direct
20 "To ___ is human . . ."
21 Seeks money damages from
22 Click and clack, e.g.
23 Nature's alarm clock
25 Attention-getter
26 Third degree?
27 Kind of rally or talk
28 Corned beef concoction
32 Alarm clock setting, perhaps
35 Boutonniere's place
37 Feed lines to
38 Town meeting site
41 Chowed down
42 What straphangers lack
43 Indian corn
44 Deliver a tirade
46 Dryly humorous
47 Hi-fi component
48 Major airports
50 "The Firm" author
54 St. Francis's home
57 Haunted house sound
58 Companion of the id
59 Surprises

62 Conjure up
63 Neighborhood
64 Gratis
65 Underground conduit
66 Lively
67 Praiseful poems

DOWN

1 Modern surgical tool
2 Conclusion's opposite
3 Famous slasher film?
4 Gasteyer of "Saturday Night Live"
5 Made a smooth transition
6 Survey choice
7 "Welcome" sites
8 Keebler cookie maker
9 Corrida de ___ (bullfight)
10 Close to personally
11 Actresses Arthur and Benaderet
12 Memo starter
13 Finds the sum
18 Narrow strip of land
19 With no assurance of payment
24 Unwanted e-mail
25 Diarist Samuel
27 Hamburger unit
29 Start of a play
30 Mideast canal
31 Roll call response
32 Unwelcome mark
33 Small amount
34 Marvel superheroes

Puzzle 89 by Peter Gordon

35 They cook up whoppers
36 Animal in a mass migration
39 Beginner, slangily
40 Siestas
45 Alan of "Growing Pains"
47 Palestinian leader
49 Wedding party member
50 Errand runner
51 Got wind of
52 Come to terms

53 Math class figures
54 They're worth 1 or 11 points
55 Computer command
56 Put away
57 Oliver's request
60 Gullible person
61 ET's craft

ACROSS

1 Dips in gravy
5 Typewriter type
9 Image on an old nickel
14 Site of the 9-Across on an old nickel
15 Economist Smith
16 Do penance
17 Grid great Graham
18 All-night party
19 On pitch
20 Question to a suspect
23 Pasture sound
24 Planet, poetically
25 Tom of "Newhart"
29 Sugar pie
31 Mosque V.I.P.
35 Sound from Sneezy
36 Pueblo Indians
38 Botheration
39 Question to a prospective bride
42 Make a boner
43 Great Lakes mnemonic
44 Alphabet ender
45 Need a bath badly
47 Kid-___ (children's shows)
48 Did figure eights, say
49 Big brute
51 News initials
52 Question to a speeder
59 Close to
61 Actress Sharon
62 "Phew!" inducer
63 Transported
64 Many a trucker
65 Lantern-jawed celeb
66 Say "@#$%!"
67 Call to Fido
68 Roaster's spot

DOWN

1 Pack overhead
2 "@#$%!," e.g.
3 Bread for gyros
4 Place for mail
5 Dolly who sang "Here You Come Again"
6 State with a panhandle
7 Stalactite site
8 Traitorous Aldrich
9 Ulan ___, Mongolia
10 Spanish pianist José
11 Walkman maker
12 Latish lunchtime
13 Nancy Drew's beau
21 Peanut butter choice
22 Gin's partner
25 Ham-fisted one
26 Autumn hue
27 Sandcastle site
28 How-___ (instructional books)
29 Sank, as a putt
30 Numbered work
32 "Glengarry Glen Ross" playwright
33 Old saw
34 Single-celled creature
36 Prefix with 48-Down

Puzzle 90 by Fred Piscop

37 Chicago suburb
40 Hang like a chopper
41 Singer Sumac
46 Hilo honcho
48 Ball
50 Ueberroth or Ustinov
51 Out-and-out
52 Got threadbare
53 Work with acid
54 Kemo ___
55 Go out of business
56 Creative spark
57 Rice-a-___
58 Libidinous deity

59 Tummy muscles
60 Item for 58-Down

ACROSS

1 "___, humbug!"
4 Funnies
10 Ed who sang "My Cup Runneth Over"
14 Prefix with puncture
15 Noah's mount
16 Telegram
17 "It's c-c-cold!"
18 Classic song from the 1913 "Ziegfeld Follies"
20 Spine-tingling
22 Hostile party
23 Mr. ___ (Shea mascot)
24 Ancient Andean
26 "My Cup Runneth Over" musical
28 Halloween decoration
33 Part of the Deep South: Abbr.
34 Prohibit
35 Performed on stage
39 Chicago phenomenon
41 Reef material
43 Sea eagle
44 Excellent buy
46 More slippery, as winter roads
48 Suffix with lemon or orange
49 Marsh light
52 Fred who played Herman Munster
55 "Get ___ writing!"
56 Live and breathe
57 Full range
61 Dark
64 "Oh, my!"
67 Shelley poem
68 Intro for boy or girl
69 Nervousness
70 Every little bit
71 Vehicle pulled by a hoss
72 Brought in, as a salary
73 Just for Men product

DOWN

1 Jesus, in the manger
2 Small farm size
3 See 11-Down
4 Bay State peninsula
5 Metallic rock
6 Wizard, old-style
7 Steel ingredient
8 Showed up
9 Frustrate
10 Bowl over
11 With 3-Down, a Florida collegian
12 Slipped up
13 Bench-clearing incident
19 Nine-headed serpent of myth
21 Tattooing fluid
25 Smart ___
27 ___ upon a time
28 1975 movie thriller with a sequel in 3-D
29 Dismounted
30 Bubbling
31 Drug agent, slangily
32 Characteristic

36 Huge quantity
37 Partner of odds
38 Bottomless
40 Sunrise
42 Where Samson slew the Philistines
45 Specialized vocabulary
47 Fixed, as a piano
50 Part of N.F.L.
51 Get the blue ribbon
52 Grand parties
53 Burning rage
54 Busybody

58 "___ Lisa"
59 Utility customer
60 Larger ___ life
62 Frivolously
63 The "T" in TV
65 Page in an appointment book
66 U-turn from WNW

ACROSS

1 When new
   TV shows debut
5 ___ Alaska
10 Lounge
14 Away from the wind
15 Manicurist's board
16 Impulse transmitter
17 Short passage from
   "Water Music"?
19 Remain unsettled
20 Schism
21 Serves, as soup
23 Snug
24 Dashboard control
25 Mickey of
   Cooperstown
28 Star of David,
   essentially
31 Greeting in Hilo
32 "___, With Love"
33 Big inits. in the record
   business
34 Mount from which
   Moses saw Canaan
35 Onetime Alaskan
   capital
36 ___ monde
37 A load off one's
   mine?
38 Rations (out)
39 "Siddhartha" author
40 Start of many classes
42 Workaholic's concern
43 Appearance
44 Poet Teasdale
45 Like "King Lear"
47 Air force unit

51 Stockings
52 Physically no match
   for Cain?
54 Pitcher
55 Nurmi, the Flying
   Finn
56 Paradisiacal place
57 Military lunchroom
58 Popular 1990's sitcom
59 Arp's art

DOWN

1 Saudi monarch
2 Jai ___
3 Camera attachment
4 Vietnamese official
   who declined a
   Nobel Peace Prize
5 British Honduras, now
6 Perth ___, N.J.
7 New Jersey university
8 Do wrong
9 Poor character
   analysis?
10 Pooch that perches
11 Lubricant for ice
   skates?
12 Part of DMZ
13 Certain linemen
18 ___ Gay (W.W. II
   plane)
22 At a distance
24 Office stations
25 Estate
26 Oldsmobile model
27 Long-winded
   acceptance speeches
   in Stockholm?

Puzzle 92 by Adam Cohen

28 Monopoly purchase
29 Tickle
30 Oblique surface in carpentry
32 Sir or madam
35 Many a Winslow Homer painting
36 Foreshadowed
38 Roman 1,102
39 Silent film star
41 German pistols
42 It can help you get a date
44 Balm

45 1954 horror film about giant ants
46 Brokerage house T. ___ Price
47 Prosperity
48 Slave girl of opera
49 Requirement
50 Dame ___ Everage
53 Account amt.

ACROSS

1 Simple adding devices
6 Starring role in a Menotti opera
11 Stake money (on)
14 Subaru Impreza, e.g.
15 Song from the past
16 Smeltery input
17 Surf serving #1
19 Sales at a box office, slangily
20 Sex ___
21 Sixth sense
22 Symbol in proofreading
23 Salt Lake City zone: Abbr.
24 Sink, as the sun
26 Sign ___ (accept, as a program)
28 Surf serving #2
33 Screenwriter/novelist Roald
36 Switchboard worker: Abbr.
37 Setting of a fire maliciously
38 Stage name
40 Solemn wedding words
41 Sort of way to run
42 Sundance Kid's partner, ___ Cassidy
43 Six o'clock broadcast
45 Sgts. and Lts. get mail at them
46 Surf serving #3
49 Start over
50 Salvador lead-in
51 Sounds of disappointment
54 Song of praise
56 Sorority letter
59 Serious fan
61 "So ___!" ("Me, too!")
62 Surf serving #4
64 Show hosts, for short
65 Steed
66 Social blunder
67 Some advanced degs.
68 Synthetic fiber
69 Step into

DOWN

1 State in NE India
2 Sonar sounds
3 Suit to the circumstances
4 Steve ___, founder of 6-Down
5 Some payments are made thus
6 See 4-Down
7 Srta., in France
8 Stirs
9 Sizable zoo animals
10 Strasbourg article
11 Saying before a big drink
12 Sandusky's lake
13 Student's book
18 Stylish Oldsmobile
22 Sci-fi film of 1984
25 Some easy baskets
27 Sports org. with a March tourney
28 Slow down
29 Sorceress of myth
30 Searches for prey
31 Slightly, in music

Puzzle 93 by Nancy Salomon and Gail Grabowski

32 Signs, as a contract
33 Smidgens, as of cream
34 School grad
35 Scattershot
39 Storage building
44 Smog relative
47 Strangelove or Kildare
48 Stressed out
51 Skyward
52 Stout detective Nero ___
53 Stay (clear of)

54 Soccer star Mia
55 Swimming pool site, for short
57 Sling
58 Supposing that
60 Straight ___ arrow
62 Schedule abbr. for cable viewers
63 Swamp

ACROSS

1 Coffee, slangily
5 Elite
11 Western treaty grp.
14 Chem. table component
15 Uproar
16 Sis's sibling
17 Shrill
19 "The Lord of the Rings" figure
20 Ask too many questions
21 ___-Magnon
22 Tiny spot in the ocean
24 Arduous
28 1966 U.S. Open champion Fred
31 Actor Greene
32 Object trivially
33 Inopportune
37 Summer quaffs
38 Basket fiber
40 Knot
41 Soap star A ___
43 Slight color
44 ___ nous
45 Like Oreos and doughnuts, often
46 Extremely sad
50 Certain daisy
51 Eggs
52 Dessert in a pan
55 Russian fighter
56 Persuasion
61 Yale student
62 Kaput
63 ___ Romeo (sports car)

64 Sycophant's response
65 Sink to the bottom, as sediment
66 Trudge

DOWN

1 Cherokee maker
2 Apple spray
3 Extremely
4 Rock concert equipment
5 Force
6 Impresario Sol
7 Like many drugs: Abbr.
8 Biol. or chem.
9 Suffix on north or south
10 Major League player before moving to S.F.
11 ÷ symbols
12 Sen. Specter
13 Sound starting "Germany"
18 "___ Your Name" (Mamas & the Papas song)
23 Winding yarn
24 Like sore hands
25 One of Santa's team
26 Dinner bread
27 ___ Stanley Gardner
28 Trick
29 "Voila!"
30 Completed
34 Member of an order
35 Nose (out)
36 Property title

Puzzle 94 by Alan Arbesfeld

38 Foreword: Abbr.
39 Dried up
42 Crying
43 Bluefins
45 What ÷ signifies, in math
46 Cozy
47 Force out
48 Auspices
49 Carpentry pin
52 Hardly the life of the party
53 Dope
54 "Omigosh!"

57 Parisian street
58 Cambridge sch.
59 It might make molehills out of mountains
60 Dancer's shoe attachment

ACROSS
1 Mouthfuls of gum
5 "Fear of Flying" author Jong
10 Flying mammals
14 Side squared, for a square
15 Outdoor employee at a restaurant
16 Salt Lake City's home
17 Matt Dillon film based on an S. E. Hinton novel
19 "___ my day!"
20 Like some kisses and unlocked bikes
21 Summer in France
22 Ran, as colors
23 Pennies
25 Deer hunter's trophy
27 Airport info: Abbr.
29 Song for two
31 Word before "I told you so!"
32 Ark builder
34 Infinitesimal bit
36 Disconcert
40 "Swan Lake" garb
41 ___ lazuli
43 Poet ___ St. Vincent Millay
44 Response to "Who's there?"
46 After-bath powder
47 Give off
48 Diner sandwich
50 Kind of tolerance
52 Resident: Suffix
53 Pertains
57 Relish
59 Bog
60 Essence
62 Fruit with a peel
65 Tiny bump on a graph
66 Doofus
68 Actress Anderson
69 Swashbuckling Flynn
70 Choir member
71 Suffix with luncheon
72 "Inferno" author
73 More or ___

DOWN
1 The "W" in V.F.W.
2 Stuck in ___
3 Political descendants of Thomas Jefferson
4 Expensive fur
5 Ultimate
6 Brit. fliers
7 Tennis's Nastase
8 Jai alai equipment
9 Site of the 2004 Olympics
10 Colorful stinger
11 "___ of Two Cities"
12 Greedy one
13 Leaves hair here and there
18 Give for a while
24 Assail
26 Oolong or pekoe
27 Not pro
28 Football score of 60-0, say

Puzzle 95 by Randall J. Hartman

30 Stone in a ring
33 Not a good thing to have to eat
35 A long way
37 Praiseworthy
38 Pique
39 Loathe
42 Game with tiles
45 Whitney of cotton gin fame
49 Got uptight
51 Like one White House office
53 Walk about

54 Jet controller
55 Not write cursively
56 Kama ___
58 Shaq of the N.B.A.
61 Scorch
63 Wacky
64 Old Testament book
67 Bon ___ (witticism)

ACROSS

1 Owl's home, maybe
5 Partner of ham
10 Increase
14 ". . . ___ saw Elba"
15 Jeweler's unit
16 Uncouth
17 Trip to Germany?
19 Rat-___
20 Makes beloved
21 Fudge ___ ice cream
23 Martinique, par exemple
24 Ivy League buddies?
26 Informed
29 Innsbruck locale: Abbr.
30 Absorb, as a cost
31 Where people arrive to split
32 Long overcoat
34 Driver's lic. and others
37 Homeless German writer?
40 Hindu honorific
41 Cousin of a conch
42 Suffix with persist
43 Bray starter
45 Archer's asset
46 One in a cast
47 Scandinavian surveillance?
50 ___ standstill
51 Metes out
52 Frontier settlement
56 Response to an insult, maybe
57 Clean B & B?

60 London gallery
61 Raring to go
62 Son of Isaac
63 Gave the once-over
64 O. Henry device
65 Cabinet div.

DOWN

1 Emmy winner Neuwirth
2 Elvis's middle name
3 Tear apart
4 Pitch-and-putt club
5 Musical arranger's work
6 Partner of means
7 Belfast grp.
8 Droop
9 Rowboat's rear
10 Italian brandy
11 One getting same-day medical service, maybe
12 1960's Interior Secretary Stewart
13 "For ___ sake!"
18 Low-lying land
22 Like krypton or xenon
24 Bulletin board fastener
25 Regard highly
26 Weaponry
27 Become threadbare
28 Wipe out
29 Director Robert
32 Prefix with cycle
33 Ballpark fig.
35 Art ___
36 Suffix with hip or quip

Puzzle 96 by Alan Arbesfeld

38 "___ My Heart in San Francisco"
39 Summarized, as a ball game
44 Fled and wed
46 Westernmost Aleutian
47 Take a nibble at
48 Set to rest
49 Japanese immigrant
50 Singing cowboy
52 Ready for business
53 Seine tributary
54 Lose it
55 Bolt holder

58 Kids' card game
59 Tripper's problem?

ACROSS

1 "The Persistence of Memory" artist
5 Powerful punch
9 Clinic complaints
14 The "A" in Chester A. Arthur
15 Lawn mower brand
16 "___ Boots Are Made for Walkin' " (1966 hit)
17 Top dog
19 Make fun of
20 Bookseller ___.com
21 Liberty
23 Work station
26 Pharaoh's cross
27 Gray
31 Fat compound
33 Delivery room doctors, for short
36 Cathedral topper
37 "National Velvet" author Bagnold
38 Chew (on)
39 Drooping
40 Bird-to-be
41 Pal
42 Sound heard in a cave
43 Omar of "The Mod Squad," 1999
44 Theater worker
45 Aug. follower
46 Drop in on
47 Pricker
48 Derriere
50 Wall Street inits.
52 Tool that may be hit with a hammer
55 Burning
60 Zones
61 Top dog
64 View from an overlook
65 Do magazine work
66 Opera set in Egypt
67 Cafeteria customer
68 Using metallic dishes in a microwave, e.g.
69 Not new

DOWN

1 Comic Carvey
2 Class reunion attender
3 Dalai ___
4 Don Juan's mother
5 Peach pit
6 "Skip to My ___"
7 Big coffee holder
8 Play around, with "off"
9 Go to
10 Place for a peck
11 Top dog
12 Exxon predecessor
13 Look
18 Dangerfield who got "no respect"
22 Surprise attack
24 Nods off
25 Top dog
27 Complete fools
28 "The final frontier"
29 Top dog

Puzzle 97 by Gregory E. Paul

30 As a result
32 Boar's abode
34 Pie maker
35 Avowed
38 Opposite of ooze
41 C₄H₈
43 Emerald Isle
46 Formerly all-women's college in Poughkeepsie
49 Thrill
51 ___ voce
52 View from the pulpit
53 Operatic song

54 Federal agts.
56 Mrs., in Munich
57 Wading bird
58 Hitchhiker's quest
59 "Goodness gracious!"
62 "If ___ say so myself"
63 Wrongdoing

ACROSS

1 What rodeo horses do
5 Campus building
9 Barfly's perch
14 Workout aftereffect
15 Bread spread
16 Antilles resort
17 Not aweather
18 Exclude
19 Smelly
20 What a judo master uses to break lights?
22 Be a ham
23 Writer Kafka
24 Item in a bag
25 Texas A & M athlete
28 There are seven in a semana
30 Emulates Eminem
33 Summit
35 Work like a beaver
37 Jean-___ Picard (Patrick Stewart character)
38 I
39 Paid player
41 "I don't think so"
42 Wrath
43 Suffering
44 Hindu wrap
46 Opera set in Seville
48 Blabbed to the feds, say
50 Longings
52 Conical home
53 Little piggies
55 Shrink with fear
57 "Oh, stop your joshin'!"
59 Headline about a newly discovered refuse site?
63 Paper deliverer's plan
64 Eyes a bull's-eye, say
65 Territory
66 Playwright Rice
67 White cheese
68 Bull's-eye hitter
69 John, Paul and John Paul
70 7-6, 3-6 and 6-4, e.g.
71 Blackthorn

DOWN

1 False god
2 Bruins' sch.
3 H.S. class
4 Stay in shape
5 Whoop-de-do
6 Morsel in many a chocolate bar
7 German city famous for fairs
8 A whole bunch
9 Morley of "60 Minutes"
10 Slight quake
11 Walking despite being injured?
12 Words in passing?
13 Put on, as cargo
21 Willies
24 Asimov or Stern
25 Swears

26 Where Columbus was born
27 Sound of a golf ball landing near a hole?
29 Late advice columnist Landers
31 Blender button
32 Part of a play
34 Looks inside?
36 "Supposing . . ."
40 Excavation find
45 Ask
47 Prepares to fire again
49 Col. Sanders feature

51 Meeting of leaders
54 Pitchers
56 Basilica parts
57 Get ready for an exam
58 Without help
59 Touches
60 Russia's ____ Mountains
61 Fiddling emperor, they say
62 "It's a ____!"

ACROSS

1 Approach with a question or remark
7 Restaurant listings
11 Sombrero, e.g.
14 Riot participant, maybe
15 Its symbol is Fe
16 Bustle
17 Metal fusers
19 Solemn promise
20 Capital on a fjord
21 Pas' mates
22 Decorate
24 Stamp sellers
27 Crop growers
31 Greek war god
32 Sign before Taurus
33 When said three times, a dance move
34 ___ to one's word
38 Peaks
42 Rams' mates
43 Topper for 60-Across
44 Opposing group
45 River to the Caspian Sea
47 Dog or cat breed
49 Be very responsive, as a car
53 Gorge
54 Glacier composition
55 Has debts
59 Hockey great Bobby
60 Kitchen vessels
64 Lawyer's payment
65 Guitarist Clapton
66 Like many a grandparent
67 Part of F.D.I.C.: Abbr.
68 Possible result of nonpayment
69 Six-line poem

DOWN

1 Besides
2 Robbers' partner
3 "Neato!"
4 Conductor Klemperer
5 Emulate Betsy Ross
6 It's earthshaking
7 Central position
8 Before, to bards
9 ". . . see hide ___ hair of"
10 Risky
11 Mayhem
12 Worship
13 Burgs
18 Girl
23 Aloof
24 Mexican moolah
25 Home to Honolulu
26 Kukla, ___ and Ollie
27 It may be tempted
28 In ___ (aligned)
29 Red, as an apple
30 Goofs
33 Fish-and-chips fish
35 Bris or confirmation
36 États-___
37 In ___ (actually)
39 Custard dessert
40 "___ 18" (Leon Uris book)

Puzzle 99 by Sarah Keller

41 It may be tall
46 Toddler's jumpsuit
47 Flexible mineral
48 Changes, as the Constitution
49 Scorn
50 Full complement of Stooges or Wise Men
51 Rowed
52 Place to do the hustle
55 Makes a choice [and one more example of this puzzle's theme]

56 "Don't go yet!"
57 Feminine suffix
58 Army N.C.O.
61 Mine find
62 Overturn
63 John ___

ACROSS

1 Shaving products
6 Wrangler's buddy
10 Deck quartet
14 Buzzards Bay, for one
15 To ___ (exactly)
16 Classic Walt Kelly strip
17 Washington flip side
18 Monticello flip side
20 Shout of adoration
22 Monkeys, apes and such
23 Is imminent
25 Zero
26 Bad to the bone
29 Bonnet securer
31 In vitro items
34 Dunce cap-shaped
36 Fill to the gills
37 San Francisco's ___ Hill
38 Memorial flip side
41 Presidential seal flip side
43 Pub order
44 Turndowns
46 Shipbuilders' woods
47 Driveway surface
48 Shows contempt
51 12/25
52 It's found in a pound
53 Bee product?
55 A Little Rascal
59 One of the Fondas
63 Sacagawea flip side
65 Roosevelt flip side
66 Thin nail
67 It's flipped in this puzzle
68 Fuss
69 Nervous
70 Extremities
71 Grain disease

DOWN

1 Dangle poles over a pier, say
2 Not deceived by
3 Word for Yorick
4 Tinny-sounding
5 Shorthand taker, for short
6 Kind of top or party
7 Polished off
8 Makes calls on the court
9 Clear-cut
10 Fool's month
11 ___ Nostra
12 Designer von Furstenberg
13 Princes, e.g.
19 ___ domain
21 Drama with masks
24 They go around the block: Abbr.
26 Great applause
27 "There!"
28 Centerward
30 Karachi's land: Abbr.
31 A wee hr.
32 Bullshot ingredient
33 Deep pit
35 Television cabinet

Puzzle 100 by John Underwood

39 Sullen expression
40 Bridal bio word
42 Like a close neighbor
45 Et ___ (and the following): Abbr.
49 "Venus and Adonis" painter
50 What to call a knight
52 Papa
54 Flexible, as a body
55 Singer Lane
56 Fat in a can
57 Stars and Stripes, e.g.
58 1957 Stravinsky ballet

60 Old-time sailor's drink
61 Bounceback
62 "___ does it!"
64 Topper

ACROSS

1 ___ Vegas
4 Fisherman
10 Hit, as one's toe
14 AOL, e.g.: Abbr.
15 Harangue
16 Llama's land
17 Building wing
18 Iroquois Indian
19 Put up, as a picture
20 Earthquake measurer
23 Bowling target
24 Story that's "to be continued"
27 Sight-related
28 Ewe's mate
31 Five: Prefix
32 Fred Flintstone and others
35 Request after an auto breakdown
36 Carry-on bags have them
41 That: Sp.
42 See "damp" instead of "clamp," e.g.
43 Run off to wed
46 However, informally
47 Wasp homes
51 Sharp comeback
53 Christie of mystery
54 "Ahhh" and "Whew, that was close!"
58 Sentence subject, usually
60 Come by
61 Basic cleaner
62 Turnpike turn-off
63 Tiny acorn, e.g.
64 RCA and Panasonic products
65 The "B" in KB and MB
66 Rounded hills
67 Word before "Go!"

DOWN

1 Isn't straight up with
2 Catching z's
3 Broken finger support
4 Consisting of tiny bits
5 Sheer fabric
6 Actor Kinnear
7 Den
8 Icelandic literary work
9 Harvests
10 Globe
11 Attack aggressively
12 Cider server
13 Locust or beetle
21 Enliven, with "up"
22 With it, man
25 Heaps
26 Subjects of Congressional debate
28 Send in payment
29 Group in Lancaster County, Pa.
30 Washington transit system, with "the"
33 Vigor's partner
34 Scot's refusal
36 Fortuneteller
37 South Seas locale
38 Snazzy 1940's attire

39 Off-topic ramblings
40 Perfect
44 Grosse ___, Mich.
45 Work unit
48 Circus props
49 "Look What ___ Done to My Song, Ma" (1970 hit)
50 Least risky
52 Show gratitude to
53 The Little Mermaid
55 "Star Trek" weapon setting
56 "Beetle Bailey" dog

57 Take a tumble
58 Omaha's state: Abbr.
59 Prefix with acetylene

ACROSS

1 Almanac contents
6 Book of memories, maybe
11 Big shot, for short
14 Love to bits
15 Numbers-calling game
16 67.5°, to mariners
17 Grant provider
18 Route to prison?
20 Campus locale
22 This very moment
23 Concertgoer's keepsake
25 English race place
28 Load of bunk
29 Fall (over)
30 Courts
31 Fracas
32 Like apples, say, during the fall
34 You can lend it or bend it
35 Blaster's need
36 Book in prison?
38 It's hailed
41 Rep.'s counterpart
42 Over again
44 Flies, ants and such
47 The Beatles' "Hey ___"
48 Like Nash's lama
49 Nay sayer
50 Neigh sayer
51 Track shape
52 Unofficial ticket source
54 Desperate
56 Money in prison?
59 X-rated, say
62 Wood-dressing tool
63 Grind, as teeth
64 Come after
65 Where to hear 10-Down
66 ___ Domingo
67 007, for one

DOWN

1 Furbys, once
2 Hoo-ha
3 Escape from prison?
4 Hot water, so to speak
5 Word repeated after "Que"
6 Epitome of simplicity
7 Celestial feline
8 Pickers' instruments
9 Full-length
10 Cows' chorus
11 Of the spring
12 Shoe part
13 Nickname for a little guy
19 Out-and-out
21 Former "Family Feud" host Richard
23 "S.N.L." bit
24 T.V.A. part: Abbr.
26 "Any day now . . ."
27 Look around a prison?
31 Chess ending
33 Ideal serves
34 Go beyond the bounds of

Puzzle 102 by Tyler Hinman

37 Puts a stop to
38 Poetry in prison?
39 Geometric calculation
40 Period ender
41 Pink-legged bird
43 Ship's securer
44 Mathematician Blaise
45 Make cryptic
46 Quatrain or sestet
47 Michael who was five-time N.B.A. M.V.P.
50 Salon color
53 Cribbage needs

55 Light bulb's signification, in cartoons
57 World record suffix
58 P on a fraternity house
60 Winery cask
61 "Is it soup ___?"

ACROSS

1 Polio vaccine developer
5 "Step aside, I'll do it"
10 Unexciting
14 Have __ to one's head
15 Bird-related
16 Where Pearl Harbor is
17 Popular cookbook author
19 "Thin" coin
20 Come into view
21 Emergency situation
23 Lock opener
24 Lock location
27 Scott Joplin's "Maple Leaf __"
28 Lad
33 Muckety-muck
36 "Bolero" composer
37 Advance in years
38 Isn't solvent
39 Dove houses
40 What's harvested
41 Remote control abbr.
42 Filmmaker Woody
43 "If you __" (words of deference)
44 Worked up
47 Fuel additive
48 Manipulative one
49 File folder feature
52 Excellence
56 Formally renounce
58 __ Minor (constellation)
59 Somerset Maugham novel, with "The"
62 Mideast's Gulf of __
63 Native Alaskan
64 Like a lime
65 Pair
66 Duke, earl, etc.
67 Three, in cards

DOWN

1 Game show host Pat
2 With mouth wide open
3 Like some gravy and mattresses
4 Midleg
5 Maze runner
6 Preceding day
7 __ Maria liqueur
8 __ Antony
9 Signs, as a check
10 Spanish grocery
11 Den
12 "Life is hard . . ."
13 Colored
18 Englishman in colonial India
22 Author Roald
25 Take a walk
26 Flat part of a chart line
28 __ Alamos, N.M.
29 Occasions
30 Differentiate
31 Modest people have small ones
32 Possible result of 40-Down nonpayment

Puzzle 103 by David Bunker

33 Exploding star
34 Delinquent G.I.
35 Carillon part
39 Nonsense
40 Auto
42 Opposing
43 Most Yugoslavs
45 Cuba, e.g.
46 Red suit
49 Elizabeth I was the last one
50 Present a case in court
51 Drunken

52 Triplet plus one
53 Language of Pakistan
54 Out of sight of shore
55 Bush's alma mater
57 Joke
60 Zuider ___
61 Your and my

ACROSS
1 Passing fancies
6 Cathedral area
10 End-of-week cry
14 Greek column style
15 Fishing rod attachment
16 Roughly
17 Split
20 M.D.'s work in them
21 "Yummy!"
22 "This means __!"
23 Home of the N.L.'s Cards
24 Sleep medication
26 Bartenders check them: Abbr.
28 Split
34 Earth tone
35 Mag. staff
36 Slap shot success
37 Not just aloof
38 Closes tight
42 Dangerous sprayer
43 Runners' units
45 601, to Nero
46 Brought on board
48 Split
52 "That means __!"
53 Actor William of "Yanks"
54 Cooking spray brand
56 Mercury, but not Mars
58 Metal container
59 Bud's comic buddy
62 Split
66 Like poor losers
67 Itsy-bitsy bug

68 Golfer Palmer, informally
69 "The Untouchables" extras
70 Wallet padding
71 Bill from a computer company?

DOWN
1 Smart-alecky
2 Happy __
3 Travelers' stopovers
4 Prefix with night or day
5 Runs like a rabbit
6 Coffee shop lures
7 Check endorser's need
8 Kelp and others
9 Island near Corsica
10 Unit of bricks
11 Wimbledon venue
12 "Winning __ everything"
13 Babe in the stable
18 Arab ruler
19 Like Death Valley
24 Corrida cry
25 Something that may be hard to hold
27 Statesman Hammarskjöld
28 Gets really steamed
29 Philosopher William of __
30 Discounter's pitch
31 Tempe sch.
32 Old sitcom maid

33 Say "Li'l Abner," say
39 One of eight Eng. kings
40 Environmental problem
41 Game "played" with answering machines
44 ___-mo
47 Suffix with Canaan
49 Gambler's need
50 Calls to mind
51 Like a skinny-dipper
54 Verbal nudge
55 It's smashed in a lab
57 BB's and bullets
59 Period of penitence
60 Something that hurts, slangily
61 Applications
63 Long time: Abbr.
64 Numbered hwy.
65 Org. for people with arms

ACROSS
1 Sultan of ___
(Babe Ruth)
5 Gaming table stacks
9 Tease
14 Roof's edge
15 Leave out
16 Performer with a
painted-on smile
17 Bygone times
18 Conceal
19 HBO deliverer
20 "You said it!"
23 September bloom
24 Royal residences
28 Knave
32 Tex-Mex snack
33 "Stop right there!"
37 Dry-as-dust
38 Short flight
39 Oceanographic
charts
42 Comedian's bit
43 Currier's partner in
lithography
45 "Uh-uh!"
47 Mother ___
(Nobel-winning nun)
50 Siesta sound
51 Stretchy, as a
waistband
53 Notre Dame's
Fighting ___
57 "I'm afraid not!"
61 Madcap
64 Seep (out)
65 Smidgen
66 Apple laptop

67 Eve's man
68 Demonic
69 Hollywood's DeVito or
Glover
70 Ballfield cover
71 Byrd and Hatch, e.g.:
Abbr.

DOWN
1 "Ta-ta"
2 Merchandise
3 "Halt!," at sea
4 Mosaic piece
5 Physicist Niels
6 Mideast prince
7 An almanac lists its
highs and lows
8 Prepare, as tea
9 Pepsi competitor
10 Mobile home?
11 Big hunk
12 "Wise" bird
13 SSW's reverse
21 Leg shackles
22 Cave dweller
25 It goes in the hold
26 Sewing machine
inventor Howe
27 Everglades grass
29 "You could've
knocked me over
with a feather!"
30 ___ Bator, Mongolia
31 St. ___ fire
33 Snowlike
34 It's no mansion
35 "Tosca," e.g.
36 Sign of boredom

Puzzle 105 by Gregory E. Paul

40 Kung ___ shrimp
41 Neighbor of Israel
44 College period
46 Axis soldiers
48 Thickset
49 Lungful
52 Zagreb resident
54 1974 Tom T. Hall hit
55 Peaceful protest
56 Gets better, as a wound
58 Mentor for Luke Skywalker
59 Ivan, for one

60 Rope material
61 Grant-in-___
62 Org. for the Nets and Nuggets
63 Ship's weight unit

ACROSS

1 Pat Boone's "___ Love"
6 Symbol of redness
10 Norway's patron saint
14 Cranberry product
15 Brand for Bowser
16 Place to stack money
17 35-Across, from 1955–61
19 Finish line, perhaps
20 Windy City trains
21 Gist
22 Hindu royal: Var.
23 35-Across in 1964
27 Syndicate head
30 Program airing
31 One who opens a can of worms?
34 Hospitalized patient's state
35 See 17-, 23-, 48- and 57-Across
41 Otherwise
42 City opposite Ciudad Juárez
43 Issues in paperback, perhaps
47 Barely managed, with "out"
48 35-Across in 1994
51 Carroll girl
52 Spawner in the Sargasso Sea
53 One way to the WWW
56 Actor Moranis
57 35-Across in 1946

61 Allot, with "out"
62 "The Morning Watch" author
63 Ear or tube preceder
64 Gofer: Abbr.
65 Marquand's Mr.
66 Approaches

DOWN

1 Court great Arthur
2 One of the Fab Four
3 Hairpieces, slangily
4 "___ bin ein Berliner"
5 Hotelier Helmsley
6 Its stakes may be a beer
7 Inventor Whitney
8 It rates m.p.g.
9 Whole bunch
10 Chief Pontiac, e.g.
11 Tropical vines
12 Trumpeter Herb
13 Admiral's force
18 Bowery ___
22 Carmaker's woe
23 Finger-in-the-socket consequence
24 Spies seek them
25 Swill
26 Fiesta Bowl site
27 Crow's sound
28 "___ number can play"
29 Links org.
32 Forever, poetically
33 Vestige
36 "It comes ___ surprise"

Puzzle 106 by Gene Newman

(grid)

37 Mimicker
38 Talk, talk, talk
39 Cleveland-to-Baltimore dir.
40 Serling of "The Twilight Zone"
43 Depends (on)
44 Forces out
45 Striker, often
46 Sound system
48 Destiny
49 Napoleonic marshal
50 Spritelike
53 Visitor to Siam

54 German border river
55 Unseen "Mary Tyler Moore Show" character
57 ___ and Swiss
58 Swelled head
59 Court divider
60 Common lunchtime

ACROSS

1 First father
5 "Voila!"
10 Vocalized
14 Characteristic carrier
15 Pass along
16 ". . . with a banjo on my ___"
17 With 59-Across, indication of caring
19 Author Turgenev
20 ___ Deco
21 Prefix with dynamic
22 Football great Favre
23 Indication of larceny
27 Declares
29 "___ Gang"
30 Caustic chemical
31 18-wheeler
32 Test, as ore
34 Indication of detachment
41 Bing, bang or boom
42 Future attorney's hurdle: Abbr.
43 Appropriate
46 U.S. or Can. money
47 Like an oboe's sound
48 Indication of opportunity
53 Plant life
54 Quark's place
55 Place to retire
58 Jazz's Fitzgerald
59 See 17-Across
62 Like some dorms
63 Patronized, as a restaurant
64 Starting from
65 It ebbs and flows
66 Tiny poker stake
67 Having an angle

DOWN

1 Turkish title
2 Does and bucks
3 Object of loathing
4 Debussy's "La ___"
5 True's partner
6 Painter Matisse
7 Rock's ___ John
8 Stadium sound
9 Watch closely
10 Blouse accompanier
11 Show, as plans
12 With precision
13 Tamed
18 Gets some color, as they say
22 Gem mineral
24 Like the Sahara
25 ". . . off ___ the wizard"
26 1950's Communist-hunting grp.
27 Cigarette's end
28 Two-finger sign
32 Leaning
33 Sounds from a librarian
35 Delhi's land
36 It follows 11
37 Butter alternative
38 Computer company's customers

Puzzle 107 by Sarah Keller

39 Father
40 Where hogs wallow
43 Have an influence on
44 Hoi ___
45 Drove (along)
47 Frolic
49 Give and take?
50 Broadway actress Uta
51 Wharton's "___ Frome"
52 Daft
56 Supply-and-demand subj.

57 Skillful
59 Perform like Salt-N-Pepa
60 Suffix with Manhattan
61 Place for beakers

ACROSS

1 Network with an eye logo
4 Call bad names
10 High school class
14 Santa ___, Calif.
15 Twist-filled Broadway musical?
16 Vito Corleone's creator
17 Bedouin at a major waterway?
20 Not-so-secret secret language
21 Pirate rival
22 Chemical suffix
23 Cracker Jack bonus
25 Cloud's place
26 Rounded lump
29 Harshly criticize
31 Light sailboat at a hotel chain?
39 Indian prince in Mobile?
40 Tales about a 1980's singing group?
41 Actress Garr
42 ___ Flynn Boyle of "The Practice"
43 Tachometer abbr.
46 Performed
47 Magazine revenue source
49 Run for one's wife?
51 Sweetie
56 Gilda Radner character's embodiment?

59 Mideast guns
60 Paparazzo's device
61 In the past
62 Pretzel topper
63 Dissertation
64 "Help!"

DOWN

1 Andy of the comics
2 ___ B'rith
3 Turned state's evidence
4 Like some noses and numerals
5 Overjoy
6 "Veni, vidi, ___"
7 Tennis great Lendl
8 Spy novelist Deighton
9 Pitcher's stat.
10 Luxury resorts
11 Smarts
12 Arkansas's ___ Mountains
13 New Orleans sandwich
18 "Open, sesame!" speaker
19 Set down
23 Japanese floor covering
24 Missouri River city
26 Snatch
27 In ___ land
28 Neighbor of Yemen
29 Chicken
30 Missouri town where Harry Truman was born

Puzzle 108 by Peter Gordon

32 Actor Aykroyd
33 Noted Italian violinmaker
34 More, in Madrid
35 Body of water between Kazakhstan and Uzbekistan
36 Hindu music form
37 Not fully shut
38 Space shuttle org.
43 Picture puzzle
44 Public square
45 Big gas brand
46 Frost relative

47 Early video game company
48 Famously temperamental singers
50 Future's opposite
51 Arrived
52 Employs
53 School orgs.
54 "Othello" villain
55 God of love
57 Play part
58 When repeated, a trombone sound

ACROSS

1 Health resorts
5 TV series with Hawkeye and Hot Lips
9 Aspirin maker
14 N.Y.S.E. listing
15 Nabisco cookie
16 Miss Doolittle of "My Fair Lady"
17 Large section in an atlas
18 Thumbtack, British-style
20 Error
22 Office message
23 Drunkard
24 Church bell spot
26 Fall in scattered drops, as rain
28 Boot camp reply
30 Not on the road
34 Sheets and pillowcases
37 Sandwich shop
69 Restaurant chain acronym
40 Immediately, after "at"
41 Job title (giving a hint to this puzzle's theme)
42 Gooey ground
43 Hearty drink made with honey
44 Center of a Christmas display
45 Hearty steak
46 Flowering shrub
48 Water at the mouth

50 One-named Irish singer
52 Avenues
56 "What's the ___?"
59 Reps.' foes
61 Bluesman ___ Wolf
62 Well-worn
65 German "a"
66 Art stand
67 Fiction teller
68 R & B/jazz singer James
69 Beach souvenir
70 Stately trees
71 Work station

DOWN

1 Rip-offs
2 Put
3 Get up
4 Seattle landmark
5 Catwalk walkers
6 The "A" in E.T.A.: Abbr.
7 Line made by a 41-Across
8 Inventor Elias and others
9 Marathon runner Joan
10 High school math: Abbr.
11 Puppy sounds
12 Operatic singer Pinza
13 Long, angry complaint
19 Damage
21 Atop

Puzzle 109 by Gregory E. Paul

A grid for a crossword puzzle is shown. The grid is 14 columns wide. The numbered cells are as follows:

Row 1: 1, 2, 3, 4, [black], 5, 6, 7, 8, [black], 9, 10, 11, 12, 13
Row 2: 14, 15, 16
Row 3: 17, 18, 19
Row 4: 20, 21, 22, 23
Row 5: 24, 25, 26, 27
Row 6: 28, 29, 30, 31, 32, 33
Row 7: 34, 35, 36, 37, 38, 39
Row 8: 40, 41, 42
Row 9: 43, 44, 45
Row 10: 46, 47, 48, 49
Row 11: 50, 51, 52, 53, 54, 55
Row 12: 56, 57, 58, 59, 60, 61
Row 13: 62, 63, 64, 65
Row 14: 66, 67, 68
Row 15: 69, 70, 71

25 Duck down?
27 White-flowered plant
29 Marry again
31 Cincinnati's home
32 Time starting at dawn
33 Fencing rapier
34 ___ Linda, Calif.
35 "Il Trovatore" soprano
36 Interscholastic sports org.
38 Lecherous looks
41 Stuck around
45 Bull in a bullring
47 Ultimate purpose

49 Additional ones
51 Walk
53 Best of the best
54 Salon jobs
55 ___ preview
56 Tableland tribe
57 Iranian "king"
58 Scots Gaelic
60 Flying jib, e.g.
63 Electric fish
64 Hit head-on

ACROSS
1 Part of Q.E.D.
5 Contradict
10 "You can say that again!"
14 Mascara site
15 Ain't correct?
16 What the fourth little piggy got
17 Take the bait
18 Construction playthings
20 Like Mickey Mouse
22 Coup ___
23 Metric measure
24 ___ Solo of "Star Wars"
25 Like some suits
31 Houston-based org.
35 Bikini, e.g.
36 Way off
37 Play starter
38 Warmed the bench
39 Author connected to this puzzle's theme
42 Sushi offering
43 Verbal assault
45 Emporium event
46 Michaels of "Saturday Night Live"
48 Literary lioness
49 Shirelles hit of 1962
51 Pathet ___
53 First U.S. color TV maker
54 Taxpayer's dread
57 Part of L.E.D.
62 Crow's-nest instruments
65 Lionel train layout, maybe
66 "Nana" star Anna
67 Fake jewelry
68 Declare "good" or "excellent," say
69 Drops off
70 Grace word
71 Snick and ___

DOWN
1 Alabama county seat named for a European island
2 Wet forecast
3 Italian wine town
4 Teen's hangout, perhaps
5 One who's up
6 Canal of song
7 Do banker's work
8 Publicity
9 When Dijon gets hot
10 Pre-cable need
11 Like some points
12 New Age singer
13 Branch headquarters?
19 Nutritional fig.
21 On ___ (doing well)
24 München mister
25 Café holder
26 Whatsoever
27 Tiny bits
28 Port near Hong Kong
29 Headed for ___ (in imminent trouble)

30 Wasn't afraid
32 Sharp-tongued
33 Pool person
34 Alvin of dance
40 Flying A competitor
41 Opt
44 Bad-mouths
47 Spellbinders
50 Pigmented eye parts
52 Part of A & P: Abbr.
54 Org.
55 Until
56 Turned blue, maybe
57 To be, to Brutus

58 1969 miracle team
59 Terrible man?
60 Hoopster Archibald
61 ___ club
63 Msg. sent to squad cars
64 Mineo of film

ACROSS

1 Put off, as a motion
6 Life stories, for short
10 Poison ivy symptom
14 Trojan War epic
15 As a twosome, musically
16 Initial stake
17 "Norma Rae" director
19 London privies
20 Extra wager
21 Tennis champ Pete
23 The "L" of L.C.D.
25 "___ to break it to you, but . . ."
26 Horticulturist who developed the Shasta daisy
31 Sky color, in Paris
32 Terra ___
33 Noted French Dadaist
37 Was remunerative
41 Princess topper
43 Writer ___ Stanley Gardner
44 1965 Roger Miller hit
48 In the midst of
50 Group of three
51 A truck may go uphill in it
53 "College" member who votes for president
58 Frist's predecessor as Senate majority leader
59 It may follow grade school
61 Ending for buck
62 Tennis score after deuce
63 City in northern France
64 Cut, as wood
65 Dems.' foes
66 Cosmetician Lauder

DOWN

1 Actors Robbins and Allen
2 Jai ___
3 Nest builder
4 After midnight, say
5 Fit to be eaten
6 Drinker's total
7 Dictator Amin
8 Surpass
9 ___ good example
10 2000 Green Party candidate
11 Polar jacket
12 Summer ermine
13 Hermann who wrote "Steppenwolf"
18 ___-do-well
22 City near Fort Lauderdale
24 "-er" or "-ing," e.g.: Abbr.
26 J.F.K.'s successor
27 Ending with sched-
28 Oolong, for one
29 Coal-mining city of West Virginia
30 Hidden means of support?

Puzzle 111 by Alan Arbesfeld

34 Former N.B.A. star Danny
35 Scott Joplin piece
36 Stick out
38 Spanish gold
39 22-Down's state: Abbr.
40 Nourished
42 Mozambique's locale: Abbr.
44 Be obsequious (to)
45 Connections
46 Ring up?
47 Channel swimmer Gertrude
48 To whom Muslims pray
49 007 player Roger
52 Barely open
54 X's, in Greece
55 Lean slightly
56 Eye amorously
57 Korean leader Syngman ___
60 Light bite

ACROSS

1 Airline to Tel Aviv
5 Soothing spots
9 Pueblo dwelling
14 Broadway Auntie
15 Strait-laced
16 Like a highway
17 Some bargains
20 ___ Sark
21 Make use of
22 Trident feature
23 Sweetie
24 Top rating, perhaps
26 ___ room
28 Diamond ___
29 Not the finest dog
31 Be an agent (for)
33 Dukes and earls
35 Prefix with graphic
37 Punk's pistol
39 Overly ominous
43 Scarsdale, e.g., to New York City
44 Dummy Mortimer
46 "Honor Thy Father" author
49 Part of S.P.C.A.: Abbr.
51 Door sign
52 Maugham's "Cakes and ___"
53 Look over
55 A bartender may run one
57 42-Down scores: Abbr.
58 Ella Fitzgerald specialty
60 "Slippery" tree
62 "___ beaucoup"
64 Reelection toast?
68 Happening
69 Devil's doings
70 Starting from
71 Turn blue, maybe
72 Cincinnati team
73 TV host who wrote "Leading With My Chin"

DOWN

1 C.P.R. expert
2 Where some suits are pressed
3 Be the equivalent of
4 Hit the road
5 More agile
6 In favor
7 "Say it ___ so!"
8 Sling mud at
9 Sitcom extraterrestrial
10 Off one's trolley
11 Tip of Massachusetts
12 Songwriter Taupin
13 Classic Fords
18 Mel of the Polo Grounds
19 Willing to try
23 Patient-care grp.
25 Associate of Gandhi
27 Yale students starting in 1969
30 Not these
32 Jury's makeup
34 Pickling need

Puzzle 112 by Richard Chisholm

36 Helpful
38 Monastery head
40 Compliant one
41 Cry heard in a 2-Down
42 Where Giants and Titans clash
45 Skid row woe
46 Wine expert
47 Dinette set spot
48 Flipped (through)
50 Desert ruminants
54 Bugs bugged him
56 Former Tunisian ruler
59 Cousin of an Obie
61 Pull up stakes
63 "Get ___!"
65 Western native
66 Free (of)
67 Bay area airport letters

ACROSS

1 Strike from a manuscript
5 Gomer Pyle's org.
9 Larger than extra-large
14 Summit
15 Talk show host Dr. ___
16 Maker of the Legend
17 Mailed
18 Linoleum alternative
19 Amber or umber
20 Joseph Conrad novel
23 Slightly
24 Ballgame spoiler
25 Actress Brigitte
28 Discharge a cannon
29 Make a choice
32 Once more
33 Pitchfork part
34 0 on a phone: Abbr.
35 Balance point
38 In the past
39 Examines closely
40 Carriers of heredity
41 To the ___ degree
42 Spit four-letter words
43 Run in
44 "___ la vie"
45 Matured
46 Neither liberal nor conservative
53 Love, to Pavarotti
54 Comedian Rudner
55 Concerning

56 Stubble remover
57 Yale students
58 Turkey, businesswise
59 Antagonist
60 Religious offshoot
61 Heavy book

DOWN

1 Short run
2 Fencing weapon
3 Melodious Horne
4 Obtain, as a suspect, from another state
5 Ready for the task
6 Typewriter key
7 Not at all spicy
8 Forest gaps
9 Chan of action films
10 Storrs school, for short
11 Stubborn beast
12 Warner ___
13 Paddles
21 Steak cut
22 Not as common
25 Breakfast sizzler
26 Ticket seller
27 Salad dressing style
28 Marching band instruments
29 Share one's views
30 "For ___ sake!"
31 Secret meeting
33 Where Barbies are bought

Puzzle 113 by Stanley Newman

1	2	3	4	■	5	6	7	8	■	9	10	11	12	13
14				■	15				■	16				
17				■	18				■	19				
20				21					22					
■	■	■	23				■	24				■	■	■
25	26	27				■	28				■	29	30	31
32				■	33			■	34					
35				36			■	37						
38			■	39				■	40					
41			42			■	43							
■	■	44				■	45				■	■	■	■
46	47	48				49					50	51	52
53				■	54				■	55				
56				■	57				■	58				
59				■	60				■	61				

34 Checking account woe
36 Get more mileage from
37 Be of one mind
42 Crunchy vegetable
43 Horrified
44 Modern encyclopedia medium
45 Storage area
46 Colt's mother
47 One-named supermodel
48 Take a nap
49 Dossier
50 Norway's capital
51 Unit of matter
52 Chucklehead

ACROSS

1 Speak off the cuff
6 ___ of Commons
11 Govt. property overseer
14 Hotelier Helmsley
15 ___ salts
16 Shoemaker's tool
17 Court filings
19 Microwave, slangily
20 ". . . ___ shall die"
21 Deprived
22 It may be cut in a studio
23 Ice down again
25 ___ Reader (magazine)
27 Some ugly ducklings, so to speak
33 Scottish hillside
36 Mme., in Madrid
37 Fear
38 Spirits
40 Picnic crasher
42 End of many a college major
43 Jobs of limited duration
45 Big part of a dinosaur skeleton
47 "Much" preceder
48 Some athletes in training
51 Fencing need
52 "Stop acting up!"
56 "Roseanne" star
59 Short compositions
62 By way of

63 Eggs, in bio labs
64 Common sight after a burglary
66 Clearasil target
67 "As You Like It" woman
68 Like a sumo wrestler
69 "___ on a Grecian Urn"
70 "Yum!"
71 Commend highly

DOWN

1 ___ nothing
2 Big name in tractors
3 Computer programmer's need
4 "___ New York minute"
5 Sighter of the Pacific Ocean, 1513
6 München "sir"
7 Mayberry boy
8 Beneficial
9 Convertible type
10 CPR pros
11 Surveyor's look
12 Did one-third of a triathlon
13 Gravy Train competitor
18 Passenger safety items
22 Total
24 Ornamental shrub
26 Neighborhood that overlaps part of Greenwich Village
28 Time in history

Puzzle 114 by Christina Houlihan

29 What a plucker may pluck
30 Black, to poets
31 Baltic capital
32 "___ who?"
33 Low pitch?
34 Baby ___
35 Song for Sills
39 "Enough!"
41 Duty
44 Popeye's son
46 Artist Max
49 Asian nut-bearing palms

50 Antique dealer's transaction
53 Turn away
54 Sign of late summer
55 Stand for something?
56 Popular clown
57 Eager
58 Appraise
60 Military group
61 6/6/1944
64 Sept. follower
65 Wane's partner

ACROSS

1 Other
5 Ping-Pong table dividers
9 Move like a lion
14 Ponce de ___
15 Mishmash
16 Send, as payment
17 "It is the ___, and Juliet is the sun!"
18 Movers' trucks
19 African antelope
20 Hot movie of 1981?
23 Poker pot starter
24 Head of a flock: Abbr.
25 Get satisfaction for
28 Siren luring sailors to shipwreck
32 Enchantress in Homer
33 Third-place finish
35 Bruin legend Bobby
36 Hot movie of 1974, with "The"?
40 Carmaker Ransom ___ Olds
41 Loony
42 ___ a million
43 Waltzing, say
46 2000 Olympics city
47 Suffix with meth-
48 Big furniture retailer
49 Hot movie of 1966?
56 Permit
57 Just minutes from now
58 Secluded valley
59 Late English princess
60 Run ___ (go wild)
61 Biblical twin who sold his birthright
62 Whom Truman defeated for president
63 Talks one's head off
64 Vermin

DOWN

1 The "E" in P.G.&E.: Abbr.
2 Wife of Jacob
3 Slugger Sammy
4 Beguile
5 "Nay"
6 Gladden
7 Pie containers
8 Nothing special
9 Lean toward
10 Experience again
11 Bradley or Sharif
12 Chianti or Chablis
13 Inc., in England
21 Actress Stevens of 60's TV
22 Displeased look
25 Performed
26 Quartet member
27 Field Marshal Rommel
28 Lane of "Superman"
29 Actress Sophia
30 Baseball Hall-of-Famer Banks
31 Twisted humor
33 Like a bug in a rug
34 Elev.

Puzzle 115 by Sheldon Benardo

37 Word with strength or sanctum
38 Entry room
39 Imperil
44 Gangster known as Scarface
45 Sort of
46 They may raise a big stink
48 Macintosh laptop
49 Tennis champ Nastase
50 Cole ___
51 "Oho, dear chap!"

52 ___ cube (popular 60's–70's puzzle)
53 Ingrid's "Casablanca" role
54 Natty
55 Wildebeests
56 Do sums

ACROSS

1 Punishment for a child, maybe
5 Ill-gotten gains
9 "The Lord of the Rings" figure
14 Notion
15 Bandleader Puente
16 Land colonized by ancient Greeks
17 Hoops contests since '38
18 "What's gotten ___ you?"
19 Zeal
20 "Just a moment . . ."
23 Pumps for info
24 Sparkler
25 Peter Graves's role on "Mission: Impossible"
28 It may be framed
29 Zealous
33 "You've got mail" co.
34 Martini's partner
36 Reason for not apologizing
37 Some training for a football team
40 100 bucks
41 Kind of checking
42 Albanian money
43 Did groundwork?
44 Ukr., once
45 Uses finger paints, say
47 Homer Simpson outburst
48 Battery liquid
49 Minivacation
57 Existence
58 Figure in academia
59 Anita who sang "And Her Tears Flowed Like Wine"
60 Range maker
61 Oklahoma city
62 French film
63 Angers
64 Jet set jets
65 Brain's site

DOWN

1 Spanish child
2 Norse deity
3 French for 65-Across
4 Land user of yore
5 Affixes with glue
6 Skid row types
7 Abbr. at the top of a memo
8 "Oh!"
9 What to do "for murder" in a Hitchcock film
10 Had on
11 Time ___ half
12 Mexican rivers
13 Subway purchase
21 Verve
22 Penthouse centerfold
25 Nicotine ___
26 "In what way?"
27 Bond on the run?
28 John Jacob ___
29 White House spokesman Fleischer

Puzzle 116 by Elizabeth C. Gorski

30 Home in Rome
31 Loafer
32 Office stations
35 Parasols
36 Early arrival, shortly: Var.
38 Cool, 60's-style
39 Falls
44 Ground cover
46 Big Apple mayor who asked "How'm I doin'?"
47 "At the Milliner's" painter

48 Expect
49 Ski lift
50 Prefix with sphere
51 Tabriz money
52 Feminizing suffix
53 Cravings
54 Falco of "The Sopranos"
55 Zola novel
56 Like Easter eggs

ACROSS

1 Rand McNally offering
6 Señor's emphatic yes
10 Poker stake
14 It's rubbed on a cue tip
15 Garden with forbidden fruit
16 "Gone With the Wind" plantation
17 Indoor antenna
19 Egyptian goddess
20 UFO crew
21 Charged particle
22 Sneaker
24 Swan song
25 "Jelly's Last Jam" dancer Gregory ___
26 Conductor of a sham trial
31 Ramadas and such
32 Spigot
33 Pooped out
35 "Mazel ___!"
36 Zoo bosses
39 A's opposite, in England
40 Former veep Agnew
42 Extra-wide, at the shoe store
43 Sorrows' opposites
44 Sellers in stalls
48 Mattress supports
49 Sizable sandwich
50 On the ___ (preparing for battle)
53 Poet's "eternally"
54 Mai ___ cocktail
57 Skin soother
58 Inedible mushrooms
61 The "D" in CD
62 Jane Austen classic
63 Paper size
64 Editor's "let it stand"
65 Paper purchase
66 Clear the boards

DOWN

1 Good-size field
2 "How 'bout ___?!"
3 Chem classes
4 Vatican vestment
5 Downhiller's sport
6 Witnessed
7 Actress Lupino
8 Italian film director Leone
9 On the same wavelength
10 Under debate
11 Ogden who wrote light verse
12 Duet plus one
13 Simplicity
18 So far
23 Cat chat
24 U.S.N.A. grad
25 What the starts of 17-, 26-, 44- and 58-Across all are
26 Big name in book publishing
27 Blacksmith's block
28 Sally Field's "Norma ___"

Puzzle 117 by Nancy Salomon and Harvey Estes

29 Gillette product
30 Deuce beaters
31 "__ show time!"
34 Football gains: Abbr.
36 Furry marsupial
37 Comics shriek
38 __ Peanut Butter Cups
41 Look up to
43 One of the Bushes
45 Mean something
46 Where telecommuters work

47 Terrapin, e.g.
50 Rolls of bills
51 Hit the ground
52 Flower for Valentine's Day
53 Red-wrapped Dutch cheese
54 Roman robe
55 Word of woe
56 Castaway's locale
59 Doc bloc: Abbr,
60 "__ the ramparts . . ."

ACROSS

1 Hefty volume
5 Utah city
9 Hammett sleuth
14 About half of binary coding
15 Zilch
16 Noncitizen
17 God wounded in the Trojan War
18 Observed
19 Fox comedy series
20 "Hurry up!" to a person putting on a jacket?
23 French fine
24 "Timecop" actress
28 "Car Talk" airer
29 "Last one ___ a rotten egg!"
32 Short sock
33 Beyond tipsy
35 A Chaplin
36 "Hurry up!" to a person sharpening a pencil?
40 Affright
41 Peyote
42 Guinea pigs and kin
45 Under the weather
46 Attorneys' org.
49 Approached stealthily
51 Military commando
53 "Hurry up!" to a person assigning spies?
56 Island northwest of Oahu
59 Designer Gernreich
60 To be, in Tours
61 ___ fours (crawling)
62 Poker declaration
63 Cold-shoulder
64 Hostess Mesta
65 Singer k. d. ___
66 London gallery

DOWN

1 Without exception
2 Highway entry
3 More sheepish
4 Ruhr city
5 Tither's amount
6 Tanners catch them
7 Perfect place
8 Palindromic title
9 Far East boat
10 Hasbro division
11 Helping hand
12 L.A.P.D. investigator
13 Ltr. holder
21 Dimwit
22 Zadora of "Butterfly"
25 Baseball's Moises
26 Monthly bill, for many
27 ___ loss for words
30 Gossip topic
31 Monica of tennis
33 Suburban shopping area
34 Lucy's guy
36 PRNDL pick
37 Gutter site
38 Adding up, as interest

Puzzle 118 by Myles Callum

39 Senegal's capital
40 TV watchdog: Abbr.
43 Prima ballerina
44 Isuzu Rodeo, e.g.
46 Dame of mystery writing
47 Lebanon's capital
48 Actress Dahl
50 Danger
52 Bikini experiment, for short
54 Arizona city
55 Chief Norse god
56 Keystone lawman

57 Hydrocarbon suffix
58 Former Mideast alliance

ACROSS
1 Book of maps
6 Lounge
10 Lounge
14 Milk purchase
15 Actress Falco
16 Word before a verb, maybe
17 Pain inside
18 Taboo
19 Not timid
20 Cruising
21 1986 Detroit debut
23 Refuses
25 Tall tale
26 E.P.A. concern: Abbr.
29 Paint over
33 Government subsidy
38 This-and-that dish
39 21-Across, e.g.
40 Bruin Bobby
41 Singer ___ James
42 Story line
43 1998 Peter Weir film, with "The"
46 Group of 100
48 "No sweat"
49 Six years, in the 46-Across
51 Period of greatest success
56 Amateurish
61 Prefix with -naut
62 Aware of
63 Without value
64 Express appreciation to
65 ___ Clayton Powell Jr.
66 Help for a detective
67 "It's the truth!"
68 Region
69 Renaissance Italian family name
70 Carried with difficulty

DOWN
1 Shades of blue
2 Oklahoma city
3 Cagney's TV partner
4 Regions
5 Narrow waterway: Abbr.
6 Late-night name
7 Olfactory stimulus
8 Dance named after an aviator
9 Dance class wear
10 Grouped
11 It may get into a jamb
12 Humdinger
13 They may be split or tight
21 An ellipse has two of them
22 "___ you sure?"
24 Take-home
27 ___ about (approximately)
28 Lash ___, who played the Cheyenne Kid in old westerns
30 Pledge
31 Concerning
32 Unfreeze
33 Openings

Puzzle 119 by Alan Arbesfeld

34 It may begin "Do not . . ."
35 Lots
36 Out
37 "___ la Douce" (1963 film)
43 Actor Stamp
44 Tennis's Arthur
45 Bill ___, TV's Science Guy
47 No. on a business card
50 Manhandles
52 "Hurray!"

53 Had control of the deck
54 Golfer Palmer, informally
55 Like farm oxen
56 Husband of Ruth, in the Bible
57 Take back
58 Funnyman Laurel
59 Oversupply
60 Peter Fonda title role
64 Explosion maker

ACROSS

1 Like a tack
6 Cape Cod town
11 Mercedes rival
14 Fencing sword
15 Tore down
16 Sculler's need
17 What to accentuate, to Bing Crosby . . .
19 Get mellower
20 Swift works
21 Gown material
23 Neat dresser's quality
27 Some radios
30 What to eliminate . . .
34 Terra ___
36 Málaga Mrs.
37 River to the Caspian
38 Home to the Jazz
39 Rocker John
41 Cost of cross
42 Abundant
43 Place to graze
44 Have a gut feeling
45 What to latch onto, with "the" . . .
49 Kobe currency
50 ___ ridgeback (hunting dog)
52 Unable to sit still
55 Pre-cable need
59 Halloween word
60 Whom not to mess with
64 Play for a sap
65 Really spooky
66 Lake ___, separating Switzerland and France
67 Mack who emceed TV's "The Original Amateur Hour"
68 Play for time
69 Bolt to unite

DOWN

1 Fliers from De Gaulle
2 "Good joke!"
3 Help in a heist
4 Adjust, as a brooch
5 Proportionately
6 See 32-Down
7 Squealer
8 Israeli weapon
9 Ministerial nickname
10 Ukrainian port
11 Ferry or wherry
12 Crèche trio
13 Small songbird
18 Genesis son
22 Shrewd
24 Administer the oath of office to
25 "I, Claudius" role
26 Alaska's first governor
27 Integra maker
28 Recurring theme
29 Shepherd's handful
31 O. Henry specialty
32 With 6-Down, Sibelius work
33 Popular 90's sitcom
35 Not ours

Puzzle 120 by Holden Baker

39 Patron saint of sailors
40 Heavy metal
44 Space Needle site
46 Rapper's improvisations
47 Sanford of "The Jeffersons"
48 Kudzu, for one
51 Staircase support
52 Border on
53 Cyrano's protrusion
54 Pigeon-___
56 Verne skipper
57 Kind of tide

58 ___ Boleyn, queen to Henry VIII
61 Emeritus: Abbr.
62 Nest egg letters
63 Nada

ACROSS

1 Office station
5 Arthur ___ Stadium
9 "Hurrah!," e.g.
14 School for princes William and Harry
15 Swing at a fly
16 Fool (around)
17 Bounce back
18 "Stop right there!"
19 Ringmaster
20 Judge's query
23 Foal's father
24 ___ League (56-Down's group)
25 Krazy ___
28 Bureaucratic stuff
31 "___, humbug!"
34 Cake topper
36 Little devil
37 Voice below soprano
38 Doctor's query
42 Sliver
43 18-wheeler
44 Desert spring
45 ___ Canals (Great Lakes connectors)
46 Light lager
49 Farm bale
50 Sidekick
51 See 40-Down
53 Bartender's query
59 See 8-Down
60 Beach composition
61 Shade of blue
63 Raise the curtain
64 Wings: Lat.
65 Deep ___ bend
66 Nose, slangily
67 Baby-sit
68 E-mailed

DOWN

1 Lousy grade
2 Carve in stone
3 Old warehouse district in New York
4 "Who ___ what evil . . ." (intro to "The Shadow")
5 On dry land
6 Moved to the music
7 Crown of light
8 With 59-Across, words before "Then fall, Caesar!"
9 Make ready for use, as library books
10 Warm and comfortable
11 SeaWorld whale
12 Not new
13 Titleist supporter
21 Sad song
22 Longstocking lass
25 Fuzzy fruits
26 Sneeze sound
27 Link with
29 Supermodel Cheryl
30 Morning hrs.
31 Turn red from embarrassment
32 Heart chambers
33 ___-totsy
35 Gun lobby, briefly

Puzzle 121 by Gregory E. Paul

37 "Eureka!"
39 Dentist's tool
40 With "of" and 51-Across, a facial moisturizer
41 Religious scroll
46 ___ leather
47 Former White House speechwriter Peggy
48 Sidestepped
50 Outdoor party site
52 Foes of Rebs
53 Chirpy bird
54 Justice Black

55 Future atty.'s exam
56 New Haven institution
57 Barn topper
58 Neck and neck
59 Air rifle ammo
62 However

ACROSS
1 Five Pillars of ___
6 Tobacco wad
10 Prez's backup
14 Impact sounds
15 Heavenly circle
16 Not prerecorded
17 It may bring you back to reality
19 Warts and all
20 Pail problem
21 Queried
22 Splinter group
23 Cowgirl Evans
25 Enter
27 Exit
30 Not the main office
32 Opposite of spicy
33 Replay option
34 ___-Locka, Fla.
37 Diamond ___
38 Running things
40 Part of WWW
41 NBC weekend comedy, briefly
42 Thoroughly thumps
43 Nerd
45 Lifers, e.g.
47 Like heaven's gates
48 Bee's bundle
50 Say coquettishly
51 Sailor's hail
52 Warning wail
55 Nada
59 Fancy marbles
60 Academic enclave
62 Algonquian language
63 Understands
64 Laker star Shaquille
65 Aesop's also-ran
66 Big Board initials
67 Full of good cheer

DOWN
1 Result of a flea, maybe
2 "Get lost!"
3 Break in the action
4 Appended
5 Ed.'s pile
6 Picked out
7 Dove's opposite
8 Downwind, at sea
9 Scrabble or Boggle
10 Pickle brand
11 President whose grandson wed a president's daughter
12 Kick out
13 Trattoria topping
18 Sentry's command
24 Loud enough to hear
26 Coming
27 OPEC units: Abbr.
28 Lena of "Havana"
29 Nonmixer at a mixer
30 Ink stains
31 Column crossers

Puzzle 122 by Nancy Salomon

33 Go over
35 Part of a lemon
36 "Dear" advice-giver
39 Advertising lure
44 Combat area
46 Parisian palace
47 Undersized
48 Antismoking aid
49 Scarlett of Tara
50 Inherently
53 Actress Judith
54 Goes bad
56 Water pitcher
57 Spot for a spanking

58 Air France locale
61 Barnyard male

ACROSS

1 Voting group
5 À la ___ (with ice cream)
9 Wedding helper
14 Singer Horne
15 "Be ___!" ("Help me out!")
16 Stockholm native
17 Horse feed
18 Actress Garr
19 Spooky
20 Popular Canadian-born game show host
23 "Nope"
24 "y" ending, in superlative form
25 Dr. Frankenstein's workplace
30 The P of PRNDL
34 Enzyme suffix
35 Seize
36 Gently shift to a new topic
37 Sony Pictures Studio in Culver City, usually
41 Taboos
42 Prefix with plasm or morphic
43 Wide shoe width
44 Dele overrider
45 Use cheap materials, say
48 Stratford's stream
50 ___ culpa
51 Response to an answer

59 Jazzman Blake
60 Songwriter Bacharach
61 Sch. with generals as alums
62 Macaroni shape
63 Pricey theater section
64 Bring up, as children
65 Buildings with lofts
66 River of central Germany
67 "___ meeny miney mo"

DOWN

1 Explode, as a volcano
2 Wife of Jacob
3 Aware of
4 Vegas attraction
5 Infamous W.W. I spy
6 European auto
7 Take risks
8 Miracle drink
9 Consumers
10 Flowering vine
11 Parsley or sage
12 Singer/actress Adams
13 Stink
21 Three-stripers
22 Mystery writer Josephine
25 Suburban expanses
26 "___ in the Dark"
27 Designer Geoffrey
28 Profs' helpers, for short
29 ___ d'art

Puzzle 123 by Patrick Merrell

31 See eye to eye
32 Less polite
33 Conservative columnist Alan
36 Ferns reproduce with them
38 24 hours, for the earth
39 Stamped return env., e.g.
40 Counter in a car
45 Comedian Bill, familiarly
46 Lacking the skill

47 Word with "second" or "laws of"
49 Vantage points
51 Hall-of-Fame coach Ewbank
52 Belly-shaking dance
53 39-Down, e.g.
54 Part of Q.E.D.
55 Basic desire
56 "So that's what you mean"
57 Mideast's Gulf of ___
58 ___ a one (zip)

ACROSS

1 Sounds from a cornfield
5 Sonny who sang "Laugh at Me"
9 "Fiddlesticks!"
14 Part of a Latin 101 trio
15 "___ calling"
16 Not in dreamland
17 "You bet!"
18 They're often on their toes
20 Capital on the Hudson
22 Being broadcast
23 Poisonous plant
25 Hockey great Phil, familiarly
28 Broke a fast
29 46-Across belonged to it
30 Mentalist's claim
32 Not 'neath
33 Golf course bend
36 "Forget it!"
38 1971 Tom Laughlin cult film
41 Conductor Mehta
44 Piece of bingo equipment
46 50's nickname
47 Not swallow easily
50 Nest egg, of a sort: Abbr.
51 Uncertainties
54 Puts in writing
56 Bungled

59 Become fond of
61 Buyer
62 Bit of forensic evidence
65 Glamour rival
66 Proximate, to poets
67 Capital of Samoa
68 Marsh growth
69 "The Creation" composer
70 Classic computer game
71 Novus ___ seclorum (phrase on a dollar)

DOWN

1 Winter melon
2 Evil-repelling charm
3 Sang like a canary
4 Hoops turnover
5 Cutie pie
6 Eggs, to biologists
7 Strikeout king Ryan
8 Surfing the Net
9 ___-mutuel
10 Slop eaters
11 Waits awhile
12 Alias
13 Director Craven
19 Big times
21 Persistent, as a backache
24 Autobahn auto
26 Unimpressive brain size
27 Suffix with deposit or reposit
31 Miner's tool

Puzzle 124 by Alan Arbesfeld

34 Geisha's sash
35 Nautilus locale
37 Classic Jaguar
39 Monopoly corner square
40 Come to
41 Nada
42 Hawaiian strings
43 Fancy British wheels
45 "Batman" villain
48 Aid in crime
49 "Batman" setting
52 Gassed up

53 Big name in swimwear
55 Dieter's fare
57 Nutty as a fruitcake
58 Año starter
60 "Show Boat" composer
62 Cry from Scrooge
63 Italian article
64 Fleur-de-___

ACROSS

1 Home planet
6 Eurasia's ___ Mountains
10 Spy Mata ___
14 Waikiki welcome
15 Granny
16 Elderly
17 "Keep going!"
19 Season for carols
20 Hanks or Brokaw
21 Singer Kristofferson
22 Dicker over a price, say
24 Simon or Diamond
25 Supermarket section
26 Follows
28 Pie topping
32 Garlic unit
33 Prefix with scope or photo
34 Fork part
35 Retired Italian money
36 Brandish
37 Icy pellets
38 Swear to
39 Aardvarks' morsels
40 Takes an apartment
41 Pudding and pie
43 Shindig
44 Gifts to the poor
45 Scrabble piece
46 Diamond-shaped pattern
49 Jim-dandy
50 "The Sopranos" network
53 Guide

54 "Keep going!"
57 ___-inflammatory
58 Armbone
59 Question with an easy answer
60 Durante's famous feature
61 Ring
62 Door holders

DOWN

1 "___ of Eden"
2 Choir voice
3 Wander
4 Your, in the Bible
5 "M*A*S*H" role
6 "___ we meet again"
7 Stadium sounds
8 Folk rocker DiFranco
9 Angry, with "up"
10 "Keep going!"
11 Wide-eyed
12 Fishing line holder
13 Not busy
18 Center of the eye
23 Foreman KO'er, 1974
24 "Keep going!"
25 Vales
26 Popeye's gal
27 Tiresome ones
28 Dates on a track team schedule
29 Midget's opposite
30 Oneness
31 Squiggly swimmers
32 Garbed

Puzzle 125 by Gail Grabowski

33 Slight colors
36 Practiced before playing
40 North Carolina's capital
42 Building wing
43 Unwanted engine sound
45 General Mills breakfast cereal
46 Comedian King
47 Janet in the Clinton White House
48 Gangsters' guns

49 O'Neill's "___ Christie"
50 Skirt lines
51 Run (into)
52 Unlocks, poetically
55 Spanish cheer
56 By way of

ACROSS

1 Muddy up
5 Fiber-___ cable
10 Vaulted area
14 Old Dodge
15 Wells ___
16 Envelope closer
17 Training in microscope use?
20 Primping
21 "Steppenwolf" author
22 90° from ESE
23 Elisabeth of "Leaving Las Vegas"
25 Ripken Jr. surpassed him
29 Mad rush
33 Big drink?
34 Bearded farm animal
35 Fraternity members
36 Taking an arctic vacation?
40 Timeworn
41 Museo contents
42 Caffè ___
43 Times to play or relax
46 Butter or oleo
47 School on the Thames
48 Kingston Trio hit, 1959
49 Hotpoint competitor
52 Enters
57 Why some people move to Massachusetts?
60 Crowd noise
61 River of Rome
62 Taxi charge
63 Nothing but
64 Some murder mystery suspects
65 Tibetan bovines

DOWN

1 Cavort
2 Actor Sharif
3 "Bus Stop" playwright
4 Field of work
5 In the ___ (soon to come)
6 John of "Miracle on 34th Street"
7 H.S. math
8 Engine starter: Abbr.
9 Gear part
10 Dead to the world
11 Potpie ingredients
12 Mouth off to
13 Otherwise
18 Scorecard division
19 Pal
23 Washington, for one
24 "What ___ God wrought?"
25 "Taras Bulba" author
26 Place to learn en français
27 Swiss miss of literature
28 Managed
29 Puts into piles
30 Ham it up
31 Triangular tract
32 Pulled the plug on

Puzzle 126 by Janice M. Putney

34 Bridge expert Charles
37 Casino game
38 Rio Grande city
39 Garage contents
44 "Halt!" caller
45 The Beehive State
46 Beef on the hoof
48 Van company
49 Bushy do
50 Phobos, to Mars
51 Asia's ___ Sea
52 Mongolian desert
53 Far from certain
54 Final Four org.

55 Peter of the Monkees
56 Pindar volume
58 Biblical suffix
59 Fanciful story

ACROSS

1 Actress Thompson of TV's "Family"
5 Ace or jack
9 How to sing, ideally
14 Israeli airline
15 Baseball's Matty, or Moises
16 Ethiopia's ___ Selassie
17 Bugs bugs him
19 "Mine!"
20 1991 Madonna hit
21 Czech-born actor Herbert
22 Discharge
23 Plummeted
28 Tierra ___ Fuego
29 Goethe character who makes a pact with the devil
30 Rock's Bon ___
31 "Vive le ___!"
33 Words of praise
35 Uncomplicated kind of question
39 Pupil
40 Expatriate
42 String after A
43 Ache (for)
44 "Silly" birds
46 Fold-up bed
49 Narrative
51 Popular clog clearer
53 Wild wild West
54 Like some vamps
56 Horrible
59 Title hero of a Melville story

60 "La Traviata" composer
61 Repetitive learning method
62 "I've Got ___ in Kalamazoo"
63 "Humble" place
64 Years in Spain
65 Marvin of Motown

DOWN

1 Get really steamed
2 Assert without proof
3 Woman hoping for a knight in shining armor
4 Baldwin and Guinness
5 Lunch site
6 Barnard graduate
7 Endured, as a hurricane
8 It fizzles
9 Cry of terror
10 Country-singing mother
11 Medic's bag
12 ___ Lilly (Fortune 500 company)
13 "Is it soup ___?"
18 Groove
21 Beatles album after "Hey Jude"
24 Georgia and Ukraine, once: Abbr.
25 Cast a ballot
26 Fifty-fifty
27 Mile or kilometer: Abbr.

Puzzle 127 by David Ainslie Macleod

29 Wangle
31 Longtime CBS/NBC newsman
32 Bobby of the Bruins
34 Tampa Bay footballer, for short
35 Slangy assents
36 Discharge
37 ___-Soviet relations
38 R.E.M.'s "The ___ Love"
41 Excitement in the air
45 Do business with
46 Iroquois confederate

47 Sometime
48 Walk like a two-year-old
50 Clinton or Bush, collegiately
51 TV actress Susan
52 Arrange in different sacks
55 Shouts to a matador
56 Actress Gardner
57 Spider's work
58 To and ___
59 Victoria's Secret purchase

ACROSS

1 Agent Mulder's show, with "The"
7 Garment that may have advertising
13 Chef's collection
15 Pythagorean ___
16 High-spirited horse
17 Get off at the terminal
18 Starchy tuber
19 Hammer features
21 Mortise's partner
22 It rides on runners
24 Hurler's stat.
25 "___ the season . . ."
26 Acting through the skin
29 Gun, as an engine
32 "Saturday Night Fever" music
35 Rat Pack cohort of Frank
36 Tennessee team, for short
37 Queen mother, e.g.
39 Pasta with pockets
41 On the road
42 Disarrange
44 The Dow, e.g.
45 Big fat mouth
46 Nixon bested him
48 Director Van Sant
49 Ginger ___
50 "___ we forget"
54 Autocrats of old
57 One of David's compositions
59 Poke fun at

60 Event for scullers
62 Falls on the border
64 Winter cap feature
65 War of 1812 hero Stephen
66 Like porn
67 Shutterbugs' settings

DOWN

1 Dental pictures
2 Wild
3 Start of a boast from Caesar
4 P.M. William Gladstone's party: Abbr.
5 Heroic saga
6 Part of S.W.A.K.
7 Everyday article
8 Kind of tank
9 Bagel centers
10 Farsi-speaking land
11 University of Nevada locale
12 Some feds
14 Percussion instrument in a combo
15 QB's aims
20 Suffix with soft or hard
23 What spots on 1-Down show
25 Singer Turner
27 Yule quaff
28 Everglades
29 Crucifix
30 Macpherson of "Sirens"

Puzzle 128 by William Schaub

31 Auto engine type
32 Make-or-break time
33 Corn Belt state
34 Cashless deal
36 Record albums, to collectors
38 Down Under birds
40 Contend (for)
43 Relaxing spots
46 Sell aggressively
47 Analgesic's promise
48 Some corruption
51 Poetic Muse
52 Flapjack topper: Var.

53 Skiers' lifts
54 Prehistoric predator, for short
55 Burn a bit
56 Taj Mahal site
57 Mushy food
58 PC alternatives
61 Little bit
63 Gangster's gun

ACROSS

1 Neighbor of Ecuador
5 Dressed
9 Identical
14 Firefighters' tools
15 Poison ivy reaction
16 Pulitzer-winning novelist Alison
17 Sales agents, briefly
18 This, south of the border
19 Decorates richly
20 Very bright
23 Prefix with center
24 Med. plan
25 Part of the foot
29 Actress Meryl
31 Motion while saying "Good dog!"
33 ___ mode
34 Showered
36 Mild, as weather
38 Very bright
40 Civil rights org.
42 In a sour mood
43 Build (on)
44 "Undoubtedly"
45 Mitchell of NBC News
49 Fly that carries sleeping sickness
52 ___ Beta Kappa
53 Coast Guard rank: Abbr.
54 Very bright
58 Mideast's ___ Peninsula
61 Singer Fitzgerald
62 "It's ___ to tell a lie"

63 Disdain
64 Prophet
65 Taboo
66 Like a tie game in overtime
67 Job
68 Shoelace problem

DOWN

1 Analyzes grammatically
2 Free (from)
3 Fix
4 Moscow's land, once: Abbr.
5 Famous Boston dessert
6 Rope, cowboy-style
7 "The Thin Man" dog
8 Boat on the Indian Ocean
9 Illinois city
10 Witticisms
11 Dot-com's address
12 Help
13 Parisian article
21 Silent character in "Little Orphan Annie"
22 Top 10 record
26 Towering
27 Shade tree
28 Salary
30 Rock's Clapton
31 Mexican moolah
32 Month in Israel
35 Epithet
36 Sarajevo is its capital
37 Impressed mightily

Puzzle 129 by Alison D. Donald

38 Walk in shallow water
39 Two-by-two vessel?
40 Singer ___ King Cole
41 TV interruptions
44 Nay opposer
46 Sanity
47 San Fernando Valley community
48 Start of a John F. Kennedy quote
50 Nicholas and Ivan, e.g.
51 Sparkle

52 Loses color
55 Part of R & R
56 Nolo contendere, e.g.
57 Aquarium
58 Speedy way to get to Paris
59 ___ cream
60 Negative in Normandy

ACROSS

1 Stranded motorist's S O S
6 Fishhook part
10 Train station
14 Set one's sights
15 Meltable spread
16 "My Friend ___" (1949 flick)
17 Showy perennials
18 Josip Broz, familiarly
19 Play, as drums
20 "Consider seriously, Bret"
23 Checkup sounds
24 Be into
25 24-hour period, in astronomy
27 Francis and Dahl
31 Novelist Umberto
32 Hotfoot it
33 "Earn straight A's, Karl"
39 Saudi or Yemeni
41 Televise
42 Final, e.g.
43 "Sing lead, Horace"
48 ___ Fail (Irish coronation stone)
49 In the style of
50 Puts in order
52 Carpet leftovers
57 Radar gun meas.
58 Bullfight bravo
59 "Stay free of discomfort, Thomas"
64 Pinocchio, for one
66 The Supremes, e.g.
67 Designer Perry
68 Sicilian smoker
69 Sloth's home
70 Brooklets
71 Brother of Cain
72 Rank above viscount
73 Final authority

DOWN

1 It's true
2 Coin in the Trevi Fountain, once
3 In a frenzy
4 Many hairlines do it
5 Cutting and pasting
6 This and that
7 Name on a police blotter
8 So out, it's in
9 Sell bathtub gin, say
10 Sis, e.g.
11 Radial pattern
12 Cornhusker's city
13 Fall guy
21 S-shaped molding
22 A pop
26 Forum city
27 Pequod captain
28 Laugh, in Lille
29 Table extender
30 "Immediately," in the O.R.
34 That guy
35 Where Tabriz is
36 Linchpin's place
37 Acid ___
38 Yule, in ads

Puzzle 130 by John Greenman

40 It's in whole wheat
44 Norwegian saint
45 Name following "No, No"
46 Verne skipper
47 Siesta takers
51 Muse of comedy
52 Cast openings
53 Typewriter type
54 Stood for
55 ___ cotta
56 More cagey
60 Holiday tune
61 In a bad way

62 Guitarist Lofgren
63 Conoco competitor
65 "Yay, team!"

SOLUTIONS

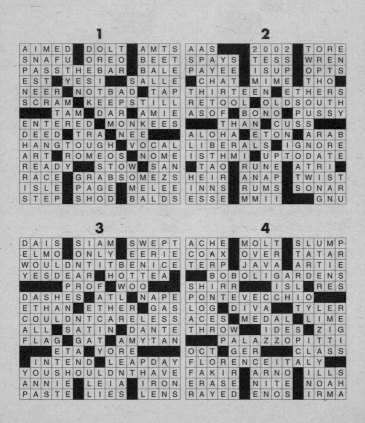

1

A	I	M	E	D		D	O	L	T		A	M	T	S
S	N	A	F	U		O	R	E	O		B	E	E	T
P	A	S	S	T	H	E	B	A	R		B	A	L	E
E	S	T		Y	E	S	I		S	A	L	L	E	
N	E	E	R		N	O	T	B	A	D		T	A	P
S	C	R	A	M		K	E	E	P	S	T	I	L	L
		T	A	M		D	A	R		A	M	I	E	
E	N	T	E	R	E	D		M	O	N	K	E	E	S
D	E	E	D		T	R	A		N	E	E			
H	A	N	G	T	O	U	G	H		V	O	C	A	L
A	R	T		R	O	M	E	O	S		N	O	M	E
R	E	A	D	Y			S	T	O	W		S	A	N
R	A	C	E		G	R	A	B	S	O	M	E	Z	S
I	S	L	E		P	A	G	E		M	E	L	E	E
S	T	E	P		S	H	O	D		B	A	L	D	S

2

A	A	S			2	0	0	2		T	O	R	E	
S	P	A	Y	S		T	E	S	S		W	R	E	N
P	A	Y	E	E		I	S	U	P		O	P	T	S
	C	H	A	T		M	I	M	E		T	H	O	
T	H	I	R	T	E	E	N		E	T	H	E	R	S
R	E	T	O	O	L		O	L	D	S	O	U	T	H
A	S	O	F		B	O	N	O		P	U	S	S	Y
			T	H	A	N		C	U	S	S			
A	L	O	H	A		E	T	O	N		A	R	A	B
L	I	B	E	R	A	L	S		I	G	N	O	R	E
I	S	T	H	M	I		U	P	T	O	D	A	T	E
	T	A	O		R	U	N	E		A	T	R	I	
I	N	N	S		A	N	A	P		T	W	I	S	T
N	U	N	S		R	U	M	S		S	O	N	A	R
	N	U	T											
E	S	S	E		M	M	I	I			G	N	U	

3

D	A	I	S		S	I	A	M		S	W	E	P	T
E	L	M	O		O	N	L	Y		E	E	R	I	E
W	O	U	L	D	N	T	I	T	B	E	N	I	C	E
Y	E	S	D	E	A	R		H	O	T	T	E	A	
			P	R	O	F		W	O	O				
D	A	S	H	E	S		A	T	L		N	A	P	E
E	T	H	A	N		E	T	H	E	R		G	A	S
C	O	U	L	D	N	T	C	A	R	E	L	E	S	S
A	L	L		S	A	T	I	N		D	A	N	T	E
F	L	A	G		G	A	T		A	M	Y	T	A	N
			E	T	A		Y	O	R	E				
	I	N	T	E	N	D		L	E	A	P	D	A	Y
Y	O	U	S	H	O	U	L	D	N	T	H	A	V	E
A	N	N	I	E		L	E	I	A		I	R	O	N
P	A	S	T	E		L	I	E	S		L	E	N	S

4

A	C	H	E		M	O	L	T		S	L	U	M	P
C	O	A	X		O	V	E	R		T	A	T	A	R
T	E	R	P		J	A	V	A		A	R	T	I	E
	B	O	B	O	L	I	G	A	R	D	E	N	S	
S	H	I	R	R			I	S	L		R	E	S	
P	O	N	T	E	V	E	C	C	H	I	O			
L	O	G		D	I	V	A			T	Y	L	E	R
A	C	E	S		M	E	D	A	L		L	I	M	E
T	H	R	O	W		I	D	E	S		Z	I	G	
			P	A	L	A	Z	Z	O	P	I	T	T	I
O	C	T		G	E	R			C	L	A	S	S	
F	L	O	R	E	N	C	E	I	T	A	L	Y		
F	A	K	I	R		A	R	N	O		I	L	L	S
E	R	A	S	E		N	I	T	E		N	O	A	H
R	A	Y	E	D		E	N	O	S		I	R	M	A

5

```
F I B S   F I L L     L A R A
A G U E   O N E A   K I T E S
N O R A   U T A H   U B O A T
G R R R R R R R R R R R R R R
      A A A   I S A
  P S A L M   J A C K   B A D
A S C A P   C O C O   S O S A
S H H H H H H H H H H H H H H
S A M S   E I N E   E U R O S
T W O   B I N S   E R N S T
    E O N   E N T
B Z Z Z Z Z Z Z Z Z Z Z Z Z Z
E I E I O   E E R Y   O B O E
S P I N S   A R A M   L A N E
T A T E     L O S E   A R E S
```

6

```
M A C K   W E A K   A K R O N
I C O N   A M M O   D I A N E
T H R E E G U Y S W A L K E D
T A K E R S     H I P N E S S
S T Y L I   S C E N T
    C O L O R   T R E N D
I N T O A B A R   T O O T O O
M O O G   E M O T E   O U R S
P A R L A Y   N E X T T I M E
S H E E R   N E A T O
    C L E R K   T E R R A
H O T S H O T   S A L O O N
I H O P E T H E Y L L D U C K
S I T A R   E R I E   E T C H
S O O T Y   R E N D   R E O S
```

7

```
O S L O   C H E F   M A M B O
A K I N   A U T O   A D I E U
T E N C O M M A N D M E N T S
S W E E P E A   T E M P E S T
    T O N E   F A T
H A D T O   E X C E L   R A P
A T R I U M   H U N   P O R E
T W E N T Y Q U E S T I O N S
E A S Y   S U M   E A T S A T
D R S   S T E E R   M A T Z O
    S U E   S A V E
A S T A I R E   M I S T A K E
T H I R T Y S O M E T H I N G
M A N G O   S L E W   O R E O
S H E E R   O D D S   R Y E S
```

8

```
A S H E   C A S S   O G L E D
P I E R   A N N O   F I L L Y
E G A N   M Y O L D F L A M E
S H R I M P   B A R S   M E R
    T E A S E   R E H E A R S
F E B   G I R L   D O R
A G U A   T A O S   O R C A S
C A R R I E S T H E T O R C H
E D N A S   E T O N   R O M E
    B A D   O R G S   S E A
L A D Y B U G   T I R E S
A R E   E M U S   N O N F A T
T R A I L B L A Z E   D I V A
C A N A L   F L O E   E R I N
H Y E N A   S E E R   D E S K
```

9

```
T O T O   E L L I S   D O D O
A P A R   N O O S E   E W E R
D E C A   C O C O C H A N E L
S C O T T I S H   E N E R O
    I O N E   R A P   D E N
Y O Y O C O N T E S T
I N I N K   A S T O   E A U
P U P S   M A N T A   E M I R
E S S   K O N G   E Y I N G
  N O N O N A N E T T E
S O D   E T A   A L O T
A R E N A   O M E L E T T E
G O G O D A N C E R   E R A S
A N A T   N I T R O   T I C S
S O S O   G L O S S   H O H O
```

10

```
B A S S O   N E S T   A D A M
A S P I N   E T T U   N A P E
N I E C E   U N E X C I T E D
J A C K S T R A W   A M A S S
O N S   T O O   A R A B
    P A I N T I T B L A C K
S P E A R   O R T S   S E A
L E V Y   B E R R Y   P E N N
A R I   F O N T   P A S T E
V I L L A G E E L D E R
    D O C S   O A R   T A S
A B O V E   W O O D C H U C K
B R E A T H E R S   H A N O I
B E R G   E R S E   E V E R T
E A S E   P E O N   D E R N S
```

11

```
H E I S T   G L A D E   A F T
A L L A H   L A T E R   L A O
L I L L E H A M M E R   B U T
    R U S E     A R E N A
F A S T E N S   N A T U R A L
A C Q U I T   S O V I E T
C H U R N   R E L I C   V A L
T E A K   S A L A D   V I S E
S S W   C O V E N   P O L K A
    V E R S E S   C A L L E R
P L A T O O N   E A S T E R N
H O L E S   A L L S
A W L   S A I N T M O R I T Z
S E E   L L A N O   U N T I E
E R Y   Y E M E N   T A S T E
```

12

```
A V I V   B E G A T   Z A P S
M I D I   A R O L E   E R A T
I V E S   S I T O N   R A G A
D O A H A T C H E T J O B O N
      N S A     H A H
B I D U P   A T M   N O C A L
E D U   C A L A I S   U R G E
H A V E A N A X T O G R I N D
A R E A   G R E E D Y   M E G
R E T R O   M R S   R E E S E
      M O P     V O N
T O M A H A W K M I S S I L E
O M A R   P A N I C   I N O N
R A N K   A R O M A   G R A D
I N X S   S E W E R   N E D S
```

13

```
A L P H A   T A L L   A J A R
B E A U T   O R E O   M U L E
U N I T E D K I N G D O M O F
T O N   C Y D   D U P E S
    T A B O O   A T A R I
U P T U R N   Q U A Y   N B A
N E H R U   P U N T   J A N
G R E A T B R I T A I N A N D
E S T   A I L S   V I C A R
R E O   F A C T   H E C K L E
    W H I S K   J O S E F
U L N A S   E A U   L A O
N O R T H E R N I R E L A N D
T R E E   W A I L   Y E S N O
O D D S   E N D S   E T H E R
```

14

```
T A C H S   H O P I   J O S E
E L I A N   A N O N   P P P S
A L T H O   L I O N   M E A T
  Y E A R O F T H E H O R S E
      H E A T   S E E R
W A W A   S O P   D I G S I N
A T E   Z I N E S   F A I R E
C H I N E S E C A L E N D A R
K O R A N   S O L A R   L T D
O L D V I C   S T Y   S E E S
      I T E M   W I S P
G U N G H A Y F A T C H O Y
A R I A   S E A T   R E N E W
P A C T   E Y R E   A R E N A
E L K E   D E E R   M E S S Y
```

15

```
R I S E S   A S I G N   S H O
A M I N O   S H O R E   C A P
T O L E T   H O N E S T A B E
E K E   H U E D   E T H N I C
  N L E R S   E N L I S T
I N T U R N   B A T E S
C Y C L E   F U S E D   T S K
E S A U   D U B Y A   T H I N
T E L   M E L B A   D E E R E
    K O A L A   B U N G E E
  G L I B L Y   C A C T I
P R E L I M   M A R K   P A M
L I T T L E B E N   P U P P Y
U F O   E I E I O   I N E P T
M T N   S N A R E   N O R T H
```

16

```
R E P E L   B A T S   O D O R
U T I L E   O N U S   C O V E
B A S E M E N T B A S E M E N
S L A V   I D E A   A L E R T
    A I R     A G O
F L A T F E E T F L A T F E E
L I M E S   T R E E S   O V A
O T O S   S H A V E   F R A T
U R N   A P A C E   E L U D E
R E G I M E N T R E G I M E N
      M I D     L O P
E S S E N   F I D O   F A T E
D I P L O M A T D I P L O M A
G L A D   A R E A   J O N A S
E T N A   E M M Y   S P E N T
```

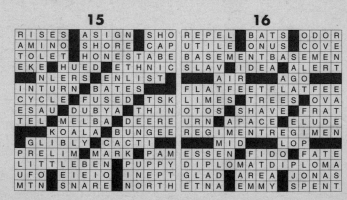

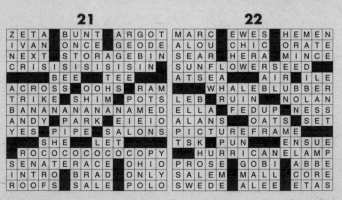

17

```
O S C A R _ S T A G _ _ B E T
K I O W A _ P A D R E _ E V E
S T O O L P I G E O N _ N I L
_ _ L E A K S _ O R A C L E _
B B C _ I T E _ A M I S H _ _
L E H I G H _ S Z E C H W A N _
A W A S H _ R E T R O _ A D O
M A I M _ D I M E S _ G R A D
E R R _ M E D I C _ D U M P S
D E P R A V E S _ P E S E T A
_ E A G E R _ R E V _ R S T _
V I R G I L _ E E R I E _ _ _
E D S _ C O U C H P O T A T O
E L O _ S P A R E _ U N I O N
P E N _ _ S W U M _ S A R G E
```

18

```
J A M I E _ P A S T E _ I M P
A T O L L _ E S Q U E _ D A R
M O U L I N R O U G E _ A R I
S P E W _ O T R A _ _ W H I Z
_ _ I N T H E B E D R O O M _
F R A N C O _ _ R U E _ _ _ _
L O R D O F T H E R I N G S _
U M A _ _ A O L _ _ R I O _
_ A B E A U T I F U L M I N D
_ _ D C L _ _ S T A T E D _
A C A D E M Y A W A R D _ _ _
Z A N Y _ E L O I _ E D G E
T I N _ G O S F O R D P A R K
E R E _ A N N I E _ V A L U E
C O X _ B O O E D _ D R I B S
```

19

```
S C A D _ T H E T A _ F O G S
O H I O _ E A T I T _ O N L Y
S I N G I N I N T H E R A I N
A C T I O N _ A L E S _ I D O
_ _ E N Y A _ E N T E R E D _
A L I _ A S A P _ S A X _ _
L O O S _ O R E S _ T E R S E
P U T T I N O N T H E R I T Z
S T A Y S _ N A P E _ T S A R
_ _ L T D _ L A D D _ E R A
B A S E H I T _ T G I F _ _
I L L _ M A R K _ E V A D E D
B L O W I N I N T H E W I N D
L I M A _ E N E R O _ N A N A
E N O S _ S E W U P _ S L A Y
```

20

```
A D M S _ S P A S M _ Z A N Y
B R I O _ H E L L O _ A L O E
Y A L U _ E P C O T _ P E W S
S M A R T A S A W H I P _ _
M A N D A R I N _ _ S A L S A
_ _ _ O R S _ _ L O U _ A O L
E T T U _ _ N I E T Z S C H E
B R I G H T A S A B U T T O N
B I G H E A D E D _ _ R O T E
E T H _ A B A _ _ U S E _ _
D E T A T _ _ A P P L E P I E
_ _ S H A R P A S A T A C K
J I M I _ L E I G H _ C L I I
A R E A _ M I N E O _ A M A N
B E A N _ A N G S T _ R A N G
```

21

```
Z E T A _ B U N T _ A R G O T
I V A N _ O N C E _ G E O D E
N E X T _ S T O R A G E B I N
C R I S I S I S I S I S I N _
_ _ _ B E E _ _ T E E _ _ _
A C R O S S _ O O H S _ R A M
T R I K E _ S H I M _ P O T S
B A N A N A N A N A N A M E D
A N D Y _ P A R K _ E I E I O
Y E S _ P I P E _ S A L O N S
_ _ S H E _ _ L E T _ _ _
_ R O C O C O C O C O C O P Y
S E N A T E R A C E _ O H I O
I N T R O _ B R A D _ O N L Y
R O O F S _ S A L E _ P O L O
```

22

```
M A R C _ E W E S _ H E M E N
A L O U _ C H I C _ O R A T E
S E A R _ H E R A _ M I N C E
S U N F L O W E R S E E D _ _
A T S E A _ _ A I R _ I L E
_ _ W H A L E B L U B B E R
L E B _ R U I N _ _ N O L A N
E L L A _ F E D U P _ N E S S
A L A N S _ _ O A T S _ S E T
P I C T U R E F R A M E _ _
T S K _ P U N _ _ E N S U E
_ _ H U R R I C A N E L A M P
P R O S E _ G O B I _ A B B E
S A L E M _ M A L L _ C O R E
S W E D E _ A L E E _ E T A S
```

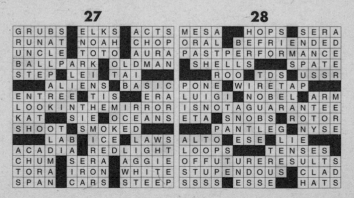

23

C	A	S	T			T	A	R		E	R	S	E
A	R	T	E		A	G	A	P	E		R	E	L	Y
C	O	A	X		D	E	C	A	L		A	J	A	R
T	U	R	A	N	D	O	T	C	O	M		O	P	E
U	N	E	S	C	O			H	A	N	O	I
S	D	S		O	N	T	H	E	D	O	T	C	O	M
			S	T	A	Y			P	I	E	T	A
D	A	M	P		O	P	A	L	S		C	R	O	P
I	S	A	A	C		T	A	T	A
M	I	C	R	O	D	O	T	C	O	M		A	P	U
	A	K	R	O	N		O	M	E	L	E	T
B	A	R		P	O	L	K	A	D	O	T	C	O	M
A	R	O	N		D	I	E	G	O		H	O	R	O
J	A	N	E		A	N	I	O	N		O	T	I	S
A	L	I	T		D	E	R			S	T	A	T

24

T	O	W	E	L		M	A	T	E	R		A	D	S
E	M	I	L	Y		A	S	I	D	E		V	E	T
T	A	L	K	I	N	G	H	E	A	D		E	V	A
E	N	D		N	O	P	E			H	O	N	O	R
			W	A	G	G	I	N	G	T	O	N	G	U	E
O	P	E	N	T	O	E		L	A	T	T	E	R
P	E	S	T	O		J	A	M	S
E	A	T	S		D	I	O	D	E		C	H	O	W
		P	A	R	E			W	H	E	R	E
P	A	Y	O	L	A		S	P	R	E	A	D	S
C	H	E	A	T	I	N	G	H	E	A	R	T
H	A	R	P	S		A	E	O	N		W	O	E
A	S	A		H	E	L	P	I	N	G	H	A	N	D
P	E	T		O	R	I	E	L		L	A	V	E	D
S	S	E		T	E	T	R	A		E	L	E	G	Y

25

W	A	G	S		R	A	M	P		R	E	A	P
E	T	U	I		S	O	N	I	A		E	R	G	O
E	R	M	A		C	O	E	D	S		D	I	E	T
D	I	M	M	E	R	S	W	I	T	C	H	E	S
S	A	Y		V	A	T			R	O	O
		A	I	M		B	L	A	S	T	O	F	F
O	H	A	R	A		D	R	A	M		S	E	E
S	E	V	E	N	Y	E	A	R	I	T	C	H	E	S
L	E	I		A	L	I	D		O	R	A	L	S
O	L	D	W	O	R	L	D		N	A	Y
	I	N	D		S	O	S		A	G	A
S	I	D	E	A	R	M	P	I	T	C	H	E	S
B	A	B	E		R	O	A	R	S		H	O	N	K
O	V	E	N		M	O	R	A	Y		A	M	I	E
W	E	T	S		S	T	E	T		R	E	E	D

26

C	A	P	P		M	E	G	A		J	A	M	E	S
A	L	E	E		A	L	A	S		A	G	E	N	T
P	I	N	K	S	L	I	P	S		N	E	R	D	Y
		N	O	E	L		A	N	I		C	U	E
M	E	Y	E	R		S	I	D	E	T	R	I	P	S
A	M	A		S	T	U	N		W	O	O
S	A	N	E		I	N	S		D	R	O	N	E
H	I	T	T	I	N	G	T	H	E	S	K	I	D	S
L	E	N	N	Y		Y	M	A		S	C	I	S
	A	F	T		L	O	L	A		E	F	T
M	U	D	S	L	I	D	E	S		S	O	N	Y	S
O	N	O		A	M	I			G	O	N	E
S	C	R	A	M		T	W	I	N	F	A	L	L	S
E	L	I	T	E		S	O	D	A		I	L	E	S
S	E	C	T	S		Y	E	O	W		R	Y	A	N

27

G	R	U	B	S		E	L	K	S		A	C	T	S
R	U	N	A	T		N	O	A	H		C	H	O	P
U	N	C	L	E		T	O	T	O		A	U	R	A
B	A	L	L	P	A	R	K		O	L	D	M	A	N
S	T	E	P		L	E	I		T	A	I
		A	L	I	E	N	S		B	A	S	I	C
E	N	T	R	E	E		T	I	S		E	R	A
L	O	O	K	I	N	T	H	E	M	I	R	R	O	R
K	A	T		S	I	E		O	C	E	A	N	S
S	H	O	O	T		S	M	O	K	E	D
	L	A	B		I	C	E		L	A	W	S
A	C	A	D	I	A		R	E	D	L	I	G	H	T
C	H	U	M		S	E	R	A		A	G	G	I	E
T	O	R	A		I	R	O	N		W	H	I	T	E
S	P	A	N		C	A	R	S		S	T	E	E	P

28

M	E	S	A		H	O	P	S		S	E	R	A
O	R	A	L		B	E	F	R	I	E	N	D	E	D
P	A	S	T	P	E	R	F	O	R	M	A	N	C	E
	S	H	E	L	L	S			S	P	A	T	E
		R	O	O		T	D	S		U	S	S	R
P	O	N	E		W	I	R	E	T	A	P
L	U	I	G	I		N	O	B	E	L		A	R	M
I	S	N	O	T	A	G	U	A	R	A	N	T	E	E
E	T	A		S	N	O	B	S		R	O	T	O	R
	P	A	N	T	L	E	G		N	Y	S	E
A	L	T	O		E	S	E		L	I	E
L	O	O	P	S			T	E	N	S	E	S
O	F	F	U	T	U	R	E	R	E	S	U	L	T	S
S	T	U	P	E	N	D	O	U	S		C	L	A	D
S	S	S	S		E	S	S	E		H	A	T	S

29

B	E	A	D		G	A	S	P		G	A	T	O	R
E	R	G	O		A	C	H	E		A	F	I	R	E
A	M	E	N		L	I	A	R		Z	O	N	E	D
M	I	N	N	I	E	D	R	I	V	E	R			
U	N	D	E	R			I	S	A	B	E	L	L	A
P	E	A		V	I	E		C	L	O	S	E	T	S
			R	I	A	L	T	O			A	I	D	S
	M	I	N	N	E	A	P	O	L	I	S			
A	B	C	S			C	R	E	W	E	D			
S	I	C	K	E	S	T		S	E	T		F	O	E
P	O	L	Y	M	E	R	S			U	T	U	R	N
	M	I	N	I	C	O	M	P	U	T	E	R		
S	P	O	O	L		C	A	P	O		R	I	G	A
L	E	A	V	E		A	L	T	O		F	L	O	P
Y	I	K	E	S		L	E	S	T		S	E	N	T

30

S	A	S	S		S	P	R	E	E		A	L	G	A
T	R	E	K		P	R	O	A	M		M	O	R	T
A	L	L	Y		R	I	P	U	P		I	G	O	R
G	O	L	D	M	I	N	E		L	U	G	O	S	I
			I	M	E	T		B	O	N	A	N	Z	A
G	O	O	V	E	R		M	A	Y	A	S			
A	N	N	E			E	A	T	E	R		G	R	R
Y	O	U	R	E	I	N	T	H	E	M	O	N	E	Y
E	R	S		G	N	A	T	S			P	A	P	A
			S	Y	N	C	S		D	R	E	W	O	N
J	A	C	K	P	O	T		R	A	I	N			
A	R	N	E	T	T		W	I	N	D	F	A	L	L
M	E	O	W		I	R	O	N	S		I	S	E	E
B	E	T	E		M	A	N	G	O		R	I	F	T
S	L	E	D		E	G	G	O	N		E	F	T	S

31

S	A	L	E	M		A	L	D	A		E	T	T	A
E	L	O	P	E		R	U	I	N		L	I	E	N
W	A	I	S	T	M	A	N	A	G	E	M	E	N	T
S	E	N	O	R	A		A	L	E	X		U	S	E
			M	I	L	E	R		L	O	P	P	E	D
T	A	M		C	A	T		M	A	T	E			
O	R	E	M		W	H	O	A		I	N	A	N	E
M	I	N	E	R	I	N	F	R	A	C	T	I	O	N
S	A	U	D	I		I	T	C	H		A	R	N	O
			E	P	I	C		I	O	N		Y	E	S
S	C	R	A	P	S		M	A	R	I	E			
A	R	E		L	O	S	E		S	K	A	T	E	S
H	O	S	T	E	L	T	A	K	E	O	V	E	R	S
I	N	T	O		D	O	N	E		L	E	A	S	T
B	E	S	T		E	A	S	Y		A	S	S	E	S

32

G	R	A	S	P		P	E	L	F		M	A	M	A
S	A	N	T	A		A	P	E	R		A	L	E	X
A	N	N	U	L		W	I	N	E		M	I	R	E
			B	O	U	N	C	I	N	G	B	A	L	L
O	R	B		M	T	S			E	R	A	S	E	S
B	O	O	K	I	E		B	I	T	E				
E	D	W	I	N		T	A	T	I		E	M	M	A
Y	E	L	L	O	W	B	R	I	C	K	R	O	A	D
S	O	S	O		E	A	T	S		I	R	A	T	E
				S	T	R	S		I	N	S	T	E	P
C	A	L	A	I	S		L	T	D			S	O	T
I	N	S	T	R	U	C	T	I	O	N	S			
V	I	A	L		I	R	O	N		E	N	A	C	T
E	S	T	A		T	O	N	E		S	I	N	A	I
T	E	S	S		S	P	I	N		S	P	A	R	E

33

W	O	O	D		P	E	W	S		B	O	Z	O	S
O	H	N	O		O	X	E	N		A	T	A	R	I
M	I	L	E		L	U	L	U		M	O	N	E	T
B	O	Y	S	W	I	L	L	B	E	B	O	Y	S	
			T	A	C	T		A	I	L				
A	D	M	I	R	E		A	D	S		E	S	P	N
C	R	A	M	S		S	L	E	E	P		T	O	E
H	O	P	E	A	G	A	I	N	S	T	H	O	P	E
O	W	L		W	A	G	E	S		B	A	R	E	D
O	N	E	S		M	A	N		F	O	L	K	S	Y
			A	T	M		G	R	A	F				
L	I	V	E	A	N	D	L	E	T	L	I	V	E	
C	O	R	A	L		C	E	O	S		I	D	E	A
U	S	A	G	E		A	L	A	N		F	L	A	T
E	S	S	E	X		A	L	T	O		E	E	L	S

34

W	A	T	T		A	S	T	I	R		A	V	I	D
E	M	E	R		V	E	R	N	E		S	A	N	E
B	O	X	I	N	G	R	I	N	G		A	C	N	E
T	R	A	C	E		B	O	E	R		R	A	S	P
V	E	N	E	E	R		R	E	R	U	N			
				P	R	O	A	M		T	I	L	T	E	D
T	A	B	S		T	H	O	M		C	E	L	L	O
A	M	I		I	C	E	P	A	C	K		O	S	U
C	E	L	L	S		M	U	L	L		S	T	A	R
O	N	L	O	A	N		P	I	E	T	A			
			Y	O	Y	O	S			F	I	N	A	L	E
S	I	C	K		P	A	C	T		E	D	W	I	N
P	A	L	S		R	U	B	B	E	R	B	A	N	D
A	G	U	E		O	N	E	A	L		A	R	E	A
R	O	B	E		B	A	R	R	Y		G	E	N	T

35

```
R O B S   T R A S H Y   A L F
O S L O   S U B L E T   G E L
T H U N D E R R O A D   I V E
S A R G E     A P R   A L E E
      S E S A M E S T R E E T
P T A   M E R   T A R
A A R P   C U P S   P I E T A
S U N S E T B O U L E V A R D
S T E A M   A L M A   E R I E
      L I P   U V A   L O N
P R I M R O S E P A T H
E O N S   L A X     T I B E T
A G O   T I N P A N A L L E Y
R U N   O C T O P I   L A R K
L E E   W E A S E L   S H O E
```

36

```
L A R U E   T A M P A   Q U M
A R E N A   A L I A R   U N A
N E P L U S U L T R A   I C H
E S S O   I T S   C R A D L E
      C H E     S H A R P E R
B A S K E T S   P E T E R
A M I   R E W A R D   S O W N
R I N S E   E R A   T O Q U E
T R E K   L A T I N I   U S A
      Q U I E T   N E T C O S T
T R U A N T S   G O O
R O A S T S   O U R   S I T E
U S N   A D I N F I N I T U M
C I O   C I S C O   I N E R T
K E N   T E T E S   P E R K S
```

37

```
A T A R I   S N I P   L U S H
R O B I N   T A D A   A R E A
K N U C K L E S A N D W I C H
S I T E   E P A   T R Y S T S
      C O M O   W H E E
  S L A P O N T H E W R I S T
S P O K E N   H E R   N C O
T I R E D   J E T   A S T R O
A C E   O A T   C L A R E T
B E N D I N G A N E L B O W
    I D O S   E L S E
P A R L O R   A T L   R E N T
S H O U L D E R H O L S T E R
S O O T   E R I E   P A R E E
T Y K E   R E A R   S W E D E
```

38

```
B E T S   P A P A S   G R I P
M A U I   A T O N E   R E N E
T U R N S L O O S E   A N T E
    A C O M P L E T E F O O L
A N N E X   L O X   I N S
R O D   F O R M   H A R E
C R O S S E Y E   T A B
  A T O T A L F A I L U R E
    A P T   E T C E T E R A
P I K A   A R E S   A I R
R O B   U L M   I S L E T
A M I L L I O N B U C K S
J E S U   B R I A N K E I T H
A L E X   R A N T O   E Z R A
H O S E   A L O S S   T E A L
```

39

```
F I L C H   A R E S   T H I N
L O I R E   G U R U   W A C O
A T L A S   A T T N   O L E S
B A T S I N T H E B E L F R Y
    S T I E S   A M I
H U T   A B S   S T U T T E R
A L I S T   I C H   E R N O
S N A K E I N T H E G R A S S
N A R Y   S E E   I S S U E
T R A L A L A   S A N   H E S
    I R A   A M I G O
F R O G I N T H E T H R O A T
O A T H   D U E L   A N K L E
G R I T   E T A L   M O R O N
S A S S   R U D Y   S T A T S
```

40

```
L I L A C   P A L E   M E A T
O D O U R   R E A L   E L L A
C O C K A D O O D L E D O O M
I L K   T E N N   S N I P E S
    S P E N T   I C E S
M A M A   T O P D O G S
E R I C A   H A R M   F R O
L I T T L E K A N G A R O O M
D A H   L E I S   S A U T E
    B O L D E S T   I R O N
  S H I V   T E L L S
A P O G E E   S E R A   C S A
C E N T R A L P A R K Z O O M
M A K O   R E A M   E E R I E
E R S E   N A R Y   R E E L S
```

41

```
A S I S   A T O Z   C R A B S
C O M P   R O P E   H A R E M
C H A I N M A I L   A C U T E
T O M E I   D U D   R E B E L
    G N P   M A I L C A L L
N I C E T R Y     S E A
C A L L H O M E   T Y R A N T
A G A   B A T C H     T E A
R O M A N O   H O M E L O A N
    M E N   M U T A N T S
L O A N W O R D   S H U
E R R E D   A R E   I G L O O
A B U S E   W O R D C H A I N
V I S T A   L O G O   I D L E
E T H Y L   S P O T   N E S S
```

42

```
A C N E   T E A S   O S C A R
D O E R   R A V I   S P O R E
I M P S   A R I Z   T A L K S
D E A T H I N V E N I C E
A T L   O P S     C A E S A R
S H I R R S   J A R   L T D
    I R E F U L   I P A N A
  D I V I D I N G I N T W O
W I N E D   S T A N C E
S E C     A H A   N U R S E S
J U L I U S     F O B   M I A
  I N T H E V I C I N I T Y
D O N U T   D A N E   E T H S
I S E R E   A L A N   W H E N
S E D E R   M E L T   T Y R O
```

43

```
H E A R D   B U B B A   M B A
A L B E E   A R E A S   R U N
M I S S M A N N E R S   B E T
    P U P A S   B A T O N S
A D M I R A L   B L U E J A Y
S O R T E R   P A E L L A
I N K E R   W O R S T   N I A
D U N S   P I P E S   A G T S
E T O   P A R I S   S P L A T
  W A R R E N   T U P E L O
S P I R I T S   T E L L S O N
N O T I M E   A B A T E
O L A   M R S M A L A P R O P
O I L   E R R O R   N I O B E
P O L   R E A R S   S E T I N
```

44

```
T H I S   S L O G S   L A Z E
R E V I E W A B L E   I R I S
O R A N G E P E E L   B I N S
D E N   R A I S E   P E A C E
    P E R S E   B A R
R E C E S S     C E N T R A L
A L I A S   F O O D   Y U L E
N A R C   B O W L S   B R I G
I T C H   A R E A   L E A V E
S E A B I R D   C A L L E R
    R M N   G N A R L
S C R A P   R A I N Y   A N A
O L I N   C O T T O N S W A B
L A N D   O V E R E X P O S E
E D D Y   P E S O S   A L A S
```

45

```
O G L E   A N D S   M A T E S
P I E R   D E E P   A R O M A
E L S E   H U L A   S L U M S
C A T C H E R I N T H E R Y E
  T A R O   Y I N
P E T   V E N T U R E   L O T
A L O N E   O R O   F E T E
S O W O N E S W I L D O A T S
S P E W   R U E   R E S E T
E E L   P A P R I K A   T R Y
    I R S   T I N S
J I M M I E C R A C K C O R N
A D O B E   H U L K   O B E Y
V E N U S   E D I E   R O D E
A S S E T   W E A R   N E S T
```

46

```
O R C A   C C C P   O P A L S
M E A D   R E A L   A R I O T
A N I L   U S N A   T O D A Y
R E N A I S S A N C E M A N
    I N O N     O R O
H O E   D E A C O N S   M P G
E N N U I   R I G   S O A R
L E O N A R D O D A V I N C I
G A L E   O N A   O C T E T
A L A   P L A T E A U   E R S
    C A L   D E C A
D A N T E A L I G H I E R I
R I C O H   L U B E   S Y S T
E R A T O   U C L A   L E V I
C E D E S   M I E N   E S P N
```

47

B A S S		U N D O		W A L D O
O P A L		P A R S		A M O U R
U S M A R S H A L		R A N E E
T E E P E E	B O O T H I L L	
	A T V		S I S	
S C A L D	I B E A M		P S T
A R R A Y	D O D G E C I T Y
L O O M		S E R G E	A T O P
T O M B S T O N E	D R A K E
S K A	T A S E R	E S S E S
	M A I		S O B	
O K C O R R A L	T I L D E S
I N A P T	W Y A T T E A R P
L E V E L	E R T E	E Z R A
S W E D E	S E E R	R E S T

48

P U M P		C A R A T		P A R A
S T A R		O V A T E		E X I T
S A R I		R E C O N		S L O E
T H E S T O C K M A R K E T
	M O N		N A Y	
O B I		F E D	A C T	B A A
C O M P U T E R S Y S T E M S
C O M A		P O I		W E B S
U N I N V I T E D P E O P L E
R E X	A S H	E A R	S E T
	F R O		R I B	
T H E Y M I G H T C R A S H
S H O T	E D W I N	A U T O
I O W A	R E E V E	G R E G
N U L L	S A N E R	S A W S

49

| C E L L O | C B E R | M A L E |
| O R I O N | H O N E | A L I T |
| C O F F E E A N D D A N I S H |
A S E T	T I E	O R I O L E
	F U R	C L E A N E R
T A I P E I	A L E S	
A S S E T	A S I N	S E N T
M E A T A N D P O T A T O E S
P A Y S	A D E S	H E N N A
	A M E N	D O W S E R
C R A M M E R	H E Y	
A E R I A L	D O E	F R E E
P E A C H E S A N D C R E A M
E L B A	S I D E	H O I S T
S S S S	S T A Y	A G N E S

50

S C U F F	S C O T	S L O G
C A V I L	N A N A	T A L L
A R E T E	A R M S	E R M A
G R A Z E G R A Y S	A V E R
	C A L C	E N L A C E
R O M P E R	A R L E S	
A X E L	D E S I	A T R I A
G E T A W A Y	S C R E A M S
A N Z I O	R E E L	E V A S
	N O M E N	E N L I S T
H O O P L A	T A R E	
E L A L	C H E C K C Z E C H
R I T A	R I R E	T I T H E
O V E N	O V E R	A N N U M
D A N E	S E R B	R E A M S

51

| U S M A | E R R E D | T A L C |
| G O I N | L E A V E | O W E S |
| H U N D R E D Y A R D D A S H |
	N I E C E S	A O R T A
J O E	S T E	R I M	D A R
A F L A C	M O U R N	S T P
W A L N U T	S T A Y S	
N I N E I N C H N A I L S
	A P N E A	I N T A K E
L A S	L E A R N	K E V I N
O A T	A S P	O D E	A P E
A C O R N	U N R E A L	
T H R E E M I L E I S L A N D
H E E D	D O N E E	O M N I
E N D S	S C A D S	E P E E

52

E G B D F	F O A M	V A M P
L A N A I	E L L A	E T U I
B R A W N	L A M A	N A S A
A B I G A I L V A N B U R E N
	L O S	D O S I D O
A T M O S T	U M P S	
C H I P	A N N L A N D E R S
C A D E T	O I L	S A M O A
T W I N S I S T E R	M I L L
	K N E E	B S A	
H O T T E A		B S A	
I N E E D S O M E A D V I C E
P I P E	N O O N	C I D E R
P O E M	I Z O D	A L O N G
O N E S	T E N S	P E L T S

53

```
E L F   P O S T S   P E O N S
L I E   O N T O P   A L P H A
I N N   S C A L E   S M E L L
J A C K I E G L E A S O N
A G E N T     C U E   D O G
H E R O   P A T H S   D A M E
  W E I G H   F E T A L
T H E H O N E Y M O O N E R S
S O L O N   M A C R O
A N E W   E R E C T   T A N G
R E V   I R E   M E T O O
  A U D R E Y M E A D O W S
M E T R E   S W I R L   N I P
O M E G A   E C L A T   E S E
B U S E S   S A L S A   D E L
```

54

```
I N T E R   T I L   G U S T O
S A U D I   U N I   A S P E R
M I L I T A N T S   N O R S E
  F I T Z G E R A L D   I T S
S P O I L S   A H I T
    R E O   H O W I T Z E R
H A D   S W O O N   T E T E
A T I L T   W O E   G O R E D
R A T A   E D S E L   S S S
I T Z W O R D S   M I R
  I N R E   B I T E R S
S U N   B A R M I T Z V A H
T R E V I   T E N S I O N A L
A S S E T   E R E   E K I N G
B A S E S   S E T   R E N E E
```

55

```
S C A M   A R A B   C R E A M
D A R E   D A L E   H A L L E
S L A G   R I L E   A B B E S
  F L A T O N O N E S B A C H
  W H I S T   L E I
D E P A R T   P A S T I M E
E L A T E   E R I N   B U N
M O S T W A N T E D L I S Z T
O P T   L I E D   A N E A R
S E E S R E D   S P U N K Y
  A I R   C O L I N
T O O H O T T O H A N D E L
E C L A T   O L A V   A T O Z
S H A R E   M O R E   T A L E
S O N A R   E R A S   E L A N
```

56

```
D O I N   E V I T A   E G A D
A R C O   M A C E S   B E D E
H E A R T B R E A K H O T E L
L O N G H A I R   A L O N E
  T E R S E   S E R I F
A S H   E S S E N C E   F A T
D E E J A Y   X O O   M O N O
O G L E D   H U B   O R F E O
R A P T   P A R   B U S M A N
E L M   D E L B E R T   Y R S
  Y M C A S   L I L A C
A S S A I   D I S A L L O W
W H E N I M S I X T Y F O U R
E E L S   D E V I L   R U S E
S A F E   S C A R Y   E D E N
```

57

```
L O P   F L A S H   A T L A S
E R A   E E R I E   D U A N E
A C U   D A R L A   E L I T E
H A L T   R A L P H N A D E R
  R A I N Y   I O N
S M E L T S   V A R I E T Y
W A V E S   F A X E D   H E F
A C E S   E R R E D   R E A L
P A R   A V A I L   T E R S E
W E L D I N G   D O N A T E
  E A T   T O M E I
J O H N M A D D E N   E D A M
A R E N A   I R A N I   E W E
B A R O N   N O S E D   R A N
S L A N T   O P E R A   S Y D
```

58

```
P A M P A S   S T E W   P T A
E T E R N E   C O D E   E A R
N O N O N A N E T T E   P R E
S M U T   M O N O   V E E P S
  E L A T E   G I L L
A M B I E N T   S A L I E N T
D U A N E   A T I T   A M E S
I N B   K I K I D E E   O V A
N C A A   D E L E   A S K E R
S H A R P E N   S A V I O R S
  U N I S   A L I E N
S T R O P   O B I S   A I D A
A A H   P U P U P L A T T E R
L I U   I R E S   E R R A N T
E L M   N I N E   S C A N T Y
```

59

```
S T A N . A G O G . . D A M E S
H I T E . D U N E . A L A M O
O N E A . M A T T . L Y S O L .
W E A T H E R V A N E . . E T O
M A S . I N D . L O Y . R I M .
E R E C T . S N I T . T A C O .
. . . H O B . O F A . I T O N .
. I N A N O T H E R V E I N .
D C O N . R H O . Y A T . . . .
R E S T . N E W S . S O L O S .
A W E . R E B . P A C . E R E .
C A R . Y O U R E S O V A I N .
U T I C A . R E E K . I D E A .
L E N I N . B I D E . V E N T .
A R G O S . S N O W . A N T E .
```

60

```
S O F A . S I T B Y . P A A R
A L U M . A D O R E . E C R U
A L T A . B E T E L . A C E S
R A Z Z Z O O O W L S . I N T
. . E A T . . S O M E D A Y
O S A . G A F F . W I R E .
R O L E . G U R U . L E N D S
C A L L L E E E C L E C T I C
A R O M A . L O L A . T A D A
. C E L L . N A V E . L O T .
P H A R A O H . . I D O . . .
L E T . W O O O S S S P I E S
A R I E . T R U T H . A G R A
Z O O T . E S T E E . R O L L
A N N A . R E S T S . T R E K
```

61

```
E G A D . S C R E W . D I E D
M A M E . A R E N A . I N R E
A R O N . R U B A D U B D U B
I D E A M A N . M E S S U P .
L E B L A N C . O B S . R T E
S N A I L . H E R O . V A I L
. . . A B E L . G E M I N I .
. R I N G A D I N G D I N G .
R E V E A L . D E S I . . . .
O D E D . A P E R . S U S H I
M S G . D C I . F R O N T O N
. C O D D L E . B A N K E R S
R A T A T A T T A T . E R N O
A R I Z . V I A L S . P E E L
P E T E . A N G L O . T O T E
```

62

```
A S P S . C O O N . U P F O R
D O O R . H A F T . S E L E S
M U S I C O F T H E H E A R T
I T S . H O S E . Y E N . . .
T H E S I S . N L E R . S T L
. . K N E E . E D I B L E S .
N A Y . R A S H . N O E N D .
A T L A S S H R U G G E D .
T O T A L . T H E N . O K S .
A M I B L U E . R U S T . . .
T I C . E R R S . S C A L E S
. . O Y S . O L E O . A L P .
F I S H C A L L E D W A N D A
A R E N A . S O F T . I C E D
T A R O T . U N T O . M E R E
```

63

```
V I S T A . D O I T . T R A Y
O O H E D . E D G E . H A L E
T W E E D L E D U M . E M M A
E A S T . I P S A . A T P A R
. H I E S . N I N O . . . . .
. I D E N T I C A L T W I N S
O N E . T O G O . K E E N O N
E D I T H . H O W . A L A M O
D I S H E S . T H A T . L A W
S A M E O L D S A M E O L D .
. . . B R R R . T A R T . . .
J O L L Y . O M N I . H A L F
A R I A . T W E E D L E D E E
M E S H . V S I X . E R A S E
B O A S . S E N T . A S Y E T
```

64

```
A P N E A . . I N B . B L U M
D R A W L . O N E A . A U R A
L A B E L . H U G H G R A N T
I D O . E P O S . A R O U S E
B O B B Y S H E R M A N . . .
. . . A S H . E A T . N S A .
A D O S . A C T I . I D E A L
C I V I L W A R G E N E R A L
D R A C O . L E N T . R O B S
C E L . V O L . H O E . . . .
. . J E S S E J A C K S O N .
P R E A M P . P E N T . A N Y
H A R P E R L E E . A S K I N
A S I A . E Y E R . N I E C E
T H E N . Y E S . . E S S E X
```

65

```
S C A B S   T A B S     I S L E
A L L O T   E L A L     N E E D
G O O D Y   N O R A     A L O E
A T T Y   S T U D M U F F I N
    B L A H       B R O
S T A L A G   S H A N G H A I
E U R O S   C H I N     I N N
D R A W S T R I N G P A N T S
E B B     H O L D   O L D I E
R O S E B O W L   D E P I C T
      M O M   C O M A
S T R I P M A L L S   C L A D
I R A N   C L E O   N I E C E
P U Z O   A S I S   I N A N E
S E E R   N O S E   P O K E R
```

66

```
B L E A T   S P E C   A J A X
A U D I O   P I E R   N O R M
E T E R N A L T R I A N G L E
Z E N   E M I T     M A S O N
      S L I T   S U E
  I N C E S S A N T N O I S E
S M E R S H   D I E   P R O G
L I V E S   U M P   V I O L A
I D E A   A S I   S I N N E D
P E R M A N E N T P R E S S
      C A R   R A T S
O R G A N   Z A S U   H I S
P E R P E T U A L M O T I O N
E L I E   O N C E   S A N T A
L Y N X   P O K E   O N T A P
```

67

```
U K E S   E L B A   A C T E D
N O A H   R E A P   L A R V A
C A R Y G R A N T   B R E E D
A L L   L A S S   W I R E R S
P A Y M E N T   M A N Y
    A N T   S A Y O N A R A
S T E R N   S H I N   A J A X
T A X I   A M A Z E   T A K E
A R I A   D O M E   T I R E D
B A T H M A T S   R I O
    C O P E   S E A N C E S
A G H A S T   F E A R   A V A
F L A R E   J I M C A R R E Y
R I L E Y   E D I T   C O N S
O B E Y S   B O S S   A L T O
```

68

```
M U R A L   F L O W N   J A M
A C U R A   A U D I O   A G O
S L I M P I C K E N S   N E O
H A N A   R T E   D O O V E R
      N I A   G U A V A
  S K I N N Y D I P P I N G
F I E   T I A R A S   N E R D
I N T E L   C E N   K E Y I N
R E T D   S H A N I A   C P A
  S L I G H T M I S T A K E
      E T H O S   A O L
R E D H O T   A D A   S K E D
O A R   S P A R E C H A N G E
D R U   T U X E S   O C E A N
E L M   S T E A K   N E E D Y
```

69

```
B R O W   P U M A S   H A S P
L O N E   I S I A H   Y O K E
O N E E I G H T H U N D R E D
B A H   N E E T   T E E T E R
    A S T O R   P S I   A T O
C A N T O N   T O O L S
E N D A T   S E L F   C O K E
O N E T O U C H O F V E N U S
S A D E   N O E S   I N E R T
    S I D L E   A S T U T E
M I A   C I D   C R I S P
A N T H E M   C A R O   P E A
O N E A R M E D B A N D I T S
R E A D   E M I L Y   O N U S
I R M A   D O V E S   A G I N
```

70

```
A D O R N   S C A R   L O S T
M E L E E   H O N E   O N T O
P E E L S   H A Y D N S E E K
S M O O T H   L O D E   T E E
      A L A S   N E W B O R N
G O O D E N P L E N T Y
A I M   S E R E   S T R A W
G L I B   S Y N O D   E A C H
A S T E R   T W I N   S H E
  N E E S O N N E P H E W
C A N T I N A   S A M E
A L I   G A M E   H E R D E R
N I X O N C U T S   S I E V E
A V E C   T E N T   I S L E S
L E S T   S L A Y   S H I R T
```

71

```
L I N U S   G E N T   P F F T
A T O N E   A G R A   U L E E
B O R I N G B O A R   F E I N T O N
        T O A S T   O F F E N D
S O M E R S   R I T A   I T S
A D E S   M A I N   T A N
L E W   T A M P A   L I G H T
V O L C A N O   P A I D F O R
O N I O N   U S E U P   L I E
    N O G   N E T S   M E S S
G I G   L A T E   T R E A T S
R O M P E R   S T E A M
E T U I   B A R I N G B E A R
T A L C   O M E N   E E R I E
A S E A   R I D E   D R A M S
```

72

```
R A M   H O P L I T E   C O W
A T E   A R O U S A L   A L E
T O N   C A S C A D E   L I B
  M U S I C I A N   V A L V E
    C E L T S   T E R S E R
E L A I N E   Z I N C
L I N E D   O P E N   H A M M
L E O N A R D O D A V I N C I
A U N T   A D D S   I T E M S
    I B I S   A C E T I C
S A S S E D   A Z T E C
P R A T T   S C U L P T O R
E E L   T I T U L A R   P A T
A N T   O V E R U S E   A K A
R A Y   R E P A S T S   L E G
```

73

```
B O C A   T S A R   J U T
A D A P T   A T T I C   O N O
W I L L A   T E M P O   N I N
L E M O N L A W   T R E A T Y
    M G T   I T C H Y
  L A B O R L E A D E R
A I L   I R R E G U L A R
M A P   M A L A I S E   O X O
P R O P A G A T E   N I T
    L I N C O L N L O G S
  T I E T O   A L B
S I T A R S   L A V A L A M P
P G A   E T H E L   M O N D E
E E L   D I A N A   A N K L E
D R Y   C M O N   G A I N
```

74

```
A S H E S   A F A R   S H O D
S T A V E   N O N E   T O M E
K O R E A   G A T E   R U I N
  P E R F O R M I N G A R T S
      A N Y   L A Y
A G L A R E   F L I P   F I B
R E E V E   O R E S   W A D E
G O V E R N M E N T B I L L S
O D E S   E A T S   A S S E T
T E E   T O N S   B R E E D S
    F I N   O A R
B A L L P A R K F R A N K S
O B O E   T O O T   C O A T S
N U K E   A B L E   K E N Y A
O T I S   L E A N   S L E E P
```

75

```
S A L S A   I R I S   S W A P
A V A I L   S I L K   L A C E
D O U B L E S O L I T A I R E
E N D   T A U T   P U T T E R
    L O S E   F O R E
S M A L L E R H A L F   P T A
N O M A D   O D E   W O E S
A T O M   G A P E S   H U R T
K O N A   R O E   R I N S E
E R G   R A N D O M O R D E R
    B O N E   T S A R
R O T U N D   N O R M   R C A
U N B I A S E D O P I N I O N
I C A L   O P A L   N I T R O
N E R D   N I K E   G L E N N
```

76

```
F U S S   F A L L   E R O D E
A R E A   A S E A   R O V E S
I D E S   T H A N   A G E N T
R U S H T H E P A S S E R
      H E N   N E T
C A E S A R   C L A D   G O P
O R L O N   L E A F   S U L U
S T E A K M E D I U M W E L L
T I C K   A G E D   O A S I S
S E T   P R O D   E L Y S E E
    B A G   B R A
  F I R E W H E N R E A D Y
S T I N T   H A Z E   W I R E
H I N G E   A L E S   E D E N
E A S E D   M E L T   R E D S
```

77

```
A L E C   R O M P S   H E L P
D I V A   I N T R O   A P E S
E V E N S T E V E N   N E T S
P E R D U E     S A D D E S T
T R Y O N   A S T R A Y
      G A L L O   M A I Z E
R A M P   I D I   F E N D E R
E M I L   R A M B O   D E A L
D E C A F S   J A R   Y A L E
S N A I L   M I K E S
      N O N A M E   T O D A Y
V A L J E A N   L A R E D O
A R I A   S I L L Y B I L L Y
N E O N   A L I E N   O H I O
S A N E   L A T E X   N I B S
```

78

```
E L M E R   R A D A R   H A J
L E O N I   A L I C E   O L E
B A N A N A P E E L S   T D S
O C T   G N P   S U N S P O T
W H E A T I E S     I T O
      R O L L E R S K A T E S
S A F E S   A H A   G A L A
E R A   S L I P O N S   T A G
R E N A   I D O   I L O N A
B A L L B E A R I N G S
      E A R   T R E N D I E R
C A T S E Y E   I R A   C E O
H S T   W A X E D F L O O R S
U T E   E L A T E   E R N I E
M A R   D E M O S   D O S E S
```

79

```
C O V E   S H U S H   C U S S
O R E L   T O R T E   A N T E
O I L S   E G G A R   I C A N
L O V E M E T E N D E R L Y
I L E   A L I     P O E S Y
T E T O N   E V I T A   S U E
    O N O   E C O   R A P S
  I H A V E R H Y T H M
I N N S   E R S   S E E
C O B   B R E E D   M A G M A
E M A I L     O O P   R O T
  I S N T T H A T A S H A M E
A N K A   R U S E S   I D E A
T E E N   A G I L E   L E N S
M E T E   M E A L S   L A T E
```

80

```
A J A X   M A S H   O F U S E
G E N E   A T E E   R A V E D
L U G S   D A T A   C L E A N
O D E   T E L   T R A L A L A
W I L D W I L D W E S T
    R O T   R A N   O T T O
T Y P E B   P A V E D   I O N
W E E W I L L I E W I N K I E
A T E   T O O N S   V O I L A
S I P S   I T E   Z I T
    W O R L D W I D E W E B
G A L I L E I   A P E   O L E
I R E N E   N E S S   Q U I T
M A N G O   E T T U   U N D O
P L A Y S   S E E P   E D E N
```

81

```
E P S O M   R U S S O   A M C
H A I K U   U N C U T   B I O
S C R A M   M A R C O P O L O
    P B S   I C E R I N K
M A R I O C U O M O   O L E S
A D A   J E S U   R P M
A L B   U N I T S   U P P E R
M A I L M E N   A C E T O N E
S I D E B   G A T O R   A N T
    T O A   L I N T   C U R
A P O S   T O L E D O O H I O
C A R G O E S     O R R
I P S O F A C T O   I G L O O
D U O   O S A K A   C A P R A
S A N   Z E R O S   O N S E T
```

82

```
T A C K Y   P Y G M Y   R N S
O L L I E   R A D I O   O A T
M O O N S   O R A N G   A M Y
B U G S B U N N Y   I N D E X
    M U T E     I B A R
R O T A T E   F I N E T U N E
H A W N   F L O R A   N O L
I K E   P L A I N E R   N B C
N E E   O U T R E   D E L I
O N T A R G E T   M O O R E D
    Y A K S   B A N G
A T B A Y   S Y L V E S T E R
C H I   P E W E E   T H O L E
T A R   I D E A S   W O O E D
S T D   G U E S S   O W N E D
```

83

BEGAT · UTAH · CAPO
AMANA · PAVE · ODOR
BURNRUBBER · AMID
ASPERSE · REPRISE
· YEAR · ASTER ·
COMA · STEPONE ·
AGAIN · DIRT · ODE
SLAMONTHEBRAKES
HEM · BONE · YPRES
· TOSTADA · TARO ·
AWARD · DISK · ·
DELAYED · VERITAS
MALI · MAKEAUTURN
AVON · IRIS · PENNA
NEWS · TENT · PREOP

84

DEVIL · ACME · PCBS
OVINE · LOOT · HORA
TENDERFOOT · OP1E
SNEEZE · DUSTPAN
· PASSBY · HOERS
PORT · TWA · FAIR
UHUH · CIR · ANDHOW
RIB · PUGNOSE · EGO
ROBBER · OPT · BARK
· ERTE · NAB · IDES
AGREE · BEHALF
GENERAL · LOOSES
INEZ · DOUBLECHIN
LICE · OCTO · SAUNA
EEKS · SKEW · SLEEP

85

OAFS · COLDS · WHET
SWAP · ONSET · HYDE
CARE · STALE · EPIC
ARMEDTOTHETEETH
RESCUE · IDOL · ·
· HELLO · SNIFFS
ESC · LEVI · TERRA
THUMBONESNOSEAT
CORER · ANTE · DYE
HOLDUP · SOUPS ·
· ISLE · RANCOR
LIVEHANDTOMOUTH
OLAV · STARS · OTTO
ASIA · MELEE · PIED
FALL · ARIES · SERA

86

SHOTS · CAMPS · SHO
HOLST · AGERS · LIB
OMAHA · SURETHING
DEFINITELY · INDY
· RDS · EELSKIN
WAFT · UAR · DOS
ABE · ZZTOP · OASIS
WITHOUTQUESTION
ATEIN · AURAE · PTA
DEL · ERS · ASAP
PAGODAS · EAR ·
ALOU · BYALLMEANS
CERTAINLY · ATSEA
ERG · SLOMO · SHINY
ROE · SEDAN · SAFES

87

PILOT · BACK · ITCH
AROSE · ELAL · CARA
SABLE · NILE · EBAN
· BONDJAMESBOND
SOY · ARI · KOOKY
TWIGGY · HELIX ·
ELSIE · RENE · POD
METARZANYOUJANE
STS · ETNA · TATAR
· PANSY · BARRIE
SAPID · RAH · ORK
CALLMEISHMAEL ·
ORAL · ANTE · GAMAL
TOTO · STAT · EVADE
SNOW · TORT · NENES

88

SHAQ · LALA · DALE
LULU · EPIC · EWERS
AMOI · HAGS · MOVIE
PEEL · ICH · AERATE
· TIGHTASADRUM
AFT · CHEATON ·
MORTE · SON · ALAS
PROUDASAPEACOCK
STYX · RAF · LEFTY
SENESCE · TIE
SHARPASATACK
TATARS · TAR · ONTO
ALONE · PHIL · OAHU
GENOA · EERO · KNOT
· REND · ERST · YAMS

89

```
L I Z A   S O M E   T I B I A
A N O N   E T A L   O N E N D
S T R A I G H T F O R W A R D
E R R   S U E S   N O I S E S
R O O S T E R   P S S T
    P H D   P E P   H A S H
S I X A M   L A P E L   C U E
C O M M U N I T Y C E N T E R
A T E   S E A T S   M A I Z E
R A N T   W R Y   A M P
    H U B S   G R I S H A M
A S S I S I   M O A N   E G O
C A T C H E S O F F G U A R D
E V O K E   A R E A   F R E E
S E W E R   P E R T   O D E S
```

90

```
S O P S   P I C A   B I S O N
T A I L   A D A M   A T O N E
O T T O   R A V E   T U N E D
W H A T S T H E S T O R Y
        M O O     O R B
P O S T O N   H O N   I M A M
A C H O O   H O P I S   A D O
W H O S T H E L U C K Y M A N
E R R   H O M E S   O M E G A
R E E K   V I D   S K A T E D
      A P E     U P I
W H E R E S T H E F I R E
A B O U T   T A T E   O D O R
B O R N E   C B E R   L E N O
S W E A R   H E R E   D A I S
```

91

```
B A H   C O M I C S   A M E S
A C U   A R A R A T   W I R E
B R R   P E G O M Y H E A R T
E E R I E   E N E M Y   M E T
    I N C A     I D O I D O
J A C K O L A N T E R N
A L A   D E B A R   A C T E D
W I N D   C O R A L   E R N E
S T E A L   I C I E R   A D E
    W I L L O T H E W I S P
G W Y N N E     I T I N
A R E   G A M U T   U N L I T
L A N D O G O S H E N   O D E
A T T A   U N E A S E   A L L
S H A Y   E A R N E D   D Y E
```

92

```
F A L L   B A K E D   L A Z E
A L E E   E M E R Y   A X O N
H A N D E L B A R S   P E N D
D I S U N I O N   L A D L E S
        C O Z Y   D E F O G
M A N T L E   H E X A G R A M
A L O H A   T O S I R   E M I
N E B O   S I T K A   H A U T
O R E   M E T E S   H E S S E
R O L L C A L L   C A R E E R
      G U I S E   S A R A
T R A G I C   W A R P L A N E
H O S E   A B E L B O D I E D
E W E R   P A A V O   E D E N
M E S S   E L L E N   D A D A
```

93

```
A B A C I   A M A H L   B E T
S E D A N   O L D I E   O R E
S E A S C A L L O P S   T I X
A P P E A L   E S P   S T E T
M S T   S E T   O N T O
    S H R I M P S C A M P I
D A H L   O P E R   A R S O N
A L I A S   I D O   A M U C K
B U T C H   N E W S   A P O S
S M O K E D S A L M O N
    R E D O   S A N   A W S
H Y M N   C H I   Z E A L O T
A M I   S T U F F E D S O L E
M C S   H O R S E   G A F F E
M A S   O R L O N   E N T E R
```

94

```
J A V A   C H O S E N   O A S
E L E M   O U T C R Y   B R O
E A R P I E R C I N G   E L F
P R Y   C R O   I S L E T
    B A C K B R E A K I N G
S T O L L E   L O R N E
C A V I L   I L L T I M E D
A D E S   I S T L E   N O D E
M A R T I N E Z   T I N G E
      E N T R E   D U N K E D
H E A R T R E N D I N G
O X E Y E     O V A   P I E
M I G   A R M T W I S T I N G
E L I   R U I N E D   A L F A
Y E S   S E T T L E   P L O D
```

95

W	A	D	S		E	R	I	C	A		B	A	T	S
A	R	E	A		V	A	L	E	T		U	T	A	H
R	U	M	B	L	E	F	I	S	H		M	A	K	E
S	T	O	L	E	N		E	T	E		B	L	E	D
		C	E	N	T	S		A	N	T	L	E	R	S
A	R	R		D	U	E	T		S	E	E			
N	O	A	H		A	T	O	M		A	B	A	S	H
T	U	T	U		L	A	P	I	S		E	D	N	A
I	T	S	M	E		T	A	L	C		E	M	I	T
			B	L	T		Z	E	R	O		I	T	E
A	P	P	L	I	E	S		S	A	V	O	R		
M	I	R	E		N	U	B		B	A	N	A	N	A
B	L	I	P		S	T	U	M	B	L	E	B	U	M
L	O	N	I		E	R	R	O	L		A	L	T	O
E	T	T	E		D	A	N	T	E		L	E	S	S

96

B	A	R	N		S	W	I	S	S		G	O	U	P
E	R	E	I		C	A	R	A	T		R	U	D	E
B	O	N	N	V	O	Y	A	G	E		A	T	A	T
E	N	D	E	A	R	S			R	I	P	P	L	E
			I	L	E		P	E	N	N	P	A	L	S
A	W	A	R	E		A	U	S		E	A	T		
R	E	N	O		U	L	S	T	E	R		I	D	S
M	A	N	N	I	N	T	H	E	S	T	R	E	E	T
S	R	I		L	I	M	P	E	T		E	N	C	E
		H	E	E		A	I	M		A	C	T	O	R
T	A	I	L	F	I	N	N		A	T	A			
A	L	L	O	T	S			O	U	T	P	O	S	T
S	L	A	P		S	W	E	P	T	U	P	I	N	N
T	A	T	E		E	A	G	E	R		E	S	A	U
E	Y	E	D		I	R	O	N	Y		D	E	P	T

97

D	A	L	I		S	L	U	G		A	C	H	E	S
A	L	A	N		T	O	R	O		T	H	E	S	E
N	U	M	E	R	O	U	N	O		T	E	A	S	E
A	M	A	Z	O	N		F	R	E	E	D	O	M	
			D	E	S	K		A	N	K	H			
A	S	H	E	N		L	I	P	I	D		O	B	S
S	P	I	R	E		E	N	I	D		G	N	A	W
S	A	G	G	Y		E	G	G		B	U	C	K	O
E	C	H	O		E	P	P	S		U	S	H	E	R
S	E	P		V	I	S	I	T		T	H	O	R	N
			R	E	A	R		N	Y	S	E			
N	A	I	L	S	E	T		O	N	F	I	R	E	
A	R	E	A	S		M	I	S	T	E	R	B	I	G
V	I	S	T	A		E	D	I	T		A	I	D	A
E	A	T	E	R		N	O	N	O		U	S	E	D

98

B	U	C	K		H	A	L	L		S	T	O	O	L
A	C	H	E		O	L	E	O		A	R	U	B	A
A	L	E	E		O	M	I	T		F	E	T	I	D
L	A	M	P	C	H	O	P	S		E	M	O	T	E
			F	R	A	N	Z		I	R	O	N		
A	G	G	I	E		D	I	A	S		R	A	P	S
V	E	R	T	E	X		G	N	A	W		L	U	C
O	N	E		P	R	O		N	A	H		I	R	E
W	O	E		S	A	R	I		C	A	R	M	E	N
S	A	N	G		Y	E	N	S		T	E	P	E	E
		T	O	E	S		Q	U	A	I	L			
P	S	H	A	W		D	U	M	P	F	O	U	N	D
R	O	U	T	E		A	I	M	S		A	R	E	A
E	L	M	E	R		B	R	I	E		D	A	R	T
P	O	P	E	S		S	E	T	S		S	L	O	E

99

A	C	C	O	S	T		M	E	N	U		H	A	T
L	O	O	T	E	R		I	R	O	N		A	D	O
S	P	O	T	W	E	L	D	E	R	S		V	O	W
O	S	L	O		M	A	S		A	D	O	R	N	
		P	O	S	T	O	F	F	I	C	E	S		
F	A	R	M	E	R	S		A	R	E	S			
A	R	I	E	S		C	H	A		T	R	U	E	
T	O	P	S	O	F	M	O	U	N	T	A	I	N	S
E	W	E	S		L	I	D		A	N	T	I	S	
			U	R	A	L		M	A	L	T	E	S	E
S	T	O	P	O	N	A	D	I	M	E				
C	H	A	S	M		I	C	E		O	W	E	S	
O	R	R		P	O	T	S	A	N	D	P	A	N	S
F	E	E		E	R	I	C		D	O	T	I	N	G
F	E	D		R	E	P	O		S	E	S	T	E	T

100

F	O	A	M	S		P	A	R	D		A	C	E	S
I	N	L	E	T		A	T	E	E		P	O	G	O
S	T	A	T	E		J	E	F	F	E	R	S	O	N
H	O	S	A	N	N	A		S	I	M	I	A	N	S
			L	O	O	M	S		N	I	L			
E	V	I	L		H	A	T	P	I	N		O	V	A
C	O	N	I	C		S	A	T	E		N	O	B	
L	I	N	C	O	L	N		K	E	N	N	E	D	Y
A	L	E		N	O	E	S		T	E	A	K	S	
T	A	R		S	N	E	E	R	S		X	M	A	S
			D	O	G		Q	U	I	L	T			
A	L	F	A	L	F	A		B	R	I	D	G	E	T
B	A	L	D	E	A	G	L	E		T	O	R	C	H
B	R	A	D		C	O	I	N		H	O	O	H	A
E	D	G	Y		E	N	D	S		E	R	G	O	T

101

```
L A S   A N G L E R   S T U B
I S P   T I R A D E   P E R U
E L L   O N E I D A   H A N G
S E I S M O G R A P H E R
T E N P I N   S E R I A L
O P T I C   R A M   P E N T A
    C A V E M E N   T O W
S I Z E L I M I T A T I O N S
E S O   M I S R E A D
E L O P E   T H O   N E S T S
R E T O R T   A G A T H A
    S I G H S O F R E L I E F
N O U N   A T T A I N   L Y E
E X I T   N U T L E T   T V S
B Y T E   K N O L L S   S E T
```

102

```
F A C T S   A L B U M   V I P
A D O R E   B E A N O   E N E
D O N O R   C O N C O U R S E
    Q U A D   J U S T N O W
S T U B   A S C O T   T A L E
K E E L   W O O S   M E L E E
I N S E A S O N   E A R
T N T   C O N T E X T   C A B
    S E N   O N C E M O R E
P E S T S   J U D E   O N E L
A N T I   H O R S E   O V A L
S C A L P E R   D I R E
C O N T E N D E R   D I R T Y
A D Z   G N A S H   E N S U E
L E A   S A N T O   A G E N T
```

103

```
S A L K   L E T M E   B L A H
A G U N   A V I A N   O A H U
J A M E S B E A R D   D I M E
A P P E A R   C O D E R E D
K E Y   H A S P   R A G
    L I T T L E S H A V E R
N A B O B   R A V E L   A G E
O W E S   C O T E S   C R O P
V O L   A L L E N   S A Y S O
A L L I N A L A T H E R
    S T P   U S E R   T A B
Q U A L I T Y   A B J U R E
U R S A   R A Z O R S E D G E
A D E N   A L E U T   S O U R
D U A D   P E E R S   T R E Y
```

104

```
W H I M S   A P S E   T G I F
I O N I C   R E E L   O R S O
S U N D A E O N A B A N A N A
E R S   M M M   W A R   S T L
    O P I A T E   I D S
B O W L E R S H E A D A C H E
O C H E R   E D S   G O A L
I C Y   S E A L S U P   U Z I
L A P S   D C I   H I R E D
S M A L L W I N E B O T T L E
    Y O U   D E V A N E
P A M   C A R   O R E   L O U
S T O C K M A R K E T N E W S
S O R E   M I T E   A R N I E
T M E N   O N E S   G A T E S
```

105

```
S W A T   B E T S   R A G O N
E A V E   O M I T   C L O W N
E R A S   H I D E   C A B L E
Y E S S I R R E E B O B
A S T E R   P A L A C E S
    R O G U E   T A M A L E
W H O A N E L L Y   A R I D
H O P   S E A M A P S   G A G
I V E S   N O W A Y J O S E
T E R E S A   S N O R E
E L A S T I C   I R I S H
    S O R R Y C H A R L I E
A N T I C   O O Z E   I O T A
I B O O K   A D A M   E V I L
D A N N Y   T A R P   S E N S
```

106

```
A P R I L   B E E T   O L A F
S A U C E   A L P O   T I L L
H U G H O B R I A N   T A P E
E L S   N U B   R A N E E
    J A M E S S T E W A R T
C A P O   T E L E C A S T
A N G L E R   C O M A
W Y A T T E A R P P L A Y E R
    E L S E   E L P A S O
    R E P R I N T S   E K E D
K E V I N C O S T N E R
A L I C E   E E L   A O L
R I C K   H E N R Y F O N D A
M E T E   A G E E   I N N E R
A S S T   M O T O   N E A R S
```

107

A	D	A	M		T	H	E	R	E		S	U	N	G
G	E	N	E		R	E	L	A	Y		K	N	E	E
H	E	A	R	T	I	N	T	H	E		I	V	A	N
A	R	T		A	E	R	O			B	R	E	T	T
	H	A	N	D	I	N	T	H	E	T	I	L	L	
A	V	E	R	S				O	U	R		L	Y	E
S	E	M	I		A	S	S	A	Y					
H	E	A	D	I	N	T	H	E	C	L	O	U	D	S
			N	O	I	S	E			L	S	A	T	
A	P	T		D	O	L		R	E	E	D	Y		
F	O	O	T	I	N	T	H	E	D	O	O	R		
F	L	O	R	A		A	T	O	M		B	E	D	
E	L	L	A		R	I	G	H	T	P	L	A	C	E
C	O	E	D		A	T	E	A	T		A	S	O	F
T	I	D	E		P	E	N	N	Y		B	E	N	T

108

C	B	S		R	E	V	I	L	E		S	H	O	P
A	N	A		O	L	I	V	E	R		P	U	Z	O
P	A	N	A	M	A	C	A	N	A	L	A	R	A	B
P	I	G	L	A	T	I	N				A	S	T	R	O
			I	N	E			T	O	Y		S	K	Y
G	L	O	B			S	L	A	M					
R	A	M	A	D	A	C	A	T	A	M	A	R	A	N
A	L	A	B	A	M	A	M	A	H	A	R	A	J	A
B	A	N	A	N	A	R	A	M	A	S	A	G	A	S
			T	E	R	I				L	A	R	A	
R	P	M		D	I	D			A	D	S			
E	L	O	P	E			C	U	T	I	E	P	I	E
B	A	B	A	W	A	W	A	S	A	V	A	T	A	R
U	Z	I	S		C	A	M	E	R	A		A	G	O
S	A	L	T		T	H	E	S	I	S		S	O	S

109

S	P	A	S		M	A	S	H		B	A	Y	E	R
C	O	R	P		O	R	E	O		E	L	I	Z	A
A	S	I	A		D	R	A	W	I	N	G	P	I	N
M	I	S	C	U	E		M	E	M	O		S	O	T
S	T	E	E	P	L	E		S	P	I	T			
			N	O	S	I	R		A	T	H	O	M	E
L	I	N	E	N		D	E	L	I		I	H	O	P
O	N	C	E		S	E	W	E	R		M	I	R	E
M	E	A	D		T	R	E	E		T	B	O	N	E
A	Z	A	L	E	A		D	R	O	O	L			
			E	N	Y	A		S	T	R	E	E	T	S
U	S	E		D	E	M	S		H	O	W	L	I	N
T	H	R	E	A	D	B	A	R	E		E	I	N	E
E	A	S	E	L		L	I	A	R		E	T	T	A
S	H	E	L	L		E	L	M	S		D	E	S	K

110

E	R	A	T		B	E	L	I	E		A	M	E	N
L	A	S	H		A	R	E	N	T		N	O	N	E
B	I	T	E		T	I	N	K	E	R	T	O	Y	S
A	N	I	M	A	T	E	D			D	E	T	A	T
			A	R	E			H	A	N				
T	A	I	L	O	R	M	A	D	E		N	A	S	A
A	T	O	L	L		A	F	A	R		A	C	T	I
S	A	T		L	E	C	A	R	R	E		E	E	L
S	L	A	M		S	A	L	E		L	O	R	N	E
E	L	S	A		S	O	L	D	I	E	R	B	O	Y
			L	A	O				R	C	A			
A	U	D	I	T			E	M	I	T	T	I	N	G
S	P	Y	G	L	A	S	S	E	S		O	V	A	L
S	T	E	N		P	A	S	T	E		R	A	T	E
N	O	D	S		B	L	E	S	S		S	N	E	E

111

T	A	B	L	E		B	I	O	S		R	A	S	H
I	L	I	A	D		A	D	U	E		A	N	T	E
M	A	R	T	I	N	R	I	T	T		L	O	O	S
S	I	D	E	B	E	T		S	A	M	P	R	A	S
				L	E	A	S	T		I	H	A	T	E
L	U	T	H	E	R	B	U	R	B	A	N	K		
B	L	E	U				F	I	R	M	A			
J	E	A	N	A	R	P		P	A	I	D	O	F	F
			T	I	A	R	A				E	R	L	E
		K	I	N	G	O	F	T	H	E	R	O	A	D
A	M	O	N	G		T	R	I	A	D				
L	O	W	G	E	A	R		E	L	E	C	T	O	R
L	O	T	T		J	U	N	I	O	R	H	I	G	H
A	R	O	O		A	D	I	N		L	I	L	L	E
H	E	W	N		R	E	P	S		E	S	T	E	E

112

E	L	A	L		S	P	A	S		A	D	O	B	E
M	A	M	E		P	R	I	M		L	A	N	E	D
T	W	O	F	O	R	O	N	E	O	F	F	E	R	S
	C	U	T	T	Y		T	A	P		T	I	N	E
H	O	N		T	E	N		R	E	C		L	I	L
M	U	T	T		R	E	P		N	O	B	L	E	S
O	R	T	H	O		H	E	A	T	E	R			
	T	O	O	F	O	R	E	B	O	D	I	N	G	
			S	U	B	U	R	B		S	N	E	R	D
T	A	L	E	S	E		S	O	C		E	X	I	T
A	L	E		E	Y	E		T	A	B		T	D	S
S	C	A	T		E	L	M		M	E	R	C	I	
T	O	F	O	U	R	M	O	R	E	Y	E	A	R	S
E	V	E	N	T		E	V	I	L		A	S	O	F
R	E	D	Y	E		R	E	D	S		L	E	N	O

113

D	E	L	E		U	S	M	C		J	U	M	B	O
A	P	E	X		P	H	I	L		A	C	U	R	A
S	E	N	T		T	I	L	E		C	O	L	O	R
H	E	A	R	T	O	F	D	A	R	K	N	E	S	S
		A	B	I	T		R	A	I	N				
B	A	R	D	O	T		F	I	R	E		O	P	T
A	G	A	I	N		T	I	N	E		O	P	E	R
C	E	N	T	E	R	O	F	G	R	A	V	I	T	Y
O	N	C	E		E	Y	E	S		G	E	N	E	S
N	T	H		C	U	S	S		A	R	R	E	S	T
			C	E	S	T		A	G	E	D			
M	I	D	D	L	E	O	F	T	H	E	R	O	A	D
A	M	O	R	E		R	I	T	A		A	S	T	O
R	A	Z	O	R		E	L	I	S		F	L	O	P
E	N	E	M	Y		S	E	C	T		T	O	M	E

114

A	D	L	I	B		H	O	U	S	E		G	S	A
L	E	O	N	A		E	P	S	O	M		A	W	L
L	E	G	A	L	B	R	I	E	F	S		Z	A	P
O	R	I		B	E	R	E	F	T		D	E	M	O
R	E	C	O	O	L			U	T	N	E			
			L	A	T	E	B	L	O	O	M	E	R	S
B	R	A	E		S	R	A			P	H	O	B	I	A
A	U	R	A	S		A	N	T		O	L	O	G	Y
S	T	I	N	T	S		J	A	W		I	N	A	S
S	H	A	D	O	W	B	O	X	E	R	S			
			E	P	E	E			B	E	H	A	V	E
B	A	R	R		E	T	U	D	E	S		V	I	A
O	V	A		O	P	E	N	D	R	A	W	E	R	S
Z	I	T		C	E	L	I	A		L	A	R	G	E
O	D	E		T	A	S	T	Y		E	X	T	O	L

115

E	L	S	E		N	E	T	S		P	R	O	W	L
L	E	O	N		O	L	I	O		R	E	M	I	T
E	A	S	T		V	A	N	S		E	L	A	N	D
C	H	A	R	I	O	T	S	O	F	F	I	R	E	
			A	N	T	E			R	E	V			
A	V	E	N	G	E		L	O	R	E	L	E	I	
C	I	R	C	E		S	H	O	W		O	R	R	
T	O	W	E	R	I	N	G	I	N	F	E	R	N	O
E	L	I			N	U	T	S		O	N	E	I	N
	D	A	N	C	I	N	G		S	Y	D	N	E	Y
			A	N	E		I	K	E	A				
I	S	P	A	R	I	S	B	U	R	N	I	N	G	
A	L	L	O	W		S	O	O	N		G	L	E	N
D	I	A	N	A		A	M	O	K		E	S	A	U
D	E	W	E	Y		Y	A	K	S		R	A	T	S

116

N	O	T	V		S	W	A	G		D	W	A	R	F
I	D	E	A		T	I	T	O		I	O	N	I	A
N	I	T	S		I	N	T	O		A	R	D	O	R
O	N	E	S	E	C	O	N	D	P	L	E	A	S	E
			A	S	K	S			G	E	M			
P	H	E	L	P	S		A	R	T		A	V	I	D
A	O	L		R	O	S	S	I		P	R	I	D	E
T	W	O	M	I	N	U	T	E	D	R	I	L	L	S
C	S	P	O	T		N	O	F	E	E		L	E	K
H	O	E	D		S	S	R		S	M	E	A	R	S
			D	O	H		A	C	I	D				
T	H	R	E	E	D	A	Y	W	E	E	K	E	N	D
B	E	I	N	G		D	E	A	N		O	D	A	Y
A	M	A	N	A		E	N	I	D		C	I	N	E
R	I	L	E	S		S	S	T	S		H	E	A	D

117

A	T	L	A	S		S	I	S	I		A	N	T	E
C	H	A	L	K		E	D	E	N		T	A	R	A
R	A	B	B	I	T	E	A	R	S		I	S	I	S
E	T	S		I	O	N		G	Y	M	S	H	O	E
			E	N	D		H	I	N	E	S			
	K	A	N	G	A	R	O	O	C	O	U	R	T	
I	N	N	S		T	A	P			W	E	A	R	Y
T	O	V		K	E	E	P	E	R	S		Z	E	D
S	P	I	R	O		E	E	E		J	O	Y	S	
	F	L	E	A	M	A	R	K	E	T	E	R	S	
			S	L	A	T	S		S	U	B			
W	A	R	P	A	T	H		E	E	R		T	A	I
A	L	O	E		T	O	A	D	S	T	O	O	L	S
D	I	S	C		E	M	M	A		L	E	G	A	L
S	T	E	T		R	E	A	M		E	R	A	S	E

118

T	O	M	E		O	R	E	M		S	P	A	D	E
O	N	E	S		N	A	D	A		A	L	I	E	N
A	R	E	S		E	Y	E	D		M	A	D	T	V
M	A	K	E	I	T	S	N	A	P	P	Y			
A	M	E	N	D	E			M	I	A	S	A	R	A
N	P	R		I	N	I	S		A	N	K	L	E	T
			S	O	T	T	E	D			O	O	N	A
	G	E	T	T	H	E	L	E	A	D	O	U	T	
F	E	A	R			M	E	S	C	A	L			
C	A	V	I	E	S		S	I	C	K		A	B	A
C	R	E	P	T	U	P			R	A	N	G	E	R
			M	O	V	E	Y	O	U	R	T	A	I	L
K	A	U	A	I		R	U	D	I		E	T	R	E
O	N	A	L	L		I	M	I	N		S	H	U	N
P	E	R	L	E		L	A	N	G		T	A	T	E

119

```
A T L A S   L O L L     I D L E
Q U A R T   E D I E     N O U N
U L C E R   N O N O     B O L D
A S E A   F O R D T A U R U S
S A Y S N O     Y A R N
      E C O L   R E C O A T
G R A N T I N A I D   H A S H
A U T O   O R R     E T T A
P L O T   T R U M A N S H O W
S E N A T E   E A S Y
    T E R M   H E Y D A Y
B U S H L E A G U E   A E R O
O N T O   N U L L   T H A N K
A D A M   C L U E   N O L I E
Z O N E   E S T E   T O T E D
```

120

```
S H A R P   T R U R O   B M W
S A B E R   R A Z E D   O A R
T H E P O S I T I V E   A G E
S A T I R E S     S A T I N
    N A T T I N E S S
A M S   T H E N E G A T I V E
C O T T A   S R A   U R A L
U T A H   E L T O N   T O L L
R I F E   L E A   S E N S E
A F F I R M A T I V E   Y E N
    R H O D E S I A N
A N T S Y     A N T E N N A
B O O   M R I N B E T W E E N
U S E   E E R I E   L E M A N
T E D   S T A L L   E L O P E
```

121

```
D E S K   A S H E   S H O U T
E T O N   S W A T   H O R S E
E C H O   H A L T   E M C E E
  H O W D O Y O U P L E A D
    S I R E   I V Y
K A T   R E D T A P E   B A H
I C I N G   I M P   A L T O
W H E R E D O E S I T H U R T
I O T A   R I G   O A S I S
S O O   P I L S N E R   H A Y
    P A L   O L A Y
  W H A T L L Y O U H A V E
B R U T E   S A N D   N A V Y
B E G I N   A L A E   K N E E
S N O O T   T E N D   S E N T
```

122

```
I S L A M   C H A W   V E E P
T H U D S   H A L O   L I V E
C O L D S H O W E R   A S I S
H O L E   A S K E D   S E C T
    D A L E     G O I N T O
B O W O U T   B R A N C H
B L A N D   S L O M O   O P A
L I L   I N P O W E R   W E B
S N L   B E A T S   D W E E B
F E L O N S   P E A R L Y
P O L L E N     P U R R
A H O Y   S I R E N   Z E R O
T A W S   I V O R Y T O W E R
C R E E   G E T S   O N E A L
H A R E   N Y S E   M E R R Y
```

123

```
B L O C   M O D E   U S H E R
L E N A   A P A L   S W E D E
O A T S   T E R I   E E R I E
W H O I S A L E X T R E B E K
    N A H   I E S T
L A B O R A T O R Y   P A R K
A S E   G R A B   S E G U E
W H E R E I S J E O P A R D Y
N O N O S   E N D O   E E E
S T E T   C U T C O R N E R S
    A V O N   M E A
W H A T I S A Q U E S T I O N
E U B I E   B U R T   U S M A
E L B O W   L O G E   R E A R
B A R N S   E D E R   E E N Y
```

124

```
C A W S   B O N O   P S H A W
A M A T   A V O N   A W A K E
S U R E   B A L L E R I N A S
A L B A N Y   A I R I N G
B E L L A D O N N A   E S P O
A T E   G O P   E S P   O E R
    D O G L E G   I X N A Y
    B I L L Y J A C K
Z U B I N   M A R K E R
I K E   G A G   I R A   I F S
P E N S   B O L L I X E D U P
  T A K E T O   V E N D E E
B U L L E T H O L E   E L L E
A N E A R   A P I A   R E E D
H A Y D N   M Y S T   O R D O
```

125

E	A	R	T	H		U	R	A	L		H	A	R	I
A	L	O	H	A		N	A	N	A		A	G	E	D
S	T	A	Y	W	I	T	H	I	T		N	O	E	L
T	O	M		K	R	I	S		H	A	G	G	L	E
		N	E	I	L		D	E	L	I				
O	B	E	Y	S		M	E	R	I	N	G	U	E	
C	L	O	V	E		T	E	L	E		T	I	N	E
L	I	R	E		W	I	E	L	D		H	A	I	L
A	V	E	R		A	N	T	S		R	E	N	T	S
	D	E	S	S	E	R	T	S		P	A	R	T	Y
			A	L	M	S		T	I	L	E			
A	R	G	Y	L	E		A	O	N	E		H	B	O
L	E	A	D		D	O	N	T	G	I	V	E	U	P
A	N	T	I		U	L	N	A		G	I	M	M	E
N	O	S	E		P	E	A	L		H	A	S	P	S

126

R	O	I	L		O	P	T	I	C		A	P	S	E
O	M	N	I		F	A	R	G	O		S	E	A	L
M	A	G	N	I	F	Y	I	N	G	C	L	A	S	S
P	R	E	E	N	I	N	G		H	E	S	S	E	
			N	N	E		S	H	U	E				
G	E	H	R	I	G		S	T	A	M	P	E	D	E
O	C	E	A	N		G	O	A	T		M	E	N	
G	O	I	N	G	F	O	R	T	H	E	C	O	L	D
O	L	D		A	R	T	E		L	A	T	T	E	
L	E	I	S	U	R	E	S		S	P	R	E	A	D
			E	T	O	N		M	T	A				
A	M	A	N	A		G	O	E	S	I	N	T	O	
F	O	R	T	H	E	L	O	V	E	O	F	C	O	D
R	O	A	R		T	I	B	E	R		F	A	R	E
O	N	L	Y		H	E	I	R	S		Y	A	K	S

127

S	A	D	A		C	A	R	D		O	N	K	E	Y
E	L	A	L		A	L	O	U		H	A	I	L	E
E	L	M	E	R	F	U	D	D		G	O	T	I	T
R	E	S	C	U	E	M	E		L	O	M			
E	G	E	S	T		N	O	S	E	D	I	V	E	D
D	E	L		F	A	U	S	T		J	O	V	I	
			R	O	I		T	R	I	B	U	T	E	S
Y	E	S	O	R	N	O		S	T	U	D	E	N	T
E	M	I	G	R	A	N	T		B	C	D			
P	I	N	E		G	E	E	S	E					
S	T	O	R	Y	L	I	N	E		D	R	A	N	O
			M	A	E		S	L	O	E	E	Y	E	D
A	W	F	U	L		B	I	L	L	Y	B	U	D	D
V	E	R	D	I		R	O	T	E		A	G	A	L
A	B	O	D	E		A	N	O	S		G	A	Y	E

128

X	F	I	L	E	S			T	S	H	I	R	T	
R	E	C	I	P	E	S		T	H	E	O	R	E	M
A	R	A	B	I	A	N		D	E	P	L	A	N	E
Y	A	M		C	L	A	W	S		T	E	N	O	N
S	L	E	D		E	R	A		T	I	S			
			E	N	D	E	R	M	I	C		R	E	V
D	I	S	C	O		D	E	A	N		V	O	L	S
D	O	W	A	G	E	R		R	A	V	I	O	L	I
A	W	A	Y		M	U	S	S		I	N	D	E	X
Y	A	P		H	U	M	P	H	R	E	Y			
			G	U	S		A	L	E		L	E	S	T
T	S	A	R	S		P	S	A	L	M		R	I	B
R	E	G	A	T	T	A		N	I	A	G	A	R	A
E	A	R	F	L	A	P		D	E	C	A	T	U	R
X	R	A	T	E	D			F	S	T	O	P	S	

129

P	E	R	U		C	L	A	D		E	Q	U	A	L
A	X	E	S		R	A	S	H		L	U	R	I	E
R	E	P	S		E	S	T	O		G	I	L	D	S
S	M	A	R	T	A	S	A	W	H	I	P			
E	P	I		H	M	O		I	N	S	T	E	P	
S	T	R	E	E	P		P	A	T		A	L	A	
			R	A	I	N	E	D		B	A	L	M	Y
	W	I	S	E	A	S	A	N	O	W	L			
N	A	A	C	P		M	O	R	O	S	E			
A	D	D		Y	E	S		A	N	D	R	E	A	
T	S	E	T	S	E		P	H	I		E	N	S	
			S	H	A	R	P	A	S	A	T	A	C	K
S	I	N	A	I		E	L	L	A		A	S	I	N
S	C	O	R	N		S	E	E	R		N	O	N	O
T	E	N	S	E		T	A	S	K		K	N	O	T

130

F	L	A	R	E		B	A	R	B		S	T	O	P
A	I	M	E	D		O	L	E	O		I	R	M	A
C	R	O	C	I		T	I	T	O		B	E	A	T
T	A	K	E	T	O	H	A	R	T	E		A	H	S
			D	I	G		S	O	L	A	R	D	A	Y
A	R	L	E	N	E	S		E	C	O				
H	I	E		G	E	T	H	I	G	H	M	A	R	X
A	R	A	B		A	I	R		E	X	A	M		
B	E	F	R	O	N	T	M	A	N	N		L	I	A
			A	L	A		N	E	A	T	E	N	S	
R	E	M	N	A	N	T	S		M	P	H			
O	L	E		F	E	E	L	N	O	P	A	I	N	E
L	I	A	R		T	R	I	O		E	L	L	I	S
E	T	N	A		T	R	E	E		R	I	L	L	S
S	E	T	H		E	A	R	L		S	A	Y	S	O